MAJOR THINKERS IN WELFARE

Contemporary issues in historical perspective

Vic George

First published in Great Britain in 2012 by

The Policy Press
University of Bristol
Fourth Floor
Beacon House
Queen's Road
Bristol BS8 1QU
UK
Tel +44 (0)117 331 4054
Fax +44 (0)117 331 4093
e-mail tpp-info@bristol.ac.uk
www.policypress.co.uk

North American office:
The Policy Press
c/o The University of Chicago Press
1427 East 60th Street
Chicago, IL 60637, USA
t: +1 773 702 7700
f: +1 773-702-9756
e:sales@press.uchicago.edu
www.press.uchicago.edu

British Library Cataloguing in Publication Data
A catalogue record for this book is available from the British Library.

Library of Congress Cataloging-in-Publication Data
A catalog record for this book has been requested.

ISBN 978 1 44730 584 2 paperback

Cover design by The Policy Press
Front cover: image kindly supplied by www.istock.com
Printed and bound in Great Britain by MPG Book Group
The Policy Press uses environmentally responsible print partners

Contents

Introduction

Like all other significant social science concepts – liberty, equality, justice, power and so on – the notion of welfare defies agreed definition. There is some agreement at the edges, at the superficial level, but this agreement disappears as one delves deeper into its detailed meaning.

At the very basic **material** level, the notion of welfare refers to the individual's basic material needs: food, water, clothing, housing, heating and suchlike needs. There is, however, no agreement on what exactly the phrase 'suchlike needs' covers or the level at which the agreed basic needs should be satisfied. There is even less agreement on what non-basic material needs should be included in the notion of welfare, even though it is generally acknowledged that such non-basic needs change over time and they vary from one society to another – that is, that non-basic material needs are relative to place and time. Many commentators would, for example, include a radio or a television set among the non-basic material needs in advanced industrial affluent societies but they are likely to exclude these items when referring to the welfare of people living in impoverished countries today. Clearly, they would not even consider them in societies before these items were invented. Economic growth and economic affluence create new physical needs all the time.

At the **non-material** level, there are some conditions which are generally accepted as being basic and hence an integral part of welfare. The best example of this is safety or security. People may have enough or even more than enough to satisfy their material needs but their welfare suffers if they are in constant physical danger or in fear of their lives. But that is as far as agreement goes. Would one include individual liberty in the same category as individual safety bearing in mind that, on one hand, millions of people over the centuries have been prepared to sacrifice their life in order to promote their liberty, and, on the other, millions have lived under tyrannies with their material needs amply satisfied? More controversially, would one include faith, happiness or justice in the notion of welfare?

Attempts to create a 'hierarchy of needs', with material needs at the base and non-material needs above it, make sense only in contemporary affluent democratic societies, but not in all societies. Many devout religious persons over the centuries have been prepared to put faith above material needs, even basic material needs; many oppressed individuals have been willing to fight and die in their quest for liberty rather than enjoy, in bondage, all the material trappings of civilisation; and many have argued that the advance of industrial civilisation has brought material abundance at the expense of individual happiness.

Human welfare, thus, depends on the satisfaction of a range of material and non-material needs, basic and relative, most of which change over time. It is not possible to provide a rigorous definition of welfare that can be used as a guide for the discussion in each chapter. Instead, we can list the main issues that each chapter will discuss, as far as is possible.

First, each chapter will discuss one or more thinkers' views on wealth, poverty and the satisfaction of basic needs. It will be seen that there is no agreement among the various authors on the satisfaction of even the most basic of needs. Many, for example, have seen the eradication of material poverty as essential to human welfare; some have seen poverty as essential to a holy life and hence to welfare; and others have claimed that it is the eradication of relative, not merely basic, poverty that is crucial for human welfare. Similarly with wealth: it has been seen as unnecessary or even harmful to individual welfare; as essential to it; and as conditional to the use to which it is being put. Thus each chapter will discuss the material and non-material needs that the thinkers consider as necessary or unnecessary for human welfare.

Second, each chapter will discuss the thinkers' views about the importance of the various sources of human welfare: the state, the family, friendly or charitable societies, and the labour market. It is true to say that non-state sources of welfare were considered the most important before the enfranchisement of the general public. It is only from the beginning of the 20th century that there was general agreement that the state should be the main or one of the main providers of welfare. There is, however, no evidence to suggest that the rise of the state as a provider of welfare has meant the decline, let alone the eclipse, of the other sources. The labour market and the payment of wages remains as strong a source of welfare as ever; the family is still a major source of welfare even though the rhetoric about the collapse of the family in advanced industrial societies may suggest differently.

Third, each chapter will show how a thinker's views on the satisfaction of the individual's welfare are influenced by how the thinker sees different social groups in society. The welfare of slaves was considered less important by many of the thinkers we discuss in this volume because they considered slaves as sub-human; similarly the welfare of women was considered less important than the welfare of men by many authors because they viewed women as inferior to men; and the satisfaction of the welfare of working-class persons was considered less essential than that of the upper classes because of the prevailing beliefs on the superiority of the upper classes. Some even insisted that high wages or high poor relief rates that were necessary to satisfy basic needs adequately would be detrimental not only to national welfare but to the individuals concerned too, because they would encourage laziness, indolence, and reliance on the state.

Fourth, each chapter will pay particular attention to the thinkers' views on the position of women in society because historical accounts of welfare have, until recently, ignored this very important issue. It will be seen that even some of the politically radical thinkers covered in this volume considered women as inferior to men and saw their place in society to be at home as wives and mothers.

Fifth, special attention will be paid to the thinkers' views on education because of the general belief that education is essential to the fulfilment of individual and societal welfare. It is a view that has lasted throughout the centuries even though many of the thinkers discussed in this volume saw education as necessary for boys and not girls, and sometimes for the boys of the middle and upper classes only.

Sixth, each chapter will discuss, where possible, the thinkers' perceptions of human nature because this perception usually influences the thinkers' views on the nature of needs and whether they should be satisfied or not, and if so how. Thinkers who believe that human beings are by nature social, cooperative and helpful to others are likely to suggest communal forms of welfare satisfaction; those who consider human beings as aggressive and individualistic are likely to argue that individuals are responsible for their welfare, either totally or predominantly; and those who take a middle position on human nature would adopt a middle line of thought, too, in relation to state welfare provision.

Seventh, each chapter will examine some of the philosophical and political science concepts because they directly and indirectly influence the satisfaction of human welfare. Thinkers who view life on planet earth as a temporary residence before the everlasting life after death will view wealth accumulation for private ends as unacceptable; those who view governments as the tool of the upper classes will have little faith in the activities of government; those who consider individual liberty as freedom from government intervention will not support substantial government provision of welfare; and so on.

Eighth, a certain amount of discussion on the historically existing social, economic and political conditions is necessary in each chapter in order to put the thinkers' views on welfare in a historical context. Plato's rejection of democracy and his espousal of strong government was a reaction to the upheavals of Athenian democracy; Hobbes' support of strong royalist government reflected his despise of the revolutions of his period; Wollstonecraft's feminist views can best be understood if one has some appreciation of the position of women in 18th-century England; Smith's views on the primacy of the market has to be seen within the expanding economy and the inefficiencies of the governments of the period; Marx's theories of the inevitable collapse of capitalism can best be understood when seen in conjunction with the rise in the radicalisation of the emerging working class; and so on.

Ninth, attention will be paid to particular contributions that an author makes outside the above eight broad categories. Cicero's views on old age were unique and relevant today even though they were made 2,000 years ago; Rousseau's emphasis on public participation is another such example; and so on.

Some of the issues that excited passionate debate in the past have been definitively resolved today: no one supports slavery and no one argues that women are inferior to men and that their place is in the home. Other issues remain as alive today as they have ever been: the causes and remedies of crime, the debate over the culture and structure of poverty, and the relevance of uncontrolled income inequality to economic growth. Still other issues ebb and flow depending on the wider economic and political conditions: the balance between private and public enterprise and the arguments for low or high levels of taxation on income and wealth are decided in favour of one or the other depending on the political climate of the day. These comments relate to the situation in contemporary advanced affluent societies and the position may be different in the less industrial and less affluent societies.

The choice of thinkers for this volume was difficult largely because it is the first volume that examines key thinkers in welfare prior to the 20th century. Not all thinkers who made significant contributions to philosophy, political science or economics are also of importance to welfare thought. Vice versa, not all authors included in this volume would necessarily appear in a volume of philosophy, economics or politics. It also goes without saying that the choice of thinkers is to some extent subjective. Some of the authors included in this volume – Plato, Wollstonecraft, Marx, for example – would be generally acceptable to most writers on welfare; others may not – St Francis of Assisi, Erasmus and so on. Personal judgement is inevitable in the selection of thinkers and, to some extent, in the interpretation of their work.

The emphasis of the volume on ideas should not be taken to imply that ideas are the major force in bringing about change in welfare provision over the years. It will become abundantly clear that the position taken in this volume is that material changes in society, ideas, wars and personalities all combine in unique ways to influence the pattern of welfare provision.

A certain amount of empathy is needed in assessing the views of early thinkers for they were writing either at the dawn or the early stages of civilisation. Only a few of the thinkers discussed in this volume – Plato, More, Rousseau and Marx – departed radically in their proposals for human welfare from the then existing reality. All the other thinkers perceived the world and made proposals for its reform within the cultural boundaries of their era.

Historical accounts of the views of prominent writers on welfare are intellectually of interest for they show how writers and societies concentrate on some issues at the expense of others; how they define some situations as social problems, how they try to solve them and with what success. It is interesting to see how some of these problems have been largely overcome while others persist to the present day. Societies sometimes learn from the experience of history although, sadly, this is not always the case. Solutions that were found to have failed in the past can still be espoused today, as with the argument that very harsh penalties reduce crime in society. Some of the debates which began thousands of years ago, such as the role of the state in public affairs, still rage on today for they are largely ideological; others, such as the debates on slavery, have been settled.

A history of welfare thought also shows that many ideas expressed centuries ago can be useful today: Plato's concerns of how to prevent corruption among politicians; Aristotle's stress that compromise and the middle way is often the best way forward; Cicero's account of the individual and social implications of old age; Wollstonecraft's belief that women should subjectively free themselves of social beliefs of inferiority; Rousseau's view that public participation is a necessary measure to combat public alienation from central governments; and Paine's claim that only those who experienced severe poverty can truly understand what poverty means, are just a few examples of the usefulness of historical accounts of welfare thought.

Hopefully, this volume will enable the reader to view contemporary issues in welfare in a historical perspective and thus get a better understanding of the issues and the complexities involved in formulating the necessary policies.

ONE

Classical Athens
Plato (427–347 BC);
Aristotle (384–322 BC)

Ideas on welfare reflect in varying ways and degrees the author's interpretation of existing reality. They can be an endorsement, a critique, a rejection, or a combination of these, of existing institutional arrangements. More often than not, ideas for reform are incremental – they depart only slightly from existing arrangements. Radical departures are rare and usually labelled utopian. But even these are reflections of existing reality – they are rejections of it in favour of some other type of arrangement that, in the eyes of the author, corrects the injustices or inefficiencies of existing society.

The views of the two major political theorists in Classical Athens, Plato and Aristotle, show how the same objective societal reality can evoke very different reactions as regards both politics and welfare. Plato's views are a rejection of Athenian democracy in favour of a communitarian society while Aristotle's views constitute a critique of but also an accommodation to, Athenian society. While they were both critical of what they considered as the inherent political instability of regimes based on democracy, they came up with different solutions to the 'problem', as they saw it.

This chapter will, therefore, discuss two contrasting approaches to human welfare: the proposals of Plato for a communitarian society as put forward in his books *The Republic* and *The Laws*; and the ideas of Aristotle for an enlightened, modestly interfering state, as they appear in his books *The Politics* and *Ethics*. It is worth stressing that their ideas on human welfare referred to small city-states with populations around 200,000 and not to large nation states. Their views must also be assessed with a degree of historical empathy for they were writing at the dawn of human civilisation. On one hand, ideas that are common knowledge today were just being discovered then. Aristotle's statement, for example, that 'man is a political animal' is taken for granted today but it was a profound statement when it was made. On the other hand, ideas that were generally accepted then may look strange and even offensive today. The views of both writers on slavery and of Aristotle on women, for example, are both odd and insulting to modern ears. Their ideas, however, on the role of education in society, the importance of social cohesion to the smooth functioning of society, the attitude of the state towards wealth and poverty in society, their debate on the relative merits and demerits of public provision, the relationship between hereditary and social factors, and so on, are still being debated today.

Social theories, including ideas about human welfare, are best understood when examined within their historical environment. Serious ideas do not emerge in a cultural vacuum. Both Plato and Aristotle were greatly influenced by the prevailing views and events in Athens – the strong emphasis on individual liberty, the prevalent practices of participatory democracy, and the role of slavery in Athenian society. Their theories were, mostly, a reaction to the Athenian environment of their time, particularly the experience of political instability. It is, therefore, important to examine briefly the political and social aspects of Athenian society before analysing their views on human welfare.

The Athenian society

Perhaps the most dominant social value of classical Athens was libertarianism: the emphasis on individual liberty that made the individual sovereign in relation to the state. All other values revolved around it. Libertarianism was the bedrock of Athenian democracy. It involved political freedom, freedom of expression and freedom under the law as well as active political participation for the select few who were recognised by that state as Athenian citizens. Women, slaves and foreign residents were not considered citizens and were excluded from taking part in politics. Out of a total population of 200,000 to 300,000, only 35,000 to 40,000 male adults were classified as citizens with the right to vote, to be elected, to act as jurors, to take part in public affairs and to be entitled to state support when in dire need (Lee, 1987, pp xxv–xxvi). Only they were considered by the state as Athenian citizens – as free men with all the duties and privileges of citizenship. Aristotle, himself, was a foreign resident, an alien, and did not possess the rights of Athenian citizenship.

The essentials of Athenian democracy are well known and need only be summarised briefly here:

- The Assembly was the heart of the political system. All citizens had the right to attend, to speak and to vote. It met about once a month and took decisions on all political issues. The Assembly elected its leader and Pericles was its elected leader for 30 years.
- The Council was made up of 500 members that were divided into committees of 50 each and it was responsible for carrying out the business of the republic.
- Council members were chosen by lot from among all the citizens; membership was limited to one year; and no one could serve more than twice.
- The Judiciary was comprised of jurors who were either elected or chosen by lot from among the citizens.
- Fees were paid to all in order to encourage attendance and participation.

Clearly this was very different from the representative forms of contemporary democracy. It was an active, participatory type of democracy of the select few where everyone's voice could carry weight. As Lee puts it: 'Such a complete system of popular control has never been known before or since' (Lee, 1987, p xxvi). Yet such a system can only be practical in a very small state, as even Rousseau, the strongest advocate of political participation, had to admit, as we shall see in Chapter 7.

This emphasis on citizen participation in public affairs was eloquently expressed by Pericles, the then elected leader of Athens: 'We are called a democracy, for the administration is in the hands of the many and not of the few', he proclaimed. He added that poverty was not a bar in the administration of the state; ordinary citizens were fair judges of public issues and they should actively participate in the affairs of the state. Non-participation in public affairs was frowned upon: 'We alone regard a man who takes no interest in public affairs, not as harmless, but as a useless character; and if few of us are originators, we are all sound judges of a policy' (Pericles' funeral oration in Thucydides, edited by Jowett, 1991, pp 127, 129).

Political practice was – as it always has been – different from political rhetoric. The administration was in the hands of a few select citizens; attendance at the Assembly was often low with the poor being the most likely absentees; demagogues swayed public opinion and votes; council members were mostly middle class; and, because the fee was very low, jurors were 'chiefly old men' (Burn, 1974, p 243).

Both Plato and Aristotle were critical of Athenian democracy, not because of these practical shortcomings, but because they considered the principle of strong emphasis on liberty as fundamentally flawed. Plato's criticisms are the more stringent and the more articulate.

Every known society, according to Plato, contained its own seeds of destruction – a view echoed by Marx two thousand years later. Wealth and avarice caused the downfall of oligarchy; excessive power concentration was the Achilles heel of tyranny; and unbridled love of liberty and individualism would always bring the downfall of democracy. Superficially, Plato argued, 'democracy is the most attractive of all societies. The diversity of its characters, like the different colours in patterned dress, make it very attractive' (Plato, in Lee, 1987, p 314). Yet, deep down, liberty is flawed because it does not select and train its leaders carefully; it leads to the collapse of self-discipline; it encourages the belief in individual rights to the detriment of individual duties; and it creates insatiable public appetites for false needs. An individual in a democracy becomes hedonistic and if anyone tells him that he is wrong, 'he won't listen but shakes his head and says all pleasures are equal and should have equal rights' (Plato, in Lee, 1987, p 319). In brief, liberty is an appealing but, fundamentally, flawed social value, claimed Plato.

Plato's communitarianism: the state is sovereign

Plato rejected the prevailing emphasis on participatory democracy in favour of a stable stratified society that is communitarian in nature. Individuals can only fulfil themselves and satisfy their welfare if they behave in accordance with the central value of justice that sets the state above the individual. Order and stability rather than freedom and change are the hallmarks of his ideal society. It is a communitarian society where the social dominates the individual, where there is more emphasis on duties than on rights.

Plato rejects previous notions that justice is just a form of self-interest or simply giving a man his due. For Plato, justice at the societal and the individual level exists when all sections of society and all individuals perform their natural tasks, work in harmony and do not question their status or that of others. Moreover, it is a society where private wealth for citizens is prohibited. It is a different form of communitarianism from subsequent versions which fully accept private property and wealth but appeal to individuals not to forget the common good in the pursuit of their individual goals.

As we shall see later, Plato's ideal society consists of three different classes each of which has different innate abilities, and this means that it is in the interests of all that each class specialises in the performance of different functions. Justice at the societal level exists when 'each of our three classes does its own job and minds its own business' (Plato, in Lee, 1987, p 146). Similarly, justice at the individual level exists when the individual performs the job for which he is naturally suited and does not interfere with the job of others. Interference either by a class or by an individual with the job of others is both inefficient and disruptive of social harmony. Both society and the individual are happy when justice, so defined, exists.

Plato's advice to the citizens of his ideal state would run as follows: perform your duties, contribute to collective welfare, accept your social status, reject notions of individual rights and do not interfere with the work of others – this is justice. You will be happier as a result. It is very different from modern approaches that see justice as equality or fairness – as a relational concept – 'a social virtue which concerns the way we behave towards each other' (Sayers, 1999, p 77).

Plato's emphasis on the supremacy of the state over the individual stemmed from his belief that excessive individualism and liberty were to blame for the collapse of successive regimes in Athens. Similarly, his emphasis on order and stability were equally a response to the constant political upheavals of Athens. The quest for the right balance between the rights of the individual vis-à-vis the rights of the community has been a recurring theme in the political and philosophical tracts over the years. Over the centuries, however, the move has been towards the rights of the individual with the rights of the community lurking in the background.

Aristotle's equity and the middle way

Aristotle spends a considerable time discussing the various values or virtues of society – happiness, equality, justice, liberality, magnanimity, friendship and so on. What is unique of his work, however, is the emphasis on the importance of moderation – 'the rule of the mean', as he calls it. All social values, or virtues as he calls them, 'are destroyed both by excess and deficiency, and they are kept alive by the observance of the mean' (Aristotle, in Thomson, 1955, p 58). In other words, every virtue is a mean between two extremes that are both vices. Thus generosity is a value or virtue in Aristotle's ideal society because it is the mean between prodigality and stinginess; courage is a virtue because it is the mean between rashness and cowardice; pride between vanity and humility; and so on.

A moral person and a moral society are guided by 'moderate' virtues in both their thoughts and their actions. He accepts that it is often difficult to decide where precisely the middle point between excess and deficiency lies in any value: at what stage of behaviour, for example, bravery degenerates into either cowardice or rashness. He acknowledges that this 'makes virtue hard of achievement, because finding the middle point is never easy' (Aristotle, in Thomson, 1955, p 73).

In Aristotle's analysis, both Athenian liberty and Platonic justice are vices rather than virtues because they are not the middle points – they are excesses. Thus he was critical of both the excessively, as he thought, libertarian Athenian democracy and the heavily solidaristic society that emerged from Plato's definition of justice. Plato's justice, he argued, obliterated individualism while the participatory form of Athenian liberty degenerated into licence.

Aristotle's emphasis on the mean was a product of his desire for consensus but not uniformity in society. It was an attempt to avoid excesses whether of the libertarian or the communitarian ilk. As we shall see below, he still felt that the individual was part of society and his welfare could only be satisfied as a member of that society. Nevertheless, he approved of private property provided it was not excessive and it was not used wholly for individual pursuits.

The value of equality is of some interest to students of human welfare. In the Periclean view of the world, all citizens were considered by the state as equal: they could all take part in the debates of the Assembly, the vote of each citizen was equal to that of another, election to public offices was often by lot to emphasise the equality of citizens, and so on. It was numerical equality. For Plato, equality was an anathema: it was an unnatural concept for people are born with unequal abilities; it was also a destructive notion for it encouraged people to behave above their stations in life. Aristotle adopted a middle position: he felt that numerical equality was useful in some situations but not in all. He, therefore, advanced the idea of proportional equality, that is equality according to merit or contribution to society:

> Now, there are two kinds of equality, the one being numerical, the other of value. I use 'numerically equal' to cover that which is equal and the same in respect of either size or quantity, and 'equal in value' for that which is equal by ratio. (Aristotle, in Saunders, 1992, p 298)

No society can function adequately by relying exclusively on one or the other of the two conceptions of equality. Societies 'must make use both of numerical equality and of equality of value' in order to progress (Aristotle, in Saunders 1992, p 299).

Aristotle, however, undermines his own argument by postulating, as we shall see below, that societies are made up of different classes whose contributions to society vary in significance and value. An accident of birth, therefore, can decide a person's contribution to society and hence the ratio of reward he can receive from society. A wealthy, educated person can expect to receive more from society because his contribution to society is deemed by the state to be greater than that of a working-class person. This type of proportional equality compounds existing inequality. Aristotle's debates on the nature of equality have been rehearsed continuously over the years, particularly in relation to education. The debates are clearer today than then but the choice between the various forms of equality – equality of opportunity, equality of merit and equality of outcome – remains a deeply political rather than a rational issue.

Origins of society

Plato and Aristotle were the first to present a viable theory of society and its origins. They both saw the development of society as something natural: it originated to satisfy human needs – food, clothing and shelter. Since Plato's writings preceded those of Aristotle (indeed he was his teacher), let us quote him first:

> Society originates because the individual is not self-sufficient, but has many needs which he can't supply himself. (Plato, in Lee, 1987, p 58)

Gradually society takes on more responsibilities such as internal and external security until ultimately it becomes responsible for ensuring the good life of its citizens – justice in Plato and happiness in Aristotle. In brief, the welfare of citizens becomes the overarching aim of society. Citizens cannot fulfil their welfare as individuals – only as members of their society.

Aristotle adds another dimension to this human interdependence. It is not merely a material but also a social interdependence that brings human beings together in organised societies. Man, he argues, 'is by nature a political animal' (Aristotle, in Saunders, 1992, p 59). Only 'subhuman or superhuman' persons can live in isolation from their fellow human beings. Thus to satisfy their material and social needs, people have no real option but to live together in organised communities. People need one another if they are to fulfil their welfare needs.

Both Plato and Aristotle adopted not only a natural but an organic view of society: in the same way that the body consists of different organs that have to function together for bodily health, society, too, is made up of different parts that need to work together in harmony for maximum efficiency. It goes without saying that some parts are more important than others both for the body and for society. Thus, although human beings are interdependent, they are also differently endowed with the result that different individuals and groups are better suited for some jobs than for others:

> We have different natural aptitudes, which fit us for different jobs. (Plato, in Lee, 1987, p 59)

This makes the division of labour not only natural but also a more efficient form of organisation in society. The satisfaction of mutual human needs and the division of labour are two of the most fundamental driving forces behind society. Stratified reciprocity and specialisation lie at the heart of society's effective and efficient functioning.

The division of labour improves not only the quantity but also the quality of production and, hence, collective human welfare, apart from the fact that it fulfils people's differing talents and abilities.

> Quantity and quality are therefore more easily produced when a man specializes appropriately on a single job for which he is naturally fitted, and neglects all others. (Plato, in Lee, 1987, p 60)

Contrary to Marx's view that it is beneficial for both the individual and society that workers should be trained to do various jobs, Plato and Aristotle maintained that attempting to perform different jobs goes against nature and it is both inefficient and socially disruptive. As society gets more complex, new needs arise, new occupations emerge and specialisation becomes even more necessary.

The division of labour thesis was accepted by many later political economists, particularly by Adam Smith in the 18th century, who made it one of the centrepieces of his theory of capitalist industrialisation, as we shall see in Chapter 9. What distinguishes Plato's thesis, however, is his assertion that certain jobs are more important than others and these can only be performed by a certain group of people with inherited ability. It is a matter of inherited ability rather than training or social circumstances that largely decides the division of labour in society. Adam Smith's division of labour was of a different nature – division of labour within jobs in factories in order to promote productivity despite the adverse effects on people's humanity, as Smith himself acknowledged.

Classes in society

We have already referred to the stratified nature of Athenian democracy whereby the majority of the population were excluded from the right of citizenship. Only a minority of men were free citizens, partaking in the affairs of the state and in cultural pursuits. The debate about the rights and duties of citizenship was central in Classical Athens, though citizenship was much more narrowly defined than in modern times.

Both Plato and Aristotle envisaged a stratified ideal society. Plato's utopian society presented in *The Republic* was a rigidly hierarchical society. The slaves and the resident aliens would be at the bottom of the ladder – Plato spends very little time on them. The rest of society would be made up of three classes: the workers, the Auxiliaries and the Guardians.

The working class would be the larger class and its function would be to provide the material wealth for the welfare of the city. It had no role to play in government but it was free of all the government regulations that applied to the other two classes. As a result, its members could own property, have families, live in their own homes and pursue their own jobs as they thought fit. They would be guided and governed by the other two smaller but wiser classes, though their daily pursuits would not be scrutinised by the state. So long as they performed well the function for which they were suited, they would be left largely to their own devices.

The Auxiliaries and the Guardians start life as one class, men and women, but they become separated through a prolonged and rigorous selection process that involves academic, civic and military testing. A small minority emerges at about the age of 50 that become the Guardians – the true rulers of society, the philosopher kings, as Plato called them. The remaining are the Auxiliaries, whose task is to implement the decisions of the Guardians. Decision-making is seen as more important than implementation – a mistake also made by contemporary welfare states in the social service sector. The two classes, however, live together, are educated together and inter-marry, as we shall discuss below.

Plato's main thrust was to ensure that the most talented, that is those who passed the various tests, should become the philosopher kings. He, therefore, provided for a certain degree – some would say far too small – of upward and downward social mobility. Exceptionally talented children of working class background could rise to philosopher-king status; vice versa, children of Guardians and Auxiliaries who showed no aptitude should be demoted to the working class. This weakens the criticism that Plato's utopia was a caste society, though his emphasis on academic talent as the sine qua non of a good politician may be faulted. Bounded meritocracy rather than hereditary privilege lies at the heart of Plato's proposals. In Lee's words:

> Belief in an aristocracy of talent may be wicked; but it is not the same
> as belief in a hereditary caste. (Lee, 1987, p xliii)

Aristotle was critical of Plato's proposal that one small class, however well selected, should rule in perpetuity. He thought that this would be 'a sure source of faction, even among those of no standing – to say nothing of those he calls warlike and spirited' (Aristotle, in Saunders, 1992, p 119). His criticism could be extended to cover the generally accepted thesis that power, particularly concentrated long-term power, corrupts, however many precautions one takes against that risk. Plato's answer would be that the philosopher kings would be so educated and their life so regulated that they would always have the welfare of society as their paramount concern.

Despite his criticisms, Aristotle's class structure is rather similar. Slaves, resident aliens, women and all those engaged in manual and commercial activity are to be excluded from holding public office, for they are not citizens – this is much like the prevailing situation in Athens. Slaves are excluded because, according to Aristotle and others, they were inferior human beings; we shall return to the position of women later in the chapter; and working-class men were excluded from citizenship because they would be busy working and would have no free time to participate in civic affairs.

Aristotle's belief that all citizens should partake in government affairs and that no one group should be allowed to dominate led him to the proposal that all citizens should perform a political function according to age: the young would be the soldiers; the older age groups would be the statesmen and judges; and the retired would be the priests. The distribution of civic tasks according to age made sense, argued Aristotle, because 'this is a division which takes into account fitness for the work' (Aristotle, in Saunders, 1992, p 416).

Slavery

Slavery was part and parcel of Athenian society: many Athenian families owned slaves for domestic and other duties; slaves were to be found in many public occupations; mines outside Athens relied almost exclusively on the work of slaves; and many rich men owned large numbers of slaves whom they hired out for a fee to others. In large concerns where citizens were not employed, slaves could rise to positions of authority; some slaves became rich enough to purchase their freedom; but the majority lived and died as slaves.

Clearly the work of slaves benefited their masters. Since slaves were legally considered as mere property, it meant that their masters could ill-treat them as they pleased; it also meant, however, that any damages or losses that slaves incurred were the liability of the master for whom they were working.

Aristotle argued that slavery is not the result of some social convention that could be changed but the outcome of biological differences that were timeless and unalterable. It is this 'natural' difference that makes slavery acceptable and beneficial to both the slave and the master:

> It is clear then that by nature some are free, others slaves, and for these it is both just and expedient that they should serve as slaves. (Aristotle, in Saunders, 1992, p 69)

Aristotle's approach to slavery was typical of the dominant view in Classical Athens, of Pericles and of Plato. It was a circular argument – slaves are inferior by nature and they can, therefore, only function as slaves in society; and they live the life of a slave because they are inferior to others by nature. It was a widely held belief based on self-interest and prejudice that was to dominate practice and debate for many centuries.

The criticism that the Athenian civilisation, despite its democratic rhetoric, was built on the backs of slaves is an exaggeration but it contains a substantial element of truth. Despite the fact that there were different types of slaves – the domestic, the policeman, the lower civil servant, the workman and the miner – and despite the fairly tolerant treatment of many slaves, the fact remains that most of the product of their toil was used by their masters and not by themselves.

Though it can be argued that slavery resembled in some respects the situation in early industrial societies where the disenfranchised working class produced the wealth of the country but gained little from it, it is fundamentally different. The worker was neither bought nor sold, he was not tortured at will by his employer and, in theory at least, he could leave his job and move elsewhere.

The position of women

Apart from in Sparta, the place of women throughout Classical Greece, including Athens, was in the home, not in the public domain. As daughters and as wives, they were under the eye of a man in the confines of their home:

> The women sat in their women's quarter at home and spun and bore children. They were married early, about the age of fifteen; and when they married they passed from the seclusion of the women's quarter in one house to the seclusion of that in another. They saw few men besides their husbands; the social gatherings of the Greeks were as masculine as the rest of their lives. (Barker, 1970, p 253)

Alien-born women enjoyed more personal freedom: they were allowed to mix with men in the marketplace and in politics and they often became mistresses to men of the citizen class in Athens. Pericles' mistress, Aspasia, was a well-known figure in Athenian society and exerted some influence on political issues. Plutarch, an Athenian historian of the times, tells us that when Pericles' marriage became unsatisfactory, 'he gave his wife over to another husband and took Aspasia and loved her very much. It is said that he greeted her with a kiss both when he went off to the Agora and when he came home' (Plutarch, quoted in Lefkowitz and Fant, 1992, p 179).

Aristotle's views on women reflected Athenian practice. He thought they were physically inferior to men, though not of the same depth of inferiority as slaves. Their greatest attribute was silence and their place was in the home as wives, mothers and house-managers. In the same way that it was unnatural for men to stay at home and not go out to work, it was also considered equally unnatural for women to be out and about in society either for work or for pleasure. Aristotle expresses the inferiority of women as follows:

> As between male and female, the former is by nature superior and rules, the latter inferior and subject. And this must be good for mankind in general (Aristotle, in Saunders, 1992, p 68)

Despite the inferior role attributed to women, they were highly thought of for bearing children, for performing their domestic duties and for being good mothers and wives. It was a paternalistic and oppressive treatment, which continued throughout the ages till modern times.

Aristotle's will brings out both his views on women and the then practices in Athens. He names the man to whom his daughter 'should be given'; he makes generous provisions for his mistress and their son; he asks that the bones of his wife be moved to be buried in his grave; he requests that some of his slaves be given their freedom; and makes financial provisions for expenses on commemorative statues (Lefkowitz and Fant, 1992, pp 59–61).

It was Plato that stepped outside Athenian convention and supported the freedom of women on lines similar to those in Sparta. He argued that the only difference between men and women was sexual/physical and this was not relevant for educational or occupational differentiation. He felt, however, that women in general were weaker than men but this should not prevent them from holding any office, including the highest office of philosopher Guardian:

> Our women Guardians must strip for exercise. They must play their part in war and in all other duties of a Guardian, which will be their sole occupation; only, as they are the weaker sex, we must give them a lighter share of these duties than men. (Plato, in Lee, 1987, p 177)

Plato's views on the status of women had significant implications for his views on marriage, the family, education and employment – all of which are discussed later. He was the first great philosopher to argue for women's emancipation, even though he was motivated primarily by his desire to use all the means available to him for the creation of his ideal society.

Private property

Plato's proposals on property and the family are extremely radical; Aristotle's ideas reflect largely the ideas of the period and they are often a reaction to and a criticism of Plato's proposals. Basically, Plato's blueprint for a communitarian society involved the abolition of both the family and private property among the Auxiliaries and the Guardian rulers – the working class and the slaves would carry on as before. The fundamental reason for the abolition of the family and private property was that these two institutions were considered as sources of individualism, selfishness and corruption – which were seen as mighty impediments to the creation of a professionally governed, harmonious, solidaristic and just society. Plato failed to recognise that the family and property could also be used to cement society together by giving people a stake in society.

Guardian rulers and Auxiliaries should live a monastic life: they should have no possessions of any substance, they should be housed in modest surroundings and they should eat simple meals. They would then be more able to concentrate on their job – how best to govern their society. Plato outlines his proposals as follows:

> First, they shall have no private property beyond the barest essentials.
> Second, none of them shall possess a dwelling-house or storehouse.

> Next, their food shall be provided by other citizens as an agreed
> wage for the duties they perform as Guardians.
> They shall eat together in private messes and live together like
> soldiers in camp.
> They must be told that they have no need of mortal and material
> gold and silver. (Plato, in Lee, 1987, p 125)

There are several differences between Plato's communitarian proposals and those of subsequent communist utopias, notably, Marxism. Unlike Marx, Plato does not aim at the vertical redistribution of wealth in order to create an egalitarian society; rather he wants to equalise wealth 'in order to remove a disturbing influence to government' (Sabine, 1963, p 58). Plato does not want to transfer political power from one class to another as Marx does; rather he wants to consolidate lasting power among the Guardian class. Marx's vision of the equalisation of power among the classes is matched by an almost contrary vision in Plato: how to ensure 'the working together of inherently unequal and hierarchically organised classes' (Sayers, 1999, p 62).

Aristotle is critical of Plato's proposals to abolish private property for three main reasons. In the first place, they will not abolish selfishness as Plato envisaged because selfishness stems not from the socio-economic environment but from 'the depravity of human character' (Aristotle, in Saunders, 1992, p 117). This, of course, begs the question of whether 'depravity' is an innate human weakness or whether it is the result of the social environment and how the two interact. We have here the first debate concerning the influence of heredity and environment on human behaviour – a debate that still goes on.

Second, while private property leads to increased effort at work, public ownership results in common neglect and the reduction of work incentives:

> People are much more careful of their personal possessions than those
> owned communally; they exercise care over common property only
> in so far as they are personally affected. (Aristotle, in Saunders, 1992,
> p 108)

Third, private property encourages liberality, that is generosity and charity to others and to society – a human quality that is essential to an ideal society. Public ownership makes this impossible and thus it morally impoverishes society.

Similar arguments against public ownership have been voiced by many subsequent writers, most recently by Hayek during the 1940s (Hayek, 1944). Aristotle's strictures of public ownership are embedded in today's neo-liberal philosophy. His solution to the problem, however, is markedly different from that offered by neo-liberalism.

For Aristotle, there is a place for both public and private ownership of property. In his ideal society, land would be divided into two parts: private and communal – the latter to be used 'to support the public service of the gods' and to 'meet the expenses of the communal feeding' (Aristotle, in Saunders, 1992, p 420). Private land should be used for both an individual and a common purpose, if possible. Of the various possible relationships between ownership and use, Aristotle favours private ownership and public use: this satisfied the best of both worlds and it was in line with his favoured value of moderation.

Despite their disagreements over the role of public ownership, both Plato and Aristotle agree that excessive wealth ownership is inimical to a virtuous life. In this, they continued a tradition that went back to Periclean democracy, if not before. They also stated a position that the Bible expresses in relation to the limited chances of the rich in entering heaven. Aristotle was particularly critical of moneylending for profit, especially to the poor who would find it difficult to pay back – a stand that made him very popular among the Church of the Middle Ages, as we shall see in Chapter 3.

The abolition of the family

Plato proposed the abolition of the family for two reasons: first, it was the only way that women would be able to partake on an equal footing with men in the affairs of the state. He wanted to relieve them of their childcare duties so that they could devote themselves fully to their work as Auxiliaries and Guardians. Second, concern with one's children not only diverted one's attention from the more important affairs of the state, but it was also a source of selfishness and possessive individualism that went contrary to the spirit of a communitarian society.

Casual sex was forbidden. Marriage was encouraged but husbands and wives would live apart and come together on certain state-arranged 'festivals' for mating. It was a form of eugenic breeding, which Plato justified on the grounds that if we apply such a system to the animals with positive results, we ought to do the same in the case of the humans.

Plato's family proposals are an early example of over-optimistic social engineering, which has made its appearance in more modified forms in the cases of the communes and the kibbutzim. His proposals can be outlined as follows:

> We must arrange for marriage, and make it as sacred as we can. (Plato, in Lee, 1987, p 179)

> We must mate the best of our men with the best of our women as often as possible, and the inferior men with the inferior women as seldom as possible. (Plato, in Lee, 1987, p 181).

> We must arrange statutory festivals in which our brides and bridegrooms will be brought together. The number of unions we will leave to the Rulers to decide. (Plato, in Lee, 1987, p 181)

Officers appointed by the state 'will take the children of the better Guardians to a nursery and put them in the charge of nurses living in a separate part of the city: the children of the inferior Guardians, and any defective offspring of the others, will be quietly and secretly disposed of'(Plato, in Lee, 1987, p 182):

> They will arrange for the suckling of the children by bringing their mothers to the nursery, taking every precaution to see that no mother recognizes her child. (Plato in Lee, 1987, p 182)

Aristotle's criticisms of Plato's family proposals resemble those on the abolition of private property. First, he felt that Plato's proposals were impractical for, if for no other reason, the attempt to conceal parenthood would not always succeed; second, they would not lead to the creation of a more solidaristic society; third, the learning that goes on within the caring environment of the family would be lost; and, fourth, they would cause considerable damage, for communally owned children are in effect neglected children:

> Each citizen acquires a thousand sons, but these are not one man's sons; any one of them is equally the son of any person, and as a result will be equally neglected by everyone. (Aristotle in Saunders, 1992, p 108)

Aristotle's views on family and marriage were a reflection of the then practices in Athens. He stressed the importance of both institutions to the well-being of individuals and of society as a whole. He felt that Plato's proposals for the abolition of private property and the family had gone too far towards drab uniformity to the detriment of diversity, which he considered a hallmark of a good society. Some things in life are best shared communally but others are best left to the individual. Plato's attempts to create harmony in society would 'reduce concord to unison' and 'rhythm to a single beat', he argued (Aristotle, in Saunders, 1992, p 116).

Poverty policies

Neither Plato nor Aristotle spent much time discussing the problem of poverty largely because the poor were not citizens. Nevertheless, they both made many passing references to poverty, usually in relation to property and wealth.

The Athenian emphasis on individual liberty encouraged everyone to look after themself but at the same time it provided the political forum for pressures to ameliorate poverty. It also stressed the social functions of wealth and hence the importance of charity. Rich people had an obligation to contribute towards the financing of state projects as benefactors:

> Wealth we consider an opportunity for service, not an occasion for boasting, and poverty no disgrace, unless we are failing to do something about it. (Pericles' funeral oration, quoted in Burn, 1974, p 262)

Pericles' views reflected practice in Athens. Taxation in Athens was rudimentary and the state relied a great deal on private finance for a good deal of its work. Thus 'the mounting of its plays, the equipment of its ships, the arrangement of its games and festivals, its chariot and horse and torch races, its musical contests and regattas were defrayed by private citizens who came forward voluntarily' (Zimmern, 1931, p 290). At the same time, the state provided cash help through both the fees paid to those who participated in democracy as well as maintenance payments to 'more than two thousand persons' (Ferguson and Chisholm, 1978, p 11).

Plato's *Republic* is a treatise for all ideologies. Its attack on the two pillars of capitalism and, some would argue, of civilised life – private property and the family – is welcomed by some radicals; its support for order and tradition in political affairs is in tune with conservatism; and its insistence on an unchanging hierarchical political and social system is supported by all authoritarian regimes. Very different types of policies in relation to poverty emerge from each of these conflicting ideological positions. The fact, however, is that Plato says very little on poverty in his *Republic* except to deplore it on the grounds that it undermines efficiency and sparks feelings of discontent that can lead to revolution, as the following quotation shows:

> Wealth and poverty: One produces luxury and idleness and a desire
> for novelty, the other meanness and bad workmanship and the desire
> for revolution as well. (Plato in Lee, 1987, p 129)

It is in his other book, *The Laws*, that Plato makes some more concrete references to poverty. He sets a ratio of four to one between the income of the richest and that of the poorest. Any income above that should be handed over to the state to be used for public purposes. He introduces the notions of the deserving and the undeserving poor, though he does not use these terms. He believes that a virtuous man, whether slave or free, should never be so neglected as to be in poverty; the law should provide for this. But vagabonds and beggars should be treated differently – they should be punished:

> It will be a matter for surprise if a virtuous person, whether slave or
> free, is ever so grossly neglected as to be in poverty. So the legislator
> will be quite safe if he lays down a law running more or less like this.
> No one is to go begging in the state. Anyone who attempts to do so,
> and scrounges a living by never-ending importunities, must be expelled
> from the market by the City-Wardens, and from the surrounding
> country by the Country-Wardens across the border, so that the land
> may rid itself of such a creature. (Plato in Saunders, 1970, p 484)

Aristotle's position on poverty is not very different from Plato's. What he says on poverty is related to his belief in moderation, on the undesirability of excessive wealth, the stress on liberality and charity, and the fear that 'inequality is everywhere at the bottom of faction' in society (Aristotle, in Saunders, 1992, p 298) – all these suggest that poverty among citizens was unacceptable to him. Neither the rich nor the poor were very appealing to him: the first 'incline more to arrogance and crime on a large scale, the latter are more than average prone to wicked ways and petty crime' (Aristotle, in Saunders, 1992, p 266). For him, the middle class is the most reasonable of the three classes and produces the best citizens and best political leaders.

The best way to help the poor is to encourage them to become independent farmers, or small business people. Simply giving cash benefits to the poor is not an answer: it merely encourages more demand for the same. Such a policy, he says, is like 'the proverbial jug with a hole in it' (Aristotle, in Saunders, 1992, p 375). The best way to deal with poverty is to encourage prosperity through a rise in self-employment:

> And, since that is to the advantage of the rich as well as the poor, all that accrues from the revenues should be collected into a single fund and distributed in block grants to those in need, if possible in lump sums large enough for the acquisition of a small piece of land, but if not, enough to start a business, or work in agriculture. (Aristotle, in Saunders, 1992, p 375)

Like Plato, however, he distinguished between the deserving and the undeserving poor, as he does in the following quotation in relation to blindness:

> Thus blindness is not an object of censure but of compassion when it is the result of a congenital defect or an illness or a blow. But if it is the result of alcoholic poisoning or general debauchery, then no one has any sympathy with the blind man. (Aristotle, in Thompson, 1955, p 91)

Poverty is a relative concept and though, by modern standards, most Athenians were in poverty, by contemporary standards poverty was concentrated among the slaves, the aliens and the working class, all of whom were not considered part of the citizenry and hence not worthy of the attention of either the legislator or the philosopher. Not unexpectedly, none of the three ideologies made any specific or detailed proposals for the reduction of poverty, though their general inclination was that a good society should attempt to reduce deserving poverty. They were, however, concerned with excessive wealth which they saw, as was pointed out earlier, as inimical to good citizenship unless it was somehow shared with the rest of society. Aristotle's favoured property arrangements, as we saw, were private ownership but common use – an arrangement that went a long way to ensure that dire needs were met and thus absolute poverty was reduced.

Education

Despite the remarkable achievements of Athens in literature, education was not a state responsibility – it was privately provided and privately paid for. It was extensive in the primary and secondary sectors but sparse in the field of higher education. Private academies, such as those established by both Plato and Aristotle, were the precursors of modern universities and attempted to fill the gap but higher education remained the privilege of the few.

Both Plato and Aristotle proposed that education should be a state responsibility; that it should be free of charge; and that it should be compulsory. Under both schemes, the slaves and the working class would be excluded and, in Aristotle's proposals, women would also be excluded. The case for state responsibility in education seemed obvious since individuals are members of society and since education was to serve collective, not simply individual, ends. Aristotle argues that:

> it is not right either that any of the citizens should think that he belongs just to himself; he must regard all citizens as belonging to the state, for each is a *part of* the state; and the responsibility for each part has regard to the responsibility of the whole. (Aristotle, in Saunders, 1992, p 452 [Aristotle's emphasis])

Both writers were also agreed that the aim of education is not utilitarian, designed to promote the material welfare of the individual. The aims of education were twofold and in some ways conflicting: to broaden the mind and to inculcate the values of the ideal society. Even physical training should be seen as part of this process, unlike the situation in Sparta where it was considered as an end in itself. Thus, they both laid more emphasis on intellectual than on physical education per se:

> In my view physical excellence does not of itself produce a good mind and character: on the other hand, excellence of mind and character *will* make the best of the physique it is given. (Plato in Lee, 1987, p 107 [Plato's emphasis])

If education was to socialise the young in the values of the ideal society, it must ensure that from an early age children are not exposed to poems, stories, myths, music and art that convey messages that are in conflict with the new ideology. Plato, more than Aristotle, favoured strong censorship in all these areas. Thus most of the existing poems, stories and myths would have to be replaced for they, according to Plato, portrayed gods as having human desires and weaknesses. For Plato: 'God is the cause, not of all things, but only of good' (Plato, in Lee, 1987, p 76). In the absence of a holy book, such as the Bible or the Koran, 'the source of morality and theology was the Greek poets', as Lee (1987, p 71) observes, and hence the need for censorship:

Socialisation of the young is an inevitable part of all educational systems and it is often a matter of opinion where socialisation ends and indoctrination begins. Plato's educational proposals, however, go beyond the generally accepted limits and this is no surprise for he was trying to use the educational system in his efforts to create a semi-closed society. Yet, Plato was also very anxious to point out that the aim of education was neither to be useful, nor to impart knowledge, but to enable the Guardians to think abstractly – hence his proposal that dialectics would be a central part of the curriculum because it enabled the individual to question long-held assumptions.

Excessive specialisation went against Aristotle's concept of moderation. Indeed, it could be harmful to the individual – mentally and physically. This, coupled with the emphasis on the arts and the humanities, meant that Aristotle's concept of higher education was what came to be known in later ages as that of a 'gentleman scholar'. In Aristotle's scheme, all citizens would go through the entire educational system: the infant school up to the age of seven; the second stage till puberty; and the third till the age of 21. After that, it was a matter left to the individual.

Plato's stages of education were the same as Aristotle's till the age of twenty-one. After that, the whole process of education was different because it was to be used as one of the criteria for selecting the Guardian rulers or, as they became otherwise known, the philosopher kings. At the age of 20, after two years of military service, some men and women will be selected for promotion and further training; the second selection stage is at the age of 30; and the third, and final, stage at the age of 50. The few men and women who are selected at the age of 50 for promotion will become the philosopher kings who will rule. All those left behind at each stage of selection will join the ranks of the Auxiliaries. The selection process took into account not only the person's educational performance but his or her record at war and at work, too.

Plato gave so much emphasis to a thorough, wide-ranging screening procedure for the selection of the future political leaders because he believed that politics is a profession just like any other and because of his belief that the quality of political leadership is central to the progress and welfare of both the state and its citizens. His ideal society will never be achieved, he felt, 'till philosophers become kings in this world, or till those we now call kings and rulers really and truly become philosophers, and political power and philosophy thus come into the same hands' (Plato, in Lee, 1987, p 203). Just to reinforce his commitment to a professional and top-class political leadership, he also, as we have already seen, argued that Guardians should own no property and should have no families of their own. In this way, philosopher kings would become the selfless servants of a rigid and unchanging social system.

The ideal citizen for Plato was someone who was well educated, interested in philosophy, willing to serve his or her country selflessly and who almost renounced all desires for self-promotion. Aristotle's ideal citizen would be a man, not a woman, also well educated and interested in philosophical pursuits, but he was also a worldly man – someone who would also 'live a full social life in the company of his family and friends and will enjoy a moderate amount of wealth and good fortune' (Muglan, 1977, p 6).

Although there are similarities between Plato's and Aristotle's views on education, they differed fundamentally as regards the main goal of education. It was Aristotle's view that came to influence Western systems of education for many centuries.

Conclusion

Athenian society championed the freedom of the individual; his active participation in public affairs and in government; and his right to seek redress in court when necessary. At the same time, it accepted wealth inequalities and poverty; it saw a limited role for the government in economic and social affairs; and it relied on charity for many of what later came to be seen as the state's functions. It tolerated and justified the suppression of women and it accepted slavery as something natural and beneficial to all, including the slaves themselves.

Plato's blueprint for a communitarian society remains to this day one of the most clearly argued and well-reasoned radical treatises. The abolition of the family and of private property, the liberation of women, the lifelong system of education and the emphasis on social harmony have the support of many a radical. Plato's insistence, however, on a professional ruling class that, in practical terms, is largely hereditary, his attack on participatory democracy, the exclusion of the working class from the affairs of the state and his support of slavery are ingredients of a conservative, unequal and oppressive ideology. Nevertheless, Plato's *Republic* remains, even to his severest critics, a classic – 'the greatest book on political philosophy which I have read. The more I read it, the more I hate it: and yet I cannot help returning to it time after time' (Crossman, 1959, p 190).

Aristotle's contribution is his insistence that extremist positions, whether in theory, in politics or in social affairs, are detrimental to human welfare. He was against excessive wealth but in favour of private property; he argued that there is a place for both the private and the public in society; he believed that liberality is a necessary quality in people for it enriches both the givers and the receivers; and his ideas on a liberal type of education greatly influenced educational developments in Europe. His support of slavery, the negation of citizenship rights to the working class and his arguments in support of the inferior position of women in his ideal society were his major conservative and reactionary ideas by today's standards.

Both Plato and Aristotle condemned great wealth inequalities for both ethical reasons and for reasons of social stability. Poverty was equally unacceptable to both but they were prepared to support poor relief for the deserving only and not for the undeserving. Poor relief was best provided through employment measures rather than through cash benefits for free men. Slaves were left to their own devices.

The contribution to ideas on human welfare made by both Plato and Aristotle lies as much on the questions they asked as on the answers they gave. The fundamental question that they asked was: 'What is the nature of a good society and a good citizen and what is the best way of achieving it?'. Perhaps, their major contribution was in the way that they set about answering this question: they moved away from theocratic, mystical explanations in favour of a reasoned, conceptual methodology as the basis for political debates. This may have been their greatest intellectual legacy to Western civilisation.

TWO

The Graeco-Roman world
Epicurus (341–271 BC), Zeno (336–263 BC), Cicero (106–43 BC), Seneca (4 BC–65 AD) and Aurelius (121–180 AD)

Continuity and change have been constant features in the development of ideologies and theories of welfare throughout history. It is rarely possible to assign specific dates to the birth or death of ideologies or theories. They tend to emerge from the past and to merge into the future in gradual ways, sometimes to reappear under different guises later on in history. In most instances, it is impossible to say whether continuity or change is the dominant feature of development. Only in very rare cases is it possible to hazard an opinion.

The development of the various ideologies of welfare during the Graeco-Roman period illustrates these difficulties quite well. Although they initially drew many of their ideas from Plato and Aristotle, they gradually became distinct enough to justify the conclusion that they were different ideologies. It would not be possible to claim with any degree of credibility that either continuity or change was the dominant feature of this development of ideas. Both processes played their part to create something new but also overlapping in several ways with the past.

The period discussed in this chapter begins with the defeat of Athens and the ascendancy of the empire of Alexander the Great and ends with the supremacy of the Roman Empire – from about the 4th century BC to the 4th century AD. It was a world that was different from that of the city-states of Greece in several significant ways and, as such, it was bound to spawn different ideologies. To begin with, it was a far larger geographical administrative unit; trade and travel were far more intense than before; the military victories of Rome ensured a long period of political order; and Rome became a far more affluent and powerful city than Athens.

Although this period witnessed the emergence of several ideologies of welfare – Scepticism, Cynicism, Epicureanism and Stoicism – we shall concentrate on the latter two because they had something special to say about welfare: Epicureanism because it was the first major ideology to put forward a taxonomy of needs for welfare that has stood the test of time, and Stoicism because it became the dominant ideology of imperial Rome. An ideology becomes dominant when it is supported by the elite groups of society, and this can only happen if the ideology serves, or at least does not contravene, the economic and political interests of the elite groups. Stoicism was gradually modified to fit with the demands of the ruling groups of imperial Rome.

The founders of these two ideologies set up their schools in Athens during the period immediately after Aristotle's death. Epicurus (341–271 BC) conducted the discussions with his followers in the garden of his own house in Athens: men and women, free and slaves, were admitted to his commune. Zeno (336–263 BC), the founder of Stoicism, established his school in an arcade, a *stoa*, in Athens and hence the name of his school.

Epicurus (341–271 BC)

Epicurus's supporters came mainly from the propertied and the cultured – they were a minority that was dissatisfied with the competitiveness of city life and the dominance of superstition and religious dogmas in society; they preferred the relaxed life in the countryside; they loved music; and they believed that knowledge could best be gained by experience, through the senses. Their contribution to welfare debates rests on their views on education and human nature, their taxonomy of needs, and their emphasis on emotional contentment as a necessary ingredient of personal welfare.

Unlike the followers of Plato, who stressed the abstract, didactic methods of accumulating knowledge; and unlike many others who believed in the divine source of ideas, Epicureans favoured the materialistic, sensual, experiential method – learning through one's senses and experiences. For this reason they were inclined to play down the importance of formal education, even though they were not against it. Formal education inculcated second-hand ideas and often superstitions to the young rather than encouraging them to acquire first-hand ideas through their own senses. In this, Epicureans shared the same approach to knowledge as Stoics and we shall return to this in the following section. The Epicurean emphasis on experiential learning was adopted by later notable educationists such as Locke, Rousseau, Pestalozzi and others.

The Epicureans rejected the Aristotelian notion of the 'political man'. Unlike Plato and Aristotle who argued that society arose in order to satisfy people's basic needs, Epicureans believed that society arose in order to provide security to its members – to ensure that people do not harm or injure others and are not harmed or injured by others. Without security, there cannot be society – a view later expressed by Aquinas and Hobbes, in particular. Most Epicureans were well off and security has always been very dear to the propertied classes – usually overriding other societal concerns.

The Epicurean view of human beings differed fundamentally from that of Aristotle. While the latter viewed human beings as largely sociable and cooperative, Epicurus saw them as individualistic and self-interested. Human beings, argued Epicurus, have no natural inclination towards community spirit and fellowship. These two conflicting views of human nature have remained, in some form or other, throughout history. The Epicurean view surfaces most clearly in the writings of Hobbes, where the state emerges to provide security because human beings are motivated primarily through aggressive self-interest and are likely to harm one another, in the absence of state intervention.

Being individualistic, human beings were in need of an agreement among themselves that would enable them to live peacefully together. They did this through a contract of justice. Thus their definition of justice differs from that of many others: it is a social contract, not an inborn characteristic, that enables humans to live together in peace:

> The justice of nature is a pledge of reciprocal usefulness, neither to harm one another nor be harmed. (Epicurus, in Morgan, 1992, p 422)

It followed from this that the main aim in life is to satisfy one's own pleasures by avoiding, easing or doing away with pain. This is the core of human welfare – the satisfaction of one's physical and spiritual pleasures. When Epicureans refer to pleasures, they do not mean the sensual or luxurious pleasures of life that have been traditionally attributed to their creed. Pleasure to the Epicureans 'is to be found pre-eminently in serenity of soul' (Copleston, 1946, p 407), as the following quotation from one of Epicurus's few surviving works shows:

> So when we say that pleasure is the goal we do not mean the pleasures of the profligate or the pleasures of consumption, as some believe but rather the lack of pain in the body and the disturbance of the soul. For it is not drinking bouts and continuous partying and enjoying boys and women, or consuming fish and the other dainties of an extravagant table, which produces the pleasant life, but sober calculation which searches out the reasons for every choice and avoidance and drives out the opinions which are the source of the greatest turmoil of men's souls. (Epicurus, in Morgan, 1992, pp 418–19)

Freedom from pain and tranquillity of mind are the essential elements of individual happiness. Human welfare consists in the achievement of these two halves of the same goal. Tranquillity of mind necessitates the rejection of all superstitions and the abandonment of goals in society that put an excessive mental strain on the individual. Involvement in politics and pursuit of wealth or luxuries as ends in themselves should be given up by anyone wishing to achieve spiritual or mental satisfaction.

Human needs are few and simple: Epicurus puts forward a three-part taxonomy of needs or desires:

> Of desires, some natural and necessary, some natural but not necessary, and some neither natural nor necessary but occurring as a result of groundless opinion. (Epicurus, in Morgan, 1992, p 422)

In the world in which Epicurus lived, the first type of need referred to bread and water because one satisfied hunger and the other thirst – they both liberated the individual from pain; the second type of need referred to such things as sumptuous food or expensive drinks, which though natural were not considered necessary for the relief of pain; and the third type of need referred to luxuries such as the erection of personal statues or the wearing of adornments, which were seen by Epicureans as totally unnecessary for human existence. The distinction between the various types of need has always been troublesome in the history of human welfare thought but, when seen in its historical context, Epicurus's taxonomy has stood the test of time. Both Adam Smith and Karl Marx, writing from opposing philosophical viewpoints, adopted a similar position and they both found it equally difficult to distinguish clearly between the various types of social needs.

The Epicurean doctrine required that only the first type of need should be satisfied in order to satisfy one's pleasures. The other two types of need were not only unnecessary for the satisfaction of human pleasures but they were also antithetical because they set up pressures that destroyed mental tranquillity. Needs or pleasures of the second and third variety are relative, they depend on public opinion; as such they are constantly changing and expanding making it difficult for people to achieve them; and thus causing mental stress. The simple life is the best, both physically and mentally:

> Simple tastes give us pleasure equal to a rich man's diet when all the pain of want has been removed; bread and water produce the highest pleasure when someone who needs them serves them to himself. And so familiarity with simple and not luxurious diet gives us perfect health and makes a man confident in his approach to the necessary business of living. (Epicurus, letter to Menoeceus, quoted in Long, 1974, p 67)

Epicurus's emphasis on the simple life inevitably meant that he did not place much value on wealth. He saw it as not only irrelevant to the good life but also as detrimental to it because of the encouragement it gave to unnecessary and unnatural desires. His acceptance of women and slaves among his followers was an advance on previous practice but it did not go much beyond that. There is no argument for the equality of the sexes or of the races in Epicureanism, only that slaves of the household should not be punished and those who prove good servants should be treated with compassion.

Epicureanism stressed three main social values: self-sufficiency, prudence and, above all, friendship. Self-sufficiency stems from the emphasis on the simple life and from the belief that the individual and the community are not interdependent in the fulfilment of their welfare. In the writings of both Plato and Aristotle, the welfare of society meant the welfare of the individual and vice versa. Not so in Epicureanism, where self-interest is the driving force behind the actions of the individual.

Prudence is important because it enables individuals to avoid those acts or situations in life that involve greater pain than pleasure. Such situations are plenty for they include not only the obvious – such as the pursuit of luxury – but also others that may appear worthy but in the end are contrary to the reduction of pain and the achievement of pleasure – an example being involvement in politics.

It is, however, friendship that attracts most praise from Epicurus. Human welfare without friendship is, to him, unimaginable:

> Of the things which wisdom provides for blessedness of one's whole life, by far the greatest is the possession of friendship. (Epicurus, in Morgan, 1992, p 422)

The value of friendship to human welfare is based on two motives: on one hand, friendship can reduce the individual's pain and increase his pleasures in a variety of direct and indirect ways and, on the other, it can also increase the welfare of others. Where there is a conflict between the two, however, Epicureanism stresses the self-interest of the individual.

In conclusion, Epicureanism was a reaction by some of the better-off people against the pressures of Athenian society. Its social values appealed to a cultured minority but not to the ordinary citizens. As such, it was destined to be short-lived as affluence and pleasure-seeking became accepted in imperial Rome. Barker sums up it nicely:

> Epicureanism charmed; but it began – and ended – in charm. (Barker, 1956, p 175)

Stoicism: Zeno (336–263 BC), Cicero (106–43 BC), Seneca (4 BC–65 AD) and Aurelius (121–180 AD)

Stoicism began in Athens, spread to other parts of the East Mediterranean and ended in Rome where it thrived among the men of wealth and social standing. During the first two Christian centuries, Stoicism became the dominant philosophy in Rome for it was able to incorporate or at least accommodate most of the dominant Roman values.

There is general agreement that Greek art, literature and philosophy dominated Rome from beginning to end: 'From very early times Rome had been washed by the tides of Greek culture' (Ogilvie, 1980, p 18). With the defeat of Athens and other Greek cities by Rome, many educated Greeks found themselves in Rome either on their own free will or as slaves to act as tutors and teachers. The Roman poet, Horace, aptly commented that 'Captive Greece captivated her barbarous conqueror' – a view shared by many. Rome's contribution to theoretical debates in philosophy or politics was negligible. Its important theoretical contribution was primarily to save and transmit much of Greek writing in its pure or blended form to the West, to develop practical projects like roads, bridges, viaducts and the like, and to lead the way for good administration.

In its long history, Stoicism had many leaders who did not always speak with one voice; inevitably there are twists and turns, repetitions and contradictions, in the philosophy of Stoicism, some of which will be highlighted here. It is true that early Stoicism 'was suckled in Cynicism', rejecting the formalities and luxuries of life (Barker, 1956, p 23) but it soon found that if it were to appeal to both the general public and the elite, it had to become respectable and useful.

Stoicism has an important place in debates on welfare: it had a good deal to say on the nature of society and government; the importance of law in human life; on debates in education, wealth and poverty; some perceptive comments on old age; and the importance of spirituality as an ingredient of human welfare.

Society and government

There is a dichotomy of views among Stoics concerning the evolution of society and government. One group relies on the notion of the 'Golden Age' in the distant past, when people lived simply and happily together and wise men ruled for the benefit of all and hence the basic needs of all were satisfied. Seneca (4 BC–65 AD) adopted this line of thinking and argued that it was greed and avarice that necessitated the emergence of state institutions. With the rise of luxuries, people became avaricious and hankered after non-essential things, inequality increased, and some people could not have even the basics of life. It, therefore, became necessary for legislation to be passed to control avarice and vice – a view not too dissimilar to Epicureanism. Other Stoics, for example Cicero (106–43 BC), followed the Aristotelian approach that the state arose out of the sociability of human nature, people's natural inclination to help one another meet basic needs.

Whatever the view of the emergence of the state, there is unanimity among the Stoics that the constitution of the Roman Republic was the ideal of all constitutions. It was widely argued that the constitution of the Roman Republic was based on a series of compromises that emerged over the years between the three competing forms of government – monarchy, aristocracy and democracy. It was not a planned constitution in the Aristotelian mould that merged the three together but rather one that contained checks and balances for political stability so that none of them dominated but all three were represented. It is doubtful whether the interests of the three major groups in Roman society were equally represented – plebeian interests often took second place while the interests of slaves were hardly noticed. Nevertheless, this view of the constitution proved influential – it is present in Burke's high opinion of the strengths of the British unplanned and unwritten constitution while the concept of checks and balances influenced Locke and through him the framing of the American constitution.

Contrary to the praises heaped on democracy in Athens by its architects, the supporters of the constitution of the Roman Republic (509–27 BC) praised the absence of democracy. Cicero's dislike of democracy is shown in his view that 'the greatest number should not have most power' in politics (Cicero, quoted in Barker, 1956, p 190). Democracy of the Athenian or even representative type never made it in Rome. As Coleman sums it up:

> Whereas the Athenians exercised equality of political 'rights' the Roman republic never intended to be a democracy. Nor did Roman citizens enjoy freedom of public speech (as did the Athenian democrats). (Coleman, 2000a, p 240)

Any traces of democracy were wiped out with the ascendancy of imperial power. Henceforth, imperial power was vested in the Emperor: it was absolute, capricious and tyrannical. The relationship between Stoicism as a creed and imperial rule was troublesome. Despite the changes in the Stoic creed and the fact that several top government officials and one emperor – Marcus Aurelius – were Stoic leaders, many Stoics died at the behest of the Emperor because of their views.

The virtuous Stoic individual

Human welfare is best served, according to Stoicism, when people live according to Nature, that is, living in association with others in society – not outside society – and according to reason, the gift that unites human beings and also separates humans from animals. All humans possess reason, though in different degrees, and all should live in accordance with Stoicism's basic values if they were to become virtuous: wisdom, courage, self-control and justice. It was a demanding doctrine that few people would manage to meet. Those few who did – the wise – achieved the highest accolade, a virtuous life. Thus in its early days, Stoicism was an elitist doctrine – it allowed for only a small number of people to become wise. With time, this was modified to make it possible for people to achieve virtue in different degrees rather than all or nothing as the initial thesis demanded – a change that made Stoicism a more accessible creed for the general public.

A number of corollaries for human welfare follow from this basic law of Nature and its accompanying value system. First, a person can be virtuous irrespective of material possessions – the rich and the poor, the free and the slave, men and women, can all become virtuous if they live their lives according to the creed. It is this belief that makes it possible for leading Stoics to include in their ranks slaves, high civil servants and emperors. Stoicism certainly discounts the importance of wealth or poverty, health or illness, as necessary parts of human welfare – a view that many have found unacceptable.

Second, personal accidents, illnesses and mishaps should be born without questioning for they are part of human life. The virtuous bear these bravely for they know that suffering is in line with the demands of Nature. It is by this feature that Stoicism is known – the quality of 'the stiff upper lip'. It was a quality that proved necessary in battle and in the aftermaths of battle. The Stoics held strongly to the view that whatever emanated from Nature had a purpose that was beneficent for society and for the individual. Nature knows best and the wise man should accept its will even if he does not understand it. The wise man is free from all passion – he bears his crosses with fortitude. This is how Marcus Aurelius (121–80 AD) put it:

> There are two reasons why you should willingly accept what happens to you: first, because it happens to yourself, has been prescribed for yourself; and secondly, because every individual dispensation is one of the causes of prosperity, success, and even survival of that which administers the universe. (Aurelius, in Staniforth, 1964, p 81)

This line of thought enabled Stoics to explain away human disasters – an approach that has been seen by many as another of the unacceptable faces of Stoicism:

> This optimistic attitude towards natural events, no matter how terrible they may seem, is one of the least palatable features of Stoicism. (Long, 1974, p 170)

Third, the wise man values self-sufficiency – very similar to the Epicurean position. Life's basic needs are few while its relative needs are unlimited. It is the first that must be satisfied for human happiness. Extravagant living should be avoided for it adds nothing to the human spirit. As Seneca rather cutely points out to his friend:

> What you must understand is that thatch makes a person just as good a roof as gold does. (Seneca, in Campbell, 1969, p 46)

Fourth, Stoicism placed a great deal of emphasis on the performance of one's duties in society, whether significant or not. In the early days, Zeno decried involvement in public affairs as a result of the stress he placed on self-sufficiency. Later Stoics, however, realised that in the growing power of Rome such a demand was unrealistic if Stoicism was to become the creed of the people. Public service became a major strand in Roman Stoicism. This could be either in the service of the state or in philanthropic, charitable work. Concern for one's fellow humans was essential for virtue even if it is somewhat contrary to self-sufficiency:

> No one can lead a happy life if he thinks of himself and turns everything to his own purpose. You should live for the other person if you wish to live for yourself. (Seneca, in Campbell, 1969, p 96)

Fifth, human welfare involved the acceptance of religion. Unlike the Epicureans, who rejected religion as nothing more than a web of superstitions, the Stoics found an important place for God in their philosophy. They rejected the ceremonial aspects of religion but accepted its usefulness in human welfare. The Stoic view of religion was also in line with that of the Roman state. Religion played a big part in the lives of ordinary Romans even though problems arose with the multiplicity of religions vying for state recognition during the imperial era. One of the notable strengths of Roman administration was its pragmatic approach to many problems, as in the case of religious diversity:

> Pressure was too great, and of necessity the state tolerated all religions provided they were not immoral, or politically dangerous. (Barrow, 1949, p 142)

Religions that were seen not to observe this were persecuted, as Christians found to their cost during the first few centuries AD. Christians refused to make 'a demonstration of loyalty to "Rome and Augustus"' and paid the penalty, as a result (Barrow, 1949, p 178).

Sixth, the belief that all human beings possessed reason so that they could act in accordance with the demands of Nature led the Stoics to conclude that a basic equality existed among all. This was not equality of genetic abilities or equality of outcome but equality of reason and of respect – in the last analysis, equality before the law. Without this legal equality, society cannot exist in concord. In his book, *The Republic*, Cicero expresses the notion of equality as follows:

> If equality of wealth is out of the question, and if, again, all cannot have an equal degree of mental ability, the rights of all citizens belonging to the same commonwealth ought certainly to be equal – for what is a State but a partnership in a system of Right. (Cicero, quoted in Barker, 1956, p 201)

Seventh, this equality of reason and of respect extends not only to all in the same society but to all citizens of the world. The distinction that the Greeks long ago made between themselves and the *barbarians* now disappears. This did not mean that national identity should be abandoned but rather that it should be supplemented by a world-view of life. Wearing his Stoic hat, Emperor Marcus Aurelius declared:

> My own nature is a rational and civic one; I have a city, and I have a country; as Marcus I have a Rome, and as a human being I have the universe; and consequently, what is beneficial to these communities is the sole good for me. (Aurelius, in Staniforth, 1964, p 101)

Natural and civil law

It is in the treatment of law rather than of philosophy that the Stoics, and indeed Rome, made their most significant contribution to human welfare. This is best epitomised in the work of Cicero first and the Roman Jurists later. They distinguish between civil law, which relates to individual nations, and natural law, which is not simply the product of the minds of legislators but the result of the workings of Nature. Natural law is, therefore, universal and eternal in character; civil law is human made and country specific:

> There will not be one law at Athens and another at Rome, or one law now and another in the future: all nations, at all times, will be bound by one eternal and immutable law: there will be one God who is common to all men and, as it were, their master and ruler; and He it is who advises, debates and enacts the law. (Cicero, *The Republic*, quoted in Barker, 1956, p 196)

Nevertheless, Cicero was enough of a politician to realise that the demands of the law of Nature were far too harsh and was prepared to modify the implementation of the law so as to make allowances for human frailties:

> The lesson is clear: the unmitigated and pure natural law may be inapplicable to the normal human situation. The natural law to which the activities of man and states are normally to be referred must be a diluted version of this law, one whose standards are necessarily lower. (Cicero, *The Laws*, quoted by Holton in Strauss and Cropsey, 1963, p 147)

The codification of law under Emperor Justinian published in 533 AD was based on the theoretical work of Cicero and of the Roman Jurists of the 2nd and 3rd centuries AD – Gaius and Ulpian, in particular. Despite the fact that Roman Emperors ruled in absolute fashion and contrary to the codified law, the spirit of the codified Roman law was preserved and was passed on to become 'a permanent factor in European political civilization' (Sabine, 1963, p 173).

Despite all efforts to make Stoicism relevant to the needs of Rome, it failed to become the doctrine of the masses (Barrow, 1949, p 160) because it overemphasised human duties and sacrifice to the detriment of human rights and material welfare. All it promised the ordinary people was a life of 'blood, sweat and tears' – in marked contrast to the opulent lifestyles of the rich. It tried to soften the blow by declaring excessive wealth as unacceptable and poverty as not being a bar to human happiness. The baton was passed on to Christianity, which eventually became the official religion of the Roman Empire – only to commit similar mistakes.

Slavery

Both the Epicureans and the Stoics parted company with the views of Plato and Aristotle on the issue of slavery. 'There is no change in political theory', says Carlyle, 'so startling in its completeness as the change from the theory of Aristotle to the later philosophical view represented by Cicero and Seneca. Over against Aristotle's view of the natural inequality of human nature we find set out the theory of the natural equality of human nature' (Carlyle, 1962, p 8).

Aristotle saw slavery as a natural social institution because some human beings are so inferior to their fellows that they are by nature servile and benefit from the tutelage of others. Epicureans and Stoics considered slavery as against Nature and hence immoral. Slavery was seen as the result of military defeats, as an accident, rather than as the result of biological differences. Slaves were simply defeated soldiers who were sold as hired labourers but none of the prevailing creeds claimed that slaves were inferior to Roman citizens in the eyes of Nature. They, too, had reason that they could develop – and many of them did it very well indeed – and could achieve virtue.

The change in attitude came about in no small measure as a result of the large number of Greeks who were brought to Rome as slaves to act as tutors and teachers. It was difficult to maintain the argument that the teachers to Roman citizens and to their children were mentally inferior! This change in attitude brought about pleas for a kinder and more humane treatment of slaves. Seneca, in a letter to his friend, explains that while slaves are not enemies to their masters when they are first acquired, they become enemies later because of the cruelty they have to endure. Treat them, he says, as human beings, if you want to retain their loyalty:

> Be kind and courteous in your dealings with a slave; bring him into your discussions and conversations and your company generally. (Seneca, in Campbell, 1969, p 93)

Yet none of the major philosophers demanded the abolition of slavery, simply because it was so important to the economy of Rome, just as it had been to that of Athens. Slaves worked as domestic servants, civil servants, on the large farms where quantity was more important than quality, in industry, as apprentices in many trades including as gladiators, and as tutors to rich families. Cruelty to slaves was not uncommon though it came under increasing criticism and was eventually constrained, though not prohibited, by law. Slaves were allowed to have their own property, many of them were freed on the death of their master, and together with the poorer free men organised social clubs, which provided social amenities and took care of the funeral of their members.

With the completion of the Roman Empire, however, it became increasingly difficult to find new supplies of slaves; masters had to ensure a greater productivity from their slaves; and it was beginning to be realised that 'the nearer the lot of the slave approached that of a free man, the more useful he was' and hence the economic justification for the abolition of slavery (Barrow, 1949, p 99). By the end of the 4th century AD, slavery was a declining institution. Some see this in pure materialist terms, that is, 'not as a result of the abolitionist movement but in consequence of complex social and economic changes' (Finley, 1972, p 165). Yet, it would be wrong to discount completely the contribution that ideology made to this. Economic forces were important, perhaps the most important factor, but 'it is not necessary to overlook the influence of the sentiment of human nature on social conditions' (Carlyle, 1962, p 50). Eventually, slavery disappeared in Europe only to be replaced by a new form of human bondage – serfdom.

Despite the changes in attitudes in some circles, and the pleas for more humane treatment of the slaves, there is no doubt about the cruelty that masters administered to their slaves. There was no effective legal protection against this either during the early or late Roman Empire, not too dissimilar from the situation in Classical Athens:

> Roman law allowed the slave-owner to punish, sell, or even kill his own slave with impunity. (Coleman, 2000a, p 268)

The fact that the law 'treated slaves as chattels who had no legal right to marry and whose parent–child relations were nonexistent in formal law' was enough justification for the maltreatment of slaves (Dixon, 1992, p 58). In real life, families among slaves did exist and they brought up their children but, legally speaking, the master was legally entitled to intervene according to his interests. The most dramatic way was that 'many children were sold at an early age without their mothers and that brothers and sisters were separated' (Dixon, 1992, p 10).

The position of women

Neither Epicureanism nor Stoicism stressed the equality of men and women as strongly as they did the equality in Nature of slaves and free men. Both doctrines made passing references to the fact that all human beings, including women, are of equal worth in the eyes of Nature but neither dwelt long enough on the implications of this principle to the position of women. All writers in both schools were men and obviously did not feel that women received a raw deal in society, despite the fact that by today's standards they evidently did.

The position of women in Rome was not that different from that of women in Athens discussed in the previous chapter. In Rome, women were at the mercy of the male head of the family:

> Save for minor exceptions, a woman was always in the power of some man – of her *paterfamilias*'. (Finley, 1972, p 127)

Women took no part in politics, in war or in paid employment. Indeed, it could be argued that the position of women was better in the early years of Rome when most women worked in the family farms than in imperial Rome when many stayed at home. It is also probably true that working-class women were in an abstract sense more free than middle-class or aristocratic women who had no work to occupy them. On the other hand, however, working-class women had a much harder life, for freedom has to include an economic dimension if it is to be fully meaningful.

Roman law paid a good deal of attention to marriage and divorce, to legitimacy and illegitimacy of offspring for primarily economic, property, child-care, inheritance and social reasons. Arranged marriages were the norm and they always made provisions for dowries. The law did its utmost to make marriages between free and slave impossible, particularly where it involved a free woman marrying a slave man. Once married, the woman ceased being in bondage to her father and became the chattel of her husband. Husbands could kill their wives for adultery and they could divorce or punish them severely for minor reasons, as the following examples illustrate:

> The husband took a cudgel and beat his wife to death because she had drunk some wine.
> He divorced his wife because he had caught her outdoors with her head uncovered.
> He became the first Roman to divorce his wife for sterility. (Cited in Lefkowwitz and Fant, 1992, pp 96–7)

Seneca denounced these punishments of women and argued for the education of women. But this was a negligible effort compared to the amount of time he allocated to slavery, self-sufficiency, living according to nature and so on. A lesser-known Stoic, Musonius Rufus, of the 1st century AD, was one of a few to make a strong defence of women's equality to men. His thesis was based on a series of propositions:

> Women have received from the gods the same ability to reason that men have.
> Women have the same senses as men, sight, hearing, smell, and all the rest.
> Women are pleased no less than men by noble and just deeds, and reject the opposite of such actions. (Rufus, quoted in Lefkowitz and Fant, 1992, pp 50–1)

In view of this commonality of abilities between the sexes, there was an unanswerable case for the education of women to be on a par with that of men, he argued. This is not just a matter of fairness but also of benefit to society: educated women will be better mothers, wives and housewives than uneducated women; they will be braver, more able to defend themselves; and will be better Stoics, able to face hardship and death.

Because of their different physical attributes, however, men and women should not be expected to do the same jobs. Since 'the males are naturally stronger, and the women weaker, appropriate work ought to be assigned to each, and the heavier tasks be given to the stronger, and the lighter to the weaker' (Rufus, quoted in Lefkowitz and Fant, 1992, p 53).

Unfortunately, Rufus does not follow through on his argument that men and women possess reason equally and how this relates to political, administrative or legal jobs where muscle power is irrelevant. He does, however, make a strong case for marriages to be based on the equality of the sexes, on mutual respect, caring and consideration, 'in health and in sickness and at all times' (Rufus, quoted in Lefkowitz and Fanti, 1992, p 54). In an uncanny way, Rufus's view of marriage depicts the Christian ideal.

Another lesser-known Stoic, Dio of Prusa, later known as Chrysostom (40–112 AD) also came to the defence of women, particularly in relation to their exploitation in the labour market and as prostitutes. He criticised the exploitation of women in the labour market and argued for prostitution to be made illegal for two basic reasons: it offended human honour; and it corrupted society rather than protecting the virtue of other women, as many others then claimed.

In brief, the defence of women by most Stoics was weak and ineffective. Similarly, the Stoic view that was reflected in the Roman legal code was concerned with the protection of patriarchal marriage, the family, inheritance issues, the bringing up of children and so on, rather than with the welfare of women.

Wealth and poverty

Stoics adopted a double standard in their conception of wealth and poverty. On one hand, they were clear that neither wealth nor poverty impeded or facilitated the achievement of virtue – the highest dream of Stoicism. On the other hand, Stoics acknowledged that if one had to choose between wealth and poverty it was rational to choose wealth because it made for a more comfortable life. After all, Cicero, Seneca and Aurelius – the three high priests of Roman Stoicism – were very rich men but they argued that this did not help or hinder them in their pursuit of virtue. Long expresses this rather unusual logic as follows:

> The value of wealth is relative to poverty, but wealth has no value relative to virtue. (Long, 1974, p 192)

Closely connected with this was the debate on private property. Some Stoics saw extensive private property as a form of historical misappropriation of common property from the days of the 'Golden Age' onwards. It was unethical and, moreover, unnecessary for human happiness. Some Stoics, Cicero and the Jurists, saw it quite differently. They acknowledged that private property might have come about in both licit and illicit ways: as a result of long use, through victory at war and through legal agreement. They also acknowledged that private property has to be put partly to social use – but not as far as Aristotle's thesis of private property and communal use. But at the end of the day, private property is sacrosanct in the eyes of the law and governments have the duty of protecting it. Governments, says Cicero, have a duty to protect the welfare of their citizens;

to treat all sections of the public fairly; but above all they have a legal and moral duty to protect private property:

> The first object to be pursued in the government of the commonwealth is that all should be secured in their property, and that private possessions should not be diminished by public action. (Cicero, in 'On Duties', cited in Barker, 1956, p 202)

It was the second view of private property – the just, rational and sacrosanct – that prevailed. Aristotle's view of ethical property ownership dominated the Middle Ages, while the Roman Jurist view served 'as an important basis for the legal doctrines and institutions of capitalism' (Roll, 1961, p 38). It was incorporated in the legal systems of the West and became one of the major pillars of capitalism.

In real life the ethical view of property never came to much because it presupposed a degree of altruism not often found in human societies. Instead of this blanket view of altruism, defenders of property, such as Cicero, saw altruism in concentric circles: beginning with the immediate family, extending to friends and then to others. The further out it travelled, the weaker it became. Its usefulness for public welfare was thus limited.

There is no outright condemnation of poverty in the writings of the major figures of Stoicism because poverty was, as pointed out above, compatible with the achievement of the ideal Stoic man – a view that was very similar to the Christian way of thinking, as we shall see in Chapter 3. It is one of the lesser-known figures of Stoicism, Dio of Prusa, later called Chrysostom, who dealt with poverty and the required policies for its reduction. One of his orations dealt with the problem of urban poverty and the need for reform, described by Barker as 'a sketch of social policy, and a plan of social welfare, which has hardly any parallel in classical literature' (Barker, 1956, p 299). He raises the well-known dilemmas of urban poverty: the shortage of jobs for the unskilled, the low pay of unskilled occupations, the hazardous nature of many of them and the difficulties of alternative employment. People with low or no wages and with 'no capital of their own except their bodies' find it difficult to meet even their basic needs – house rent, clothes, furniture, food and 'the wood to keep a fire going' (Dio of Prusa, quoted in Barker, 1956, p 295).

What then is to be done? Ideally, jobs should be created in the city but as this was not an immediate possibility, other policies were needed. He was against the practice in Athens where the authorities attempted to deal with the problem by paying fees to the public in order to attend public meetings, to act as jurors or to serve as clerks in the civil service. Such a scheme only bred 'a mob at one lazy and vulgar' (Barker, 1956, p 999). He, therefore, proposed the resettlement of the poor in the immediate countryside where they would be given land, free from rent for the first 10 years and thereafter at a small part of their annual produce. The employment approach was certain to produce men 'who were in all respects better and soberer' than the mob produced by the cash welfare payments. This is perhaps the first recorded comparison between the two approaches to the relief of poverty – cash benefits versus employment policies – one to be despised and the other to be applauded.

The sparseness of debate on poverty was not due to the absence of the problem, objectively speaking. Rome amassed wealth of unprecedented proportions but it was highly concentrated and was used for a life of luxury for the few. Poverty was widespread and grossly ignored, as the following quotation shows:

> Such luxury went hand in hand with the degradation of the poor and the underprivileged, the slaves who provided the labour, the gladiators and others who provided the amusement, the peasants who provided the means of existence. (Ogilvie, 1980, p 187)

The neglect of the poor by governments in imperial Rome was worse than it was in Athens despite the legal requirement that 'destitute parents were entitled to maintenance by their children'. It was an ineffective requirement because, then as now, it is usually the case that destitute parents have destitute children (Dixon, 1992, p 58).

Education

Stoics valued education but did not dwell on it for long. Cicero discussed at length the kind of education that existed in the Roman Republic and spoke highly of its contribution to society or at least to the ruling groups of society. Seneca valued practical education but condemned too much theorising. Rome, in brief, contributed very little to either the theory or the practice of education.

During the days of the Roman Republic, education was a family affair. It was the responsibility of the parents to teach their children how to read and write, how to be religious and how to obey their elders and the laws of the state. This was in contrast to the kind of education that existed in Greek cities that concentrated not only on the basics but also on music widely defined to include literature, poetry and singing.

The growth of the Roman Empire witnessed, as we have seen, the arrival of large numbers of Greek teachers to educate both adults and children. Indeed, the Greek language became the medium of teaching and learning in Rome until it was itself replaced by Latin, which, in turn, became the scholarly language of Western Europe:

> Greek methods, Greek models, Greek ideas came to be dominant in Roman education; and these largely in the hands of Greek teachers. (Wilkins, 1914, p 3)

Despite all this, the Athenian education system with its strong emphasis on the development of both body and mind never flourished in Rome for at least two reasons. As an imperial power, Rome needed a good supply of soldiers, administrators, builders of roads and bridges rather than an abundance of men of letters. Secondly, the authoritarian and often capricious rule of many Emperors acted as a strong impediment to the flowering of ideas. This is not to suggest that Rome has nothing to say in the literary field – rather that its record was disproportionately inferior to its achievements in the areas of law and government.

The arrival of Christianity had a mixed effect on education in Rome. On one hand, it encouraged the growth of a new wave of religious teachers but, on the other, it viewed with hostility the literature of the past because of its 'pagan' nature. Many eminent Christians of the period 'came to regard the literature of Greece and Rome as pagan and immoral, and its charms as a sinful temptation' (Knowles, 1973, p 67). It was not until Christianity itself felt secure that it was able to accept and to benefit from 'pagan' knowledge – but this was not to happen until the end of the first Christian millennium.

Old age

Despite the fact that people died young, discussions on old age can be found in both the Greek and the Roman literature. Cicero's essay on old age written in 44 BC is one of the best of its kind. It draws upon the writings of several Greeks, including Plato, and it anticipates many of the debates in today's gerontology.

He identified and criticised four reasons that were commonly given to explain and justify old people's lives. First, old age involves withdrawal from work that gives people income and status and this happens because there are no jobs suitable for old people. He accepts that many occupations need physical strength but points out that 'there are also occupations fitted for old men's minds and brains even when their bodies are infirm' (Cicero, 1971, p 219). Politics and farming are the two occupations *par excellence* for old people, he argued. The early Romans had recognised this and that is why they named 'their highest council the "Senate" – which means the assembly of old men' (Cicero, 1971, p 221). It was farming, however, that appealed to him most. With their knowledge and experience, their love of the countryside, old people were ideally suited to farming – an honourable occupation. As he puts it, 'the cultivation of the soil is one of the activities which age does not impede up to his very last days' (Cicero, 1971, p 237).

The second reason, closely related to the first, is that withdrawal from work was both biologically necessary and beneficial to the individual. Cicero accepts that old age does involve a gradual reduction in physical and mental ability but this is neither as rapid nor as undifferentiated as it is often made out. The physical deterioration argument also ignores the important point that many vital jobs in society require thought and wisdom – qualities that increase rather than decrease with age:

> Great deeds are not done by strength or speed or physique: they are
> the products of thought, character, and judgement. And far from

diminishing, such qualities actually increase with age (Cicero, 1971, p 220).

As for the mental deterioration, he agrees that memory declines with age but this only happens 'if you fail to give it exercise, or if you are not particularly intelligent' (Cicero, 1971, p 221). Old people have a selective memory for the things that are relevant to their life. His strong advice is for people to keep active, particularly mentally, during their life, for this is the surest way to prevent faculty decline.

He rejects the conventional Roman view that early retirement from work improves and prolongs one's life:

> I never agreed with that much-praised ancient proverb which advises taking to old age early, if you want it to last long. Personally, I should rather stay old for a shorter time than become old prematurely! (Cicero, 1971, p 225)

The third reason why people complain about old age is that it involves an extinction of sexual activity. He agrees that there is a reduction, though not extinction, of sexual activity in old age but he considers this a blessing rather than a curse. He quotes no less an authority than Plato to reinforce his argument that the sexual lust of the young 'will drive men to every sin and crime under the sun' – rape, adultery and crime (Cicero, 1971, p 228). Old age should therefore be welcomed for it reduced the biological sexual drives of lust. There are more important things in life, anyhow; and as an intellectual nothing competed with learning, he claimed.

Fourthly, old age is feared because of its proximity to death. True enough, death is a natural event in human life and cannot be avoided but he cautions against the belief that death is restricted to the old. Many people die young, even though they expect to reach a ripe old age. His tentative belief in the immortality of the soul gave him more strength to face death calmly and with his usual intellectual sharpness, he remarks:

> Even if I am mistaken in my belief that the soul is immortal, I make the mistake gladly, for the belief makes me happy, and is one which as long as I live I want to retain. (Cicero, 1971, p 247)

In Cicero's view, most of the problems attributed to old age are socially constructed. In the first place, the way people live their adult lives affects the quality of life in old age. Money, wealth and status are potential advantages to happiness in old age but they are insufficient in themselves – they need to be complemented with proper work and good life habits. In the second place, there are many misconceptions about old age, often shared by old people themselves, which need to be corrected before old age is seen as what it is – a period in life with its pluses and minuses.

Activists today will be heartened by his call to self-help action to change the status of old age:

> Age will only be respected if it fights for itself, maintains its own rights, avoids dependence, and asserts control over its own sphere as long as life lasts. (Cicero, 1971, p 227)

Cicero's essay remains fresh and relevant to this day. Its main failing is none other than the failing of many debates in ancient times: their concern with the few in society and their neglect of the majority – the slaves and the workers. What Cicero wrote about old age rings largely true but he grossly underplayed the significance of low income to the quality of life in old age.

Conclusion

The Epicureans' major contributions to welfare debates were, first, their taxonomy of needs and their insistence that human welfare could best be met by adhering to basic needs only. Chasing after other needs only increased the stresses of everyday life. Second, they were among the first to stress education through experience rather than through abstract reasoning – a view that found support among many progressive theorists in subsequent centuries; third, their love of nature and their belief that serenity of spirit was an integral part of human welfare; and, fourth, their departure from the Classical Greek view that human beings are by nature social and cooperative animals and their adoption of the competitive view of human nature that was to become the hallmark of Hobbes' work, as we shall see in Chapter 5.

Stoicism made two major and related contributions to the world of ideas on human welfare: first, it introduced the powerful notion of human equality in marked contrast to the Platonic and Aristotelian view of human inequality. Its immediate benefits may have been limited but it was the yeast that fermented the radical ideas of individual liberty that proved so potent in later centuries in relation to politics, slavery, gender relations and class aspirations.

Second, the work of the legal Jurists of Rome, and the codification of Roman law in line with the ideas of natural justice, formed the basis of later work and had a profound effect on the relationship between government and citizens in later periods. There was, the Jurists argued, a natural law of justice that was over and above national laws, and which rulers must observe in dealing with their subjects. The rulers received their authority to rule from the general public – an essential germ for democracy – a view that was rejected by early Christian thought, as we shall see in Chapter 3, and which did not resurface until the writings of Locke in the 17th century.

The Stoics' view of poverty and wealth rested on the assumption that human welfare does not depend on the possession or consumption of material goods. They argued most strongly that poverty was not a handicap and wealth was not an advantage to the good life – the virtuous life. The downside of this approach was an acceptance of poverty and a lack of interest in debates as to how best to prevent and ameliorate poverty or how to reduce wealth inequalities.

THREE

Early Christianity
St Augustine (354–430), St Francis (1182–1226) and St Thomas Aquinas (1225–74)

The advent of Christianity has been one of the most significant events in the history of Europe and Western civilisation. Its teachings have had a profound influence on the lives of individuals and societies; and on ideas concerning the satisfaction of welfare needs. The New Testament and subsequent leading churchmen had a great deal to say about welfare, which affected people's lives then and since.

In this chapter, we are covering the first 13 centuries AD – from the very early period of Christianity, through the Middle Ages and down to the years immediately prior to the Renaissance. It is a highly eclectic discussion focusing on human welfare issues. The chapter is divided into four sections: The New Testament and human welfare; St Augustine; St Francis; and St Thomas Aquinas. It is a period that was dominated by the ideas of churchmen viewing individuals and their problems from a Church perspective (Russell, 1991, p 303).

The New Testament and human welfare

The Christian value system

Like all other religions, Christianity, through the New Testament, is preoccupied with social values, with perceptions of the ideal, that is, with discussion of what is desirable and what is not, how humans should behave and how they should not and how they should live their life in accordance with God's will.

The value system of the New Testament differs fundamentally from the value system of advanced industrial societies in the sense that it is more divine than secular, it emphasises the importance of God in people's lives above all else. Human welfare is perceived more in religious than in secular terms. Human needs are both spiritual and physical but the first are primary to the second. It is a hierarchy of needs that is different from those put forward in modern times where physical needs – food, clothing, housing and so on – are seen as primary while spiritual needs are considered secondary with the implication that physical needs must be satisfied first before other needs can be considered (Maslow, 1970).

We will concentrate on the four Christian values that had direct implications for welfare: faith, love, equality and obedience. Faith is the paramount social value of

Christianity as, indeed, of all other religions – faith in God through Jesus Christ. The ideal human being is someone who has a strong faith in God through Jesus Christ and who lives his or her life according to God's teaching. Faith in God through Jesus Christ demands the acceptance of proposals that may appear harsh or illogical to the human mind. God's wisdom is all-embracing, far-reaching and sometimes beyond human understanding. Faith demands that one's daily life is, first and foremost, in line with God's word rather than with earthly affairs. Put in a different way, an individual who has no faith in God through Jesus Christ is not someone to be highly esteemed even if he or she may be excellent in other aspects of life; nor is he or she likely to go to Paradise.

The second social value – the one most crucial to welfare as it is understood today – is love for one's enemies as well as one's neighbours. Christ was unequivocal on this: there is no point in loving and helping one's friends and neighbours only. A true Christian must extend their love and helpful hand to their enemies as well. Love involves willingness to make sacrifices for the benefit of others. Only by doing so can a peaceful and religious Christian world be created where basic needs are met for all:

> But to you who are listening to me I say, Love your enemies; seek the welfare of those who hate you; bless those who curse you; pray for those who revile you. To him who gives you a blow on one side of the face offer the other side also. (Luke VI: 27–30)

Jesus illustrates the love of one's enemies through the story of the Good Samaritan urging his followers to act in the same way. Jews and Samaritans were bitterly hostile to each other but when a Jew was robbed and beaten half-dead on an isolated road, he was ignored by Jewish passers-by while a Samaritan passer-by took pity on him, 'dressed his wounds with oil and wine and bound him up', then took him to an inn 'where he bestowed every care on him', and paid the innkeeper enough to carry on caring for him as well as promising to pay any further expenses incurred (Luke X: 30–7).

The value of charity may be seen as an integral part of the value of love. Giving to those in need without any material benefit to oneself was seen as an expected duty of Christians. Paying one's taxes for the provision of benefits and services to all is a modern implication of the value of love; giving to charities is in line with the value of charity.

The third social value is that of equality, interpreted in a different way from previous ways. In the State of Innocence, in their life in the Garden of Eden, humans were equal and lived happily together. It was the original sin committed by Adam and Eve that led to the Fall of human beings from God's grace and hence to the collapse of the happy, egalitarian way of life.

Despite the Fall, however, all human beings remained equal in the eyes of God as far as salvation was concerned. St Paul expresses this in one of his letters, perhaps more clearly than others, as follows:

> In Him, the distinctions between Jew and Gentile, slave and free
> man, male and female, disappear; you are all one in Christ Jesus.
> (Galatians III: 28)

This does not mean that early Christianity argued for the equality of human beings in their everyday life – merely that they all have an equal chance of becoming good Christians and of being accepted by God.

The fourth social value of Christianity that features strongly in the New Testament is that of obedience. Three facts must be borne in mind in order to understand the Christian emphasis on obedience: first, Christians were under suspicion for seditious activities, they were persecuted, and many of them died at the hands of the Roman authorities during the first few centuries. St Paul was therefore anxious to show that there was no good reason for this hostility to Christianity. Second, the emphasis on the importance of life after death of necessity downplayed the significance of political affairs in this world. It is not that this world was ignored; rather that the next world was seen as more important and obedience to God was paramount. Third, social order was essential to the achievement of welfare, religious and secular, and obedience played a significant part in it.

Unlike the Roman Jurists who claimed that the ruler's authority was derived from the people and could legitimately be questioned, Christianity insisted that it derived from God. The ruler was God's representative and, as such, he should be obeyed even at times when people may have doubts about the rightness of his actions. Obedience rather than questioning of the ruler's authority was the central message of the early Christian doctrine. It was a view that would dominate political affairs during the Middle Ages, as we shall see later in the chapter:

> Let every individual be obedient to those who rule over him; for no
> one is a ruler except by God's permission, and our present rulers have
> had their rank and power assigned to them by Him. Therefore the man
> who rebels against his ruler is resisting God's will; and those who thus
> resist will bring punishment upon themselves. (Romans XIII: 1–3)

This obedience to the ruler, however, was confined to the affairs of this world and not to those of the next. For the first time, a major conflict point was created regarding the relative authority and influence between Church and state. Christ's word on this issue is clear in theory but full of ambiguities in its practical application, for it is not always clear what issues are religious rather than secular. Many human actions contain elements of both and it is a matter of opinion how to categorise them:

> Render therefore unto Caesar the things which are Caesar's; and unto
> God the things that are God's. (Matthew XXII: 21–2)

The next few hundred years were dominated in Europe by the debate over the exact boundaries between the authority of Church and state. The debate was resolved in favour of the Church with the result that the Pope's authority overshadowed that of the king's – a situation that lasted until the Reformation, when the state began gradually to assume the upper hand.

In brief, the early Christian value system was rather different from that of today – it was more divine than secular; it emphasised the importance of God more than the consumption of material goods in people's lives. Human welfare was perceived more in religious than in secular terms – a hierarchy of needs different from today's where physical needs are seen as primary and spiritual needs as secondary.

Slavery

The early Christian view of slavery follows closely on the Stoic position discussed in Chapter 2. In the same way that Stoics saw slavery as the result of the collapse of the State of Nature and of the growth of human greed, Christians saw it as the consequence of the Fall from God's grace after the Original Sin. To the Stoics, the cause of slavery was not to be found, as Aristotle argued, in the inborn inequalities among humans but in the newly created social conditions where exploitation of one human by another became acceptable. Slavery was a socially created condition and not a biological necessity. To the Christians, too, slavery was not the result of biological differences but a condition that was created by human misbehaviour and which was sanctioned by God.

The stress on obedience in the Christian creed reinforced the institution of slavery. This applied to all aspects of life – the family, the political arena, gender relationships, as well as to slavery. St Paul's advice to slaves and to their masters bears a strong resemblance to that of Seneca discussed in Chapter 2:

> Slaves, be obedient to your earthly masters, with respect and eager anxiety to please and with simplicity of motive as if you were obeying Christ. (Ephesians VI: 5–6).

He counters this by counselling the masters to be kind to their slaves – much as Cicero and Seneca did but supporting his advice by reference to God:

> And you masters, act towards your slaves on the same principles, and refrain from threats; for you know that in heaven there is One who is your master as well as theirs, and that merely earthly distinctions there are none with Him. (Ephesians VI: 9)

Several other Christian pronouncements had the effect of strengthening the hold of slavery on society. It was considered illegal for slaves to run away from their masters; for anyone to aid and abet such escapes; for slaves to become ministers of religion; and so on.

Although the early Christians fully accepted the institution of slavery; they also made it clear that slaves could live a virtuous life; they could become good Christians; and they could be accepted by God, in much the same way as free persons. Not unsurprisingly early Christianity did not consider slavery as a social problem – an attitude very similar to that found in the Classical Greek literature. The connection between slavery and Original Sin became part of the Christian tradition and it took many centuries before people ceased thinking of 'slavery as sin' (Davis, 1966, p 90).

Whatever the dominant view on slavery was, practice was always more complex as the following story involving St Paul shows:

The story of the slave Onesimus

Onesimus was a slave to Philemon, a friend of St Paul's. He ran away from his master taking with him some of his master's possessions that would help him on his travels. He made his way to Rome where he could more easily avoid detection and where he could enjoy the pleasures of a big city. After a while, however, he attached himself to St Paul where he became a Christian and a most trusted servant. Loath as he was to lose him, St Paul felt it was his duty to send him back to his master. He did this giving Onesimus a letter in which he asks his friend Philemon to forgive Onesimus and to treat him not as a slave but as a fellow Christian and a trusted servant.

(Summarised from St Paul's Letter to Philemon, written in about 63 AD)

The position of women

Unlike slavery, which was seen as the result of the Original Sin, the subordination of women to men was considered to be the result of biological factors and in keeping with God's will for He created man and woman. Most of the quotations concerning gender relationships come from St Paul, who, in several ways, reflected the then prevailing ideas and practices on gender relationships. The perennial problem in interpreting the New Testament is to decide which parts of the teaching are perennial and which are ephemeral.

The primary reason why women were inferior to men, according to St Paul, was that they were made so by God in the first place:

Man does not take his origin from woman, but woman takes hers from man. For man was not created for woman's sake, but woman for man's. (I Corinthians XI: 7)

The secondary reason was that Eve, it was argued, shared more of the blame than Adam for the Original Sin, an indication of women's greater weakness and a justification for the heavier punishment that they should receive.

As a result, women should show their inferiority in a variety of ways: they should cover their heads and they should keep silent in church. Above all, they should obey their menfolk — fathers and brothers; married women should obey their husbands without questioning in the same way that husbands should obey Christ:

> Married women, submit to your own husbands as if to the Lord; because a husband is the Head of his wife as Christ also is the Head of the church. And just as the church submits to Christ, so also married women should be entirely submissive to their husbands. (Ephesians V: 21–4)

If wives were to show blind obedience, husbands had a duty to love and cherish their wives in the same way that they looked after their own selves and as Christ sacrificed himself for the benefit of the Church. Gender relationships should at one and the same time be both unequal and loving — a blend of emotions that may be acceptable to men but which is hardly appealing to women — the weaker member of this relationship:

> Married men, love your wives, as Christ also loved the church and gave Himself up to death for her…. So too married men ought to love their wives as much as they love themselves. (Ephesians V: 25–30)

Christ's approach to women, unlike that of St Paul, was one of acceptance, judging from some of his actions. Two such situations can be quoted: the first is the fact that women were the first to witness Christ's resurrection which, it can be argued, was symbolic of Christ's more enlightened view of women. The second case concerned Christ's conversation with a Samaritan woman who had been separated from her previous five husbands and who cohabited with a sixth. He showed acceptance of a stigmatised form of behaviour, particularly behaviour from a woman of a hostile ethnic group.

Marriage and divorce

The institution of marriage existed long before the arrival of Christianity. What Christian doctrine did was to try to regulate marriage according to its own morality that was far more stringent than the prevailing Roman morality. A good deal of disagreement surrounds the interpretation of the numerous statements in both the Old and the New Testament regarding the nature of marriage, its dissolution and its reconstitution (Adams, 1980). Here, we shall simply summarise what we consider the main conclusions from this debate.

Several reasons are given for the desirability of marriage. First, and foremost, marriage is the institution that meets the needs of both parents and children – the implication being that single status is, for most people, not the desirable way to live:

> And man shall leave his father and his mother and shall cleave to his wife and the two shall become one flesh. (Genesis, 2: 24).

There are exceptions to this rule. Some men and women have the capacity and God's blessing to live a single life – or rather a life of celibacy – in order to serve God's will. This is strongly emphasised by St Paul who seems at times to argue that a life of celibacy is preferable to marriage for it provides both men and women better opportunities to serve God:

> An unmarried man concerns himself with the Lord's business – how he shall please the Lord; but a married man concerns himself with the business of the world – how he shall please his wife. (I Corinthians VII: 33–5)

Second, marriage provides the only acceptable way for procreation, in the eyes of God. Children born out of marriage are, therefore, stigmatised and also find themselves at a legal disadvantage with regard to such family matters as inheritance.

Third, marriage provides the only acceptable method for sexual satisfaction to Christians, since 'fornication', adultery and homosexuality are roundly condemned:

> It is well for a man to abstain altogether from marriage. But because there is so much fornication every man should have a wife of his own, and every woman should have a husband. Let a man pay his wife her due, and let a woman also pay her husband his. (I Corinthians VII: 2–4)

Fourth, marriage provides the ideal way for human companionship. After all, God provided Eve not simply as a helper of Adam but as his companion, and vice versa. Indeed, some argue that companionship was the major reason that God intended marriage for (Adams, 1980, pp 11–12).

Since marriage is a divine institution, it follows that it must be permanent and broken only in rare and exceptional cases through divorce. Adultery is the only reason that can be used as adequate grounds for divorce:

> Whoever divorces his wife for any reason except her unfaithfulness, and marries another woman, commits adultery. (Matthew XIX: 9)

St Paul referred to divorce several times in his letters and his words indicate that divorce should be rare and that it should not immediately lead to remarriage – time should be allowed for reflection with a view to reconciliation:

But to those already married my instructions are – yet not mine, but the Lord's – that a wife is not to leave her husband; or if she has already left him, let her either remain as she is or be reconciled to him; and that a husband is not to send away his wife. (I Corinthians VII: 10–12)

The situation is different in cases of widowhood where remarriage is acceptable:

A woman is bound to her husband during the whole period that he lives; but if her husband dies, she is at liberty to marry whom she will, provided that he is a Christian. (I Corinthians VII: 39)

Although Christian teaching on marriage and divorce was based on the philosophy of women's inferiority to men, many of the proposals were an advance over existing ideology and practice such as abandonment of wives at will and polygamy – two practices that were condemned by Christianity.

Wealth and poverty

Christian thought on wealth began by downplaying the usefulness of wealth because life on this earth, important though it is in itself, is essentially a preparation for eternal life. Although they are both important to the individual Christian, the second takes precedence, and this should be taken into account in his or her daily activities:

Do not lay up stores of wealth for yourself on earth; but amass wealth for yourself in heaven. For where your wealth is, there also your heart be. (Matthew VI: 19–21)

Unlike Stoicism, which was prepared to accept wealth under certain conditions, early Christian thought saw it simply as a disadvantage to a person's eternal life. The accumulation and the ownership of wealth run counter to the Christian way of life. It is for this reason that Christ referred very explicitly to the difficulties that rich people have in going to Heaven:

It is easier for a camel to go through the eye of a needle than for a rich man to enter the Kingdom of God (Mark X: 25)

On the other hand, a simple way of life is a much better basis for preparing for God's Kingdom. Jesus Christ's words on the occasion of the blessing of young children point to this:

It is to those who are childlike that the Kingdom of Heaven belongs. (Matthew XIX: 14)

Wealth is a handicap to salvation but like other handicaps it can be put right, as evidenced in Christ's reply to a rich man's question as to what he should do to go to Heaven. Having first advised him to obey the Commandments, Christ added the following when the young man said that he had already done all that:

> If you desire to be perfect, go and sell your possessions, and give to
> the poor, and you shall have wealth in Heaven; and come, follow me.
> (Matthew XIX: 20–2)

Related to this is Christ's advice on helping the sick, the hungry, the homeless, those in prison and other groups of the dispossessed. Those who helped the dispossessed would secure their place in the 'Life of the ages' while those who did not 'shall depart into the Punishment of the ages' (Matthew XXV: 31–46).

Not only did early Christianity adopt a hostile view to wealth and a very sympathetic view of poverty but it also implied that poverty would always exist. When a woman poured over Christ's head some expensive ointment, and his disciples protested at the waste because the money could be better spent on the poor, Christ commented:

> The poor you always have with you, but me you have not always.
> (Matthew XXVI: 11–12)

On the practical side, there is enough evidence that some of the early Church communities were organised on a communistic basis. This is well documented in relation to the Church in Jerusalem where membership was open to all Christians but on the presupposition – though not an obligatory requirement – that new members would share their property with all the others so that everybody's needs were met:

> And all the believers kept together, and had everything in common.
> They sold their lands and other property, and distributed the proceeds
> among all, according to every one's necessities. (Acts II: 44–6)

Alms-giving featured strongly in early Christianity partly because it was the only practical way of relieving poverty and partly because it would ease the donor's path to salvation, provided it was given willingly and altruistically:

> Let each contribute what he has decided upon in his own mind, and
> not do it reluctantly or under compulsion. It is a cheerful giver that
> God loves. (II Corinthians IX: 7)

St Paul, however, was anxious to stress that people should not remain idle and simply rely on charity for their living. People, he argued, had a responsibility to work, to look after themselves and their families, as well as to lead clean lives. Those who willingly avoided work should receive no charity and should be allowed to starve – one of the strongest condemnations of the 'undeserving poor', as the following quotation shows:

> But, by the authority of the Lord, we command you, brethren, to stand aloof from every brother whose life is disorderly. If a man does not choose to work, neither shall he eat. For we hear that there are some among you who live disorderly lives and are mere idle busybodies. (II Thessalonians III: 6–12)

St Augustine (354–430)

St Augustine has been one of the most controversial as well as most influential of ecclesiastical philosophers. His two main books, *Confessions* and *City of God*, are classics in Christian literature. His major contribution to debates on welfare stems from his fundamental premise that spirituality is the most essential ingredient of human welfare; the fulfilment of secular pastimes is secondary to human welfare. He was not the first to say this – Epicureans and Stoics also stressed it – but he was the first to make it the centrepiece of his philosophy.

He firmly believed that human reason was limited and insufficient by itself to bring about the satisfaction of a spiritual form of human welfare. In his *City of God*, he portrays human beings as 'wretched creatures tossed by impulses which they can struggle to subdue but will never master' (Haddock, 1988, p 71). Like Hobbes after him, he saw human beings as self-centred, pursuing their own desires irrespective of community interests. Human beings had to be controlled if peace in society was to be maintained. Unlike Plato and Aristotle, he did not believe that this could be achieved through educational means alone. It had to be reinforced by the coercive powers of the state – 'deprivations of property, liberty, and life' (Deane, 1963, p 235).

As a result of his pessimistic view of human nature, he downplayed the importance of politics in human welfare and, as one of his admirers describes him, he was a 'minimalist' in political affairs (Von Heyking, 2001, p 16). Governments were important but there was a limit to what they could achieve. Politicians and human beings have such a strong capacity to self-destruct that we should not have high expectations from governments. We should be pleased with even modest political achievements. As Von Heyking puts it, 'finding a political order that at least provides clean drinking water and functioning public utilities should be maintained and cherished' according to Augustine's views (Von Heyking, 2001, p 16).

A minimalist rather than a comprehensive welfare state is in line with Augustine's views. He would also counsel against any political strategy that was based on the belief that changing political institutions could by itself improve society. This could only happen if people's mindsets changed and that could only be achieved through faith in God.

The inherent sinfulness of human beings coupled with their limited powers of reasoning lead to the only conclusion possible: human beings need God's guiding hand if they are to create a tolerable way of life. God's intervention in human affairs can take both rewarding and punitive forms. In his *City of God*, St Augustine explains the rise of Rome as being due not only to the hard work of the Romans themselves but to God's decision to reward them for their endeavours. Vice versa, the decline of Rome was the result of the corruption of Roman society as well as of God's decision to punish the Romans for their irreligious behaviour. Like the Stoics before him, he viewed human suffering as a necessary means to redemption. Suffering is like medicine – unpleasant but necessary. Unless this is clearly understood, there is the danger that the Christian God may appear vengeful, just like some of the Greek and Roman deities.

He carried his belief in the usefulness of punishment to extremes when he advocated the wholesale coercion of heretics – justified, of course, as being for their own long-term good. It is for this reason that he has been called 'the father of the Inquisition and the prince of prosecutors' (Markus, 1988, p 113).

As a result, he saw slavery as the inevitable result of the Fall from Grace: it was an unnatural institution but necessary both as a punishment and a remedy for sin. For St Augustine:

> Slavery is penal; it is both the just punishment for man's sin and a remedy for sin. (Deane, 1963, p 114)

Slaves should obey their masters and the latter should show consideration to their slaves. They should both remember that they are the children of God. Moreover, slavery to sin is far worse than slavery to another human being – a view that would have found few, if any, supporters among the slaves!

On gender issues, he followed closely the biblical line: women are inferior to men and they should obey men; he approved of strong discipline within the family but insisted that it should aim at benefiting all the members of the family; he strongly supported the institution of marriage and strongly opposed easy divorce.

His views on poverty are noteworthy, for he argued clearly in support of state poor relief as a matter of right. In a religious society, private property should be used not only for the welfare of its owners but for the support of the poor, too. In his *City of God*, he argues that only in societies dominated by worldly preoccupations are the rich allowed to dominate the poor. He often refers to the unjust treatment of the plebs in Rome and advocates 'feeding those without their own land from the public treasury' (quoted in Von Heyking, 2001, p 103). In brief, the poor had a *right* to state poor relief – this was a major contribution to welfare debates. Like many others before him, he distinguished between the deserving and the undeserving poor, using the degree of shame felt by the poor as the criterion. Those who felt no shame should be treated less generously than those who did.

His attitude towards private property and wealth was 'neither favourable nor completely hostile' (Deane, 1963, p 108). It was not so much the possession of wealth that was the issue but the use to which wealth was put and whether covetousness entered the equation. A wealthy man that used wealth simply to accumulate more was committing a sin. This is why St Augustine was so critical of moneylending, which he saw as simply usury. Wealth should be put to the service of God. But if the poor had a right to state support, they also had a duty to ensure that they were not envious of others; that their desires were not inflated; and they did not feel aggrieved because they were poor.

St Francis of Assisi (1182–1226)

The 800 years that separate St Augustine and St Francis were marked by a number of major changes that inevitably had strong implications for debates on welfare: the collapse of the Roman Empire, the consequent emergence of a plethora of states, the replacement of slavery by serfdom, the ascendancy of the Church over the state and the suppression of free debate by Medieval Church authorities. The latter part of this period witnessed a number of major socio-economic changes: a rapid growth in commerce, banking and wealth; an increase in population and a movement from the rural to the new urban centres even though the vast majority still lived in the rural areas; a growth in schooling and a rise in literacy; and the first signs of a value system that was less traditionalist and more in tune with the growth of the new urban-based market forces – 'the seed of capitalism was sown' (Coleman, 1988, p 608).

Religious sects

This new social, political and economic environment of the towns proved a fertile ground for the rise of a number of lay and religious sects that were troubled by the opulent lifestyles and behaviour of many of the new rich and high Church dignitaries.

The 12th century saw at least three such sects. First there were the Waldensians, otherwise known as the Poor Men of Lyons, who gave up their property to live in poverty, criticised the power of the Pope and the presumption of clerical superiority over the laity, asserted that women as well as men were capable of preaching and demanded the adoption of ecclesiastical poverty. The second was the Cathari, otherwise known as the Pure or the Albigenses, who favoured common ownership, renounced marriage and sex, adhered to a strict diet and fasting, stressed monasticism, and relied for their living on alms and charity. The third was the Amalrichites, who taught gender equality and appealed to both the restless serfs and ambitious townsfolk. They all drew their inspiration from the early biblical teachings, discussed at the beginning of this chapter, and in their different ways they were demanding a more egalitarian society and a return to Christ's teachings and lifestyle.

All these and other sects lacked organisation and they were easy preys to Papal persecution. They were attacked and defeated by the Church and the state, and many of their members were imprisoned or executed. The fundamental reasons behind the rise of these sects, however, remained – the disillusionment with the established Church and the search for a more satisfying religious way of life.

The Franciscan friars

St. Francis began his Order with a few supporters who were prepared to follow his example: sell their property, give the proceeds to the poor, rely for their daily livelihood on the food given to them by others as payment for their work, live a humble life, and preach the Gospel. He wanted his friars 'to cut adrift entirely from the commercial system of the world' (Lambert, 1961, p 38). The basic principles of his movement were:

> Humility, Simplicity, Poverty, and Prayer are the four foundation stones on which St Francis built; and each was worked out on the basis of a literal obedience to the recorded sayings of Christ. (Moorman, 1968, p 3)

Almost out of sheer necessity all his early followers were of wealthy background for, as Lawrence astutely observes, voluntary poverty has no appeal to those who are already poor. Indeed, the poor by birth have a different ambition: they 'dream of getting rich' (Lawrence, 1994, p 34). As the Order expanded, however, it recruited from a wider social background and became one of the largest religious Orders of the times.

St Francis was no philosopher; he was a humble practical man. He did, however, lay down the rules that his followers should adopt. The Rule, which he enunciated in 1221, prescribed a life of destitution that went beyond any of the demands made by other Orders. The main demands of the Rule for all friars were as follows:

- sell your property and give the proceeds to the poor;
- work daily for your living;
- accept no money for payment;
- accept only food as payment;
- dress simply and wear your clothes till they are threadbare;
- sleep rough;
- seek alms when no work is available;
- have no regular place of abode of your own;
- be on equal terms with the poor and the dispossessed;
- preach the Gospel – particularly repentance and penance;
- all friars are equal in the Order.

St Francis was anxious that his Order did not become a monastic Order where the monks had no individual property but they shared the common property of the monastery. In other words, he envisaged the apostolic type of poverty rather than the poverty of the Church of Jerusalem where all the members pooled their wealth with each other so that no one was in need. It was a far more demanding type of poverty because communal ownership can easily provide a very comfortable way of life – as, indeed, happened in many monasteries. Individual monks owned nothing but they lived a very comfortable life (Lawrence, 1994, p 60).

Four profiles of poverty

The Franciscan movement highlighted the issue of poverty at the very beginnings of a commercial, capitalist society. It is worth summarising the various profiles of poverty that emerged during the period coved by the first three chapters in this volume – from Plato to St Francis – for they continued through the subsequent centuries. They were: the deserving poor, the undeserving poor, the apostolic poor and the criminally minded poor.

From the very early days, both Plato and Aristotle distinguished between the 'deserving' and the 'undeserving' poor. The 'deserving' merited sympathy and charity, for it was not their fault they were in poverty; and they were also ashamed of their poverty. They should be rewarded for all this: help should be given willingly, liberally, tactfully and, preferably, in secret. The 'undeserving' were themselves to blame for their poverty; they were brazen with their impoverishment; and they should either be made to look after themselves or, if helped, they should be constantly reminded of their responsibility for being poor. This distinction continued throughout the period we covered. It is, indeed, a distinction that has survived to the present day.

The third category of the poor – the apostolic poor – emerged with Christianity. They were those who made a conscious decision to give up their wealth, either to share it with others or to distribute to the poor, in order to follow Christ and to live a simple and religious life. Like the undeserving poor, they brought the poverty unto themselves and they were quite contented, if need be, to rely on the charity of others for their daily living. Unlike them, however, they had wealth that they willingly gave up for a very moral and religious reason, they were prepared to work, and they were men of character ready to suffer physically so as to serve their God and improve their chances for spiritual salvation.

The fourth category – the criminally minded poor – made its appearance at the end of the feudal era and the beginning of commercialisation – the end of the 13th and the beginning of the 14th centuries – when many of the landless rural poor, usually young males, made their way to the towns in search of work and money. Many found themselves in trouble with the authorities, eruptions of violence were not uncommon and 'poverty came to be a synonym for drifting and uprootedness' (Coleman, 1988, p 626). Like the 'undeserving' poor, they were to be ostracised and treated harshly, for they were seen to be themselves responsible for their condition. Additionally, they were considered as either seasoned or potential violators of the law – a dangerous species worthy of all the attention that the law could inflict on them.

Poverty at around this time was on the increase due to the disintegration of the feudal system and the rural migration to the towns. Coleman defines the poor during this period 'as those who do not possess a minimum of arable land sufficient to support a family; a family of four, say in the 13th century required 4 hectares'. With this definition, she estimates that at around 1300, 'between 40% and 60% of the European peasantry had insufficient land to maintain a family' (Coleman, 1988, p 625).

The apostolic poor, as a category, lapsed with the commercialisation and industrialisation of European society. The other three categories have survived down to the present day, though the 'criminally minded' poor are to be found not so much in the cities of the affluent world as in the expanding cities of the impoverished, developing countries. Traditional ideas of the causes of poverty have survived over the centuries despite the plethora of research evidence that contradicts some of them. What has changed, however, is the language used to describe these categories today – a softer, less stigmatising discourse.

St Thomas Aquinas (1225–74)

Aquinas's importance to welfare debates stems from his views on the nature of government, the contrast between private and public property, his taxonomy of needs, and his views on poverty, wealth, slavery and gender. His two major books, *Summa Theologiae* and *On Kingship*, combine Aristotle's analytical approach with the prescriptive thrust of St Augustine. While Aristotle used reason as the best way of understanding the world, Augustine stressed faith. Aquinas attempted to combine reason and faith in his treatment of both political and social issues in order to arrive at conclusions that combined rationality with faith:

> It enables him to develop a theory that maintains a middle position
> between faith and reason, rationalism and empiricism, individualism
> and collectivism, and authority and participation. (Sigmund, 1988,
> p xxiii)

Government and welfare

Aquinas parts company with the Christian Fathers, who maintained that in the ideal early society there was no government simply because there was no need for it. He adopts Aristotle's view that human beings are sociable creatures but they are also unequal in many ways and have a tendency of disagreeing among themselves in the pursuit of their goals. It is evidently true that 'the private good and the common good are not the same. Private concerns divide the community, while common concerns unite it' (Aquinas, *On Kingship*, ch 1, in Sigmund, 1988, p 15). The need for government is, therefore, inherent in any society.

Aquinas is clear that the primary aim of government is 'to promote the welfare' of its people: this includes not only material needs but also security and peace because:

> Without peace life in society is no longer beneficial and its divisions make social life burdensome. (Aquinas, *On Kingship*, ch 2, in Sigmund, 1988, p 17)

He rejects both tyranny and democracy: the first leads to the government being used for the benefit of one person, while the second means discord and lack of direction. Following Aristotle, the best form of government is monarchy, preferably with the king being elected either by the community or by a council so that he can be held to account and be asked to resign if he flouts his mission. This, however, must be the very last resort because, like the Christian Fathers, Aquinas believed that the ruler derives his power from God. The ruler has a duty to serve the interests of the community while the ruled have a duty to obey the ruler. Only in very extreme cases are demands, let alone actions, for the resignation of the ruler justified.

Aquinas stresses, however, that there are limits to what governments can achieve through legislation alone. This is not the same as the pessimism of Augustine with regard to government action; rather he is anxious to stress, first, the importance of other institutions concerned with welfare, the most important of which is the family; and, second, the significance of social conscience that stems from the Christian value of 'love thy neighbour as thyself'. Government action must always be supplemented with familial and community support if it is to be effective in dealing with the various social problems.

Private versus public property

Aristotle saw private property as natural to human beings while the Christian Fathers saw it as the result of the Fall. Aquinas attempts to combine these two positions by arguing that though property may have, at some time in the past, been held in common, it became private 'by the inventiveness of human reason' (Aquinas, *Summa Theologiae* II-II, q. 66, in Sigmund, 1988, p 72). In other words, private property exists not by natural or by divine law but by laws made by human beings for practical reasons.

He does not merely tolerate private property; he sees it, as Aristotle did, as superior to common property for three reasons: it encourages incentives, efficiency and order in society:

> First, because everyone is more careful to procure something that concerns himself alone than something that is common to all or to

many others; second because human affairs are handled in a more orderly fashion when each one goes about his own business, there would be complete confusion if everyone tried to do everything; third, because this leads to a more peaceful condition for man, while everyone is content with what he does. Hence we see that among those possessing something in common, disputes arise more often. (Aquinas, *Summa Theologiae*, II-II, q.66, in Clark, 1988, p 383)

Private possession does not, however, mean exclusive private use of property. Bearing in mind that natural or divine law is superior to human law, it means that the use of property must be common to some extent even though it is privately owned. Thus, Aquinas is led to the conclusion that basic human needs must be satisfied for all out of existing private property before anyone makes any profit out of it. As he puts it:

> the division and ownership of things that proceed from human law must not interfere with the alleviation of human needs by those things. (Aquinas, *Summa Theologiae*, II-II, q.66, in Clark, 1988, p 384)

Many have interpreted Aquinas's views on private property as eternal and as relevant to today's world. Some, however, have questioned this because the practical reasons given by Aquinas for private ownership have been lost in contemporary societies where ownership of large businesses is in the corporate hands of shareholders who take no active part in the daily running of organisations (Solar, 1988, p 180).

Poverty and a taxonomy of needs

In order to make some sense out of this double principle of private possession but common use, Aquinas classifies resources and needs into three kinds: first, those resources required to satisfy basic needs for physical survival; second, resources required for secondary needs – for the education of one's children, the support of one's relatives, the continuation of one's business and for paying one's debts; and, third, whatever resources are then left over to be used for other purposes.

People whose resources are not sufficient to satisfy their basic needs are entitled to take anything from other people's property to meet their needs and this does not constitute a theft, morally or legally. Moreover, someone whose resources exceed those for basic needs has a duty to give assistance to others whose basic needs are not satisfied, unless he knows that the needy persons have relatives who can help them.

Those in secondary poverty are morally entitled to relief from those whose resources exceed both basic and secondary needs. This, however, is very difficult to establish because secondary needs are very vague and flexible and hence enable anyone wishing to evade their duties to do so quite easily. The same applies to basic needs but to a far lesser extent. Aquinas acknowledges these problems but believes that they cannot be settled by legislation – only through the spirit of liberality and of common sense on behalf of everyone. He is a great believer in the value of communal social responsibility encouraged by the state to act where the law cannot. Internal controls are necessary for the regulation of human behaviour.

The formula of private possession but common use always raised the question of incentives. Why should any private property owner try to improve the productivity of his property if its proceeds were to be used to meet common needs first? The question may not have been that relevant during Aristotle's or St Paul's days because self-sufficiency was the guiding principle of production but one could argue that it assumed more urgency during Aquinas's times when commercialism and profit-making were on the rise. Aquinas does not seem to be concerned with this because he argues that profit-making, though legitimate, should not be excessive because it encourages avarice, which, in turn, dehumanises people.

He lays a great deal of emphasis on the Christian value of 'love they neighbour' and he calls for the development of a community spirit where men would be willing to share their wealth with the poor. Although he ends up with charity as the main method of relieving poverty, it is a form of charity based on the rights of the needy and the duties of the dispensers. He did not make a case for legally enforceable individual rights but perhaps his clear call for the support of the poor and the right of the poor to take property when in dire need may have been a step in the direction of individual rights to and state responsibilities for poor relief.

Slavery

Aquinas's view on the origin of slavery is very similar to that of the Stoics and of the Christian Fathers and different from Aristotle's. In their original state all men were equal but the Original Sin meant that slavery became acceptable as an institution for private gain. This is despite his view that even in Paradise there were inequalities of both physical and mental power. This kind of inequality is part of nature but slavery is not – slavery, like property, is conventional, created by human decision and action. It exists by human law and not by divine or natural law.

Like all Christian Fathers, he asks for obedience on behalf of the slaves and good treatment on behalf of the masters. But he also adds that slaves, too, have such basic human rights as 'the right not to be killed, deliberately harmed, raped or used for any extra-marital sexual services' (Finnis, 1998, p 185). On the other hand, a slave cannot enter Orders unless and until he becomes a free man; the marriage of a slave to a free person can only be valid if the free person had prior knowledge of the impediment of slavery; and a slave could not enter politics.

Despite the fact that slavery was very much on the wane by Aquinas's time, he defends it because he sees its origins in theological terms. As was said at the beginning of the chapter, faith is a fundamental value to Christianity and one of its implications is that God's decisions must be accepted even if their justification is not always clear to humans. Aquinas was first and foremost a Christian and then a philosopher. Faith rather than reason is the medium for comprehending the implications of the Original Sin.

The position of women

Aquinas accepts the sexism inherent in the writings of the New Testament and the Christian Fathers. He rejects Aristotle's view of the woman as 'a misbegotten man' but accepts St Paul's view that women were made by God to be inferior to men, and that Eve's responsibility for the Original Sin was greater than Adam's. Women's inferiority is thus the result of both the Original Sin and of nature – religious and physical reasons – a combination that makes change even more difficult.

With this gender inequality taken for granted, he accepts the scriptural view that woman was made as a helpmate for man, and he adds: 'not to help him in other work as some have said – since he can get more effective help from another man – but as a helpmate in reproduction' (Aquinas, *Summa Theologiae* I-I, q. 92, in Sigmund, 1988, p 37). As if that was not enough to highlight women's inferiority, he adds that even in reproduction the woman's role is inferior to that of man:

> Perfect animals possess the active power of reproduction in the male sex and the passive power in the female sex. (Aquinas, *Summa Theologiae* I-I, q. 92, in Sigmund, 1988, p 37)

This inequality continues into marriage: wives are to obey their husbands; although both parents are responsible for the upbringing of their children, the father has the ultimate responsibility. Aquinas justifies this on the grounds that men are physically, intellectually and emotionally stronger than women.

Although he is not against women becoming queens, he supports the existing practices whereby women were totally excluded from any political participation either as voters or as candidates.

As with slavery, however, Aquinas accepts that women are equal with men in the eyes of God and as a result they are entitled to some basic rights – physical security, satisfaction of basic needs, ownership of property and choice of religion. These are small concessions to an otherwise very sexist approach. Writing from a feminist perspective, Archibald argues that women's position in Aquinas's theory (and indeed in all the Christian literature discussed in this chapter) is in one important respect inferior to that of the slaves:

> For the slave there is the possibility of escape from dependence and tutelage to freedom; for the woman there is none. (Archibald, 1988, p 141)

In brief, one cannot but agree with the wry comment of one of Aquinas's sympathetic critics that his theory on gender relationships is 'open to notable improvement' (Finnis, 1998, p 176).

Conclusion

The emphasis that the New Testament placed on faith and obedience was stressed throughout the period covered by this chapter and had the obvious effect of creating a conservative society with advantages and disadvantages. Its main advantage was that it helped to reinforce social order in society that was fundamental to human welfare; its main disadvantage was that it stifled intellectual debates and innovatory practices thus helping to create an intolerant society that culminated in the persecutions and executions of the Inquisition.

The Christian attitude to slavery and gender was full of contradictions from the start, though it remained pretty constant throughout the period. On one hand, it preached the equality of all human beings in the eyes of God, and, on the other, it stressed the inferiority of slaves and women. Christian teaching and practice helped to strengthen the bonds of slavery though it failed at the end, for the new commercial economic forces were undermining the very institution of slavery until it disappeared altogether only to be replaced by serfdom. Christianity may have provided more security to women through the institution of marriage for life but at the cost of encouraging the belief and the practice of male superiority. It can be argued that Christianity simply reflected current practices in these two fields but this raises the obvious question of what is ephemeral and what is eternal, what is secular and what is divine – the dilemmas of all religions.

The truly radical idea of Christianity was the value of extending one's love not only to friends and neighbours but to strangers and enemies as well. Modern redistributive taxation policies and universal welfare state provisions can be justified on this principle both at the national and international level. Christian teaching during the period under discussion in this chapter interpreted the principle in much narrower terms – generous charitable giving by the wealthy to the poor. It accepted wealth provided it was put not only to individual use but also to the service of the community. The Church made no sustained effort to reduce poverty and in the end came to accept the opulence not only of laymen but also of the high-ranking clergymen in the midst of widespread misery. The Popes and the upper clergy lived a life of corruption and luxury alongside the nobility and the rising commercial class.

FOUR

The Renaissance
Desiderius Erasmus (1467–1536) and Thomas More (1478–1535)
The Reformation
Martin Luther (1483–1545) and Jean Calvin (1509–64)

The late Middle Ages were 'the threshold and the foothold' of the Renaissance and the Reformation (Lindberg, 1996, p 24) for they witnessed the societal changes that contained the seeds for a gradual break with the past: the rise in trade and banking, the rural migration to the towns, the rediscovery of Greek learning, the impact of Arabic culture through the crusaders, the rise in literacy, the increased public perception of Church corruption and hence of anti-clericalism, the emergence of social values in support of wealth accumulation, the growth in nationalism that was anxious to reduce the power of the papacy, the near abolition of serfdom, and the explorations that led to the discovery of the New World.

Despite these changes, early 16th-century Western Europe was still a primarily rural society with a subsistence economy where most people earned their living from agriculture. The household was still the basic economic unit, producing primarily for consumption, and selling and buying only at the margin. It was a strictly hierarchical society where social mobility was at its bare minimum; it was also a grossly unequal society where most of the land was owned by the nobility and the Church. The dominant spirit of the age was still obedience to those above you in the social hierarchy – people knew their status in life and tried to behave accordingly. The endless pursuit of wealth was still 'tainted with the sins of covetousness and avarice' (Wrightson, 2000, p 57). Poverty was endemic and semi-starvation was never far away for the masses in both the towns and the countryside. Western Europe may have been on the verge of entering the new world but was still largely in the world of the Middle Ages.

It is within this broader socio-economic environment that the ideas discussed in this chapter should be understood: the ideas of two Renaissance humanist writers – Erasmus and More – who argued for moderation, tolerance, open-mindedness and the enhancement of public welfare; and of the two main leaders of the Protestant Reformation – Luther and Calvin – who wanted to replace one religious orthodoxy with another, perhaps less worldly and opulent and more concerned with public welfare.

Desiderius Erasmus (1467–1536)

Many of the major literary figures of this period belonged to that branch of the Renaissance that has come to be known as humanism, an intellectual movement that was concerned with the emancipation of the human spirit from the narrowness of Church morality in all aspects of life; and with the promotion of the idea that life on this earth need not be 'simply a vale of tears, a wearisome journey that the Christian must take on his or her way to the kingdom of God in heaven' (Ball and Dagger, 1991, p 31). Erasmus, writes McGrath, 'stands head and shoulders above other northern European humanists' (McGrath, 1988, p 53); he is 'more than any other man, the symbol of humanism' (Bronowski and Mazlish, 1960, p 84). His place in a discussion of welfare is warranted by his work in education, his criticism of religious narrow-mindedness, and his belief in the goodness of human beings.

His proposals both in the field of education and poor relief stem from his fundamental belief that human beings are good by nature and can be guided both by their reason and by education to become community-minded (Spinka, 1953, p 291). In contrast to St Augustine and Luther, he asked his fellow Christians to use their reasoning in their everyday life but always remembering the teachings of Jesus, particularly the fundamental value of love thy neighbour.

> Where Luther was convinced of the utter helplessness of the human creature, Erasmus believed in the perfectibility of man by his own effort. (Caspari, 1968, p 61)

This basic belief in human goodness informs Erasmus's views on education. He argued for an educational system along the Classical Greek lines that took account of the physical, intellectual and moral needs of the individual. He believed that classical education 'aids spiritual growth and minimizes the importance of elaborate dogma' (Spitz, 1963, p 201). He wrote a large number of educational books that were widely used in schools, all advocating the importance of both the classics and the scriptures. He saw no major difficulties in combining classics and scriptures, reason and religion in the curriculum of schools. His model of a liberal Christian education was ahead of its time and influenced only a minority of elite schools. English public school education remained, until recently, as Erasmus would have wished: 'a thorough grounding in Greek and Latin, involving not only translation, but verse and prose composition' (Russell, 1991, p 502).

Education for Erasmus had that magical quality, first advanced by Plato, of shaping the minds and the attitudes of both rulers and ruled to the benefit of the whole community. The good society can be achieved through the appropriate educational system. Unlike Plato, he spent little time discussing the details of his educational system and had no time for explicitly rigid indoctrination in the school curriculum. Like Plato, however, he overemphasised the power of education in structuring society. He ignored the other side of the argument, that is, that education reflects society and, as a result, educational proposals that run openly counter to the spirit of the times are unlikely to be accepted.

He argued for universal education although his views on the education of girls were progressive by the standards of his period but not necessarily by contemporary perspectives on gender. Education for women was necessary, he argued, not only as a matter of 'social justice and for women's own well-being' but also in order to prepare them for their major role in life as wives, mothers and house managers. His writings, along with those of other humanists, 'contributed to the advocacy of female education but did so ambiguously at best' (Cousins, 2004).

Unlike many humanists of his period, he was not a nationalist. He put his faith in cosmopolitanism and pacifism. He travelled widely, visiting England several times where, according to Russell, 'he liked the fashion of kissing girls' (Russell, 1991, p 500). He did not identify with any nationality and he considered himself a citizen of the world. Like his friend, More, he was against war except in self-defence, and argued for the peaceful resolution of national conflicts through arbitration and compromise. The title of his pamphlet *War is sweet to those who do not know it* became a slogan for subsequent pacifists (Spitz, 1963, p 228). His position on both issues – nationalism and war – was personally uncomfortable at a time of emerging nationalism and spreading national conflicts in Europe.

Like other humanists, he was concerned with the rise in poverty and argued for the reorganisation of poor relief so that lay authorities could assume more responsibility. Many humanists were involved in the reorganisation of social welfare, including the Church poor relief system of Nuremberg in 1522, which set the scene for similar reforms in other cities in Germany and elsewhere. Humanism, however, was an intellectual movement propounded by learned people many of whom, including Erasmus, were dependent on the nobility and the Church for their livelihood. Their views on political and social welfare issues were always within the bounds of acceptability of their benefactors. Erasmus, for example, was quick to condemn the Peasants' Revolt in Germany, despite its very modest demands, on the grounds that it encouraged anarchy, that is, it undermined the authority of the Princes. He repeatedly argued that tyranny is preferable to what he considered 'mob rule'.

His satire on the institutions of his time, particularly the Church and the clergy, expresses his humanism in a way that could, he hoped, be conducive to change and reform. He poured scorn on the foibles of all social classes, professions, husbands and wives but he aimed his most penetrating arrows at the abuses of the Church leaders, the clerics and, above all, the celibate monks. He earnestly believed that in this way he would shame the Church into reforming itself into a more caring and less corrupt institution. Like many other humanists, he felt that the Church was in dire need of reform but this should be achieved without splits, let alone violence. His belief in the power of education again led him to underestimate the difficulties of such a project. Humanism was an intellectual movement addressing itself to the cultured classes and it was prone to accept the cosy but mistaken message that 'the pen is mightier than the sword'; reform can best be achieved through rational persuasion. Reality, however, has proved different over the years: political pressure, actual and potential, may have to join forces with reason and persuasion in order to bring about reform.

Thomas More (1478–1535)

More's claim for inclusion in this volume rests solely on his book *Utopia* – 'one of the great books of all time' (Gray, 1946, p 61); 'one of the boldest declarations of a political creed ever uttered by an English statesman on the eve of his entry into a king's service' (Seebohm, 1896, p 390). The book falls into two parts: the first is a structural analysis of the social problems of poverty, bad housing and crime in England and the harsh but futile policies adopted by the government in these areas; the second is a description of an ideal society where these problems are dealt with humanely and successfully. More acknowledged that these problems could only be solved in a non-existing society, a utopia (meaning a no-place, in Greek), a term that has since come to be used as a description of all idealistic projects and futuristic societies.

A critique of 16th-century capitalist society

The capitalist state

More's major thesis was that the social system that prevailed in the 16th century was, in his words, simply 'a conspiracy of the rich to advance their own interests under the pretext of organizing society. They think up all sorts of tricks and dodges, first for keeping safe their ill-gotten gains, and then for exploiting the poor by buying their labour as cheaply as possible' (More, 1965, p 130). These 'tricks and dodges' are gradually officially recognised and 'they acquire the force of law' with the result that 'an unscrupulous minority' reaps the benefits of the labour of the majority rather than use them to satisfy the needs of all (More, 1965, p 130). Kings and nobility were only interested in protecting and extending their interests; and they had all the power to do this, particularly in the face of public inertia and cowed submission. Most kings, he argued, 'are far more anxious, by hook or by crook, to acquire new kingdoms than to govern their existing ones properly' (More, 1965, p 42). As for the nobility, they live 'like drones on the labour of other people, in other words, of their tenants, and keep bleeding them white by constantly raising their rents' (More, 1965, p 44).

The King, in particular, is to be held responsible for this state of affairs for he is at the head of the ruling class. He does not deserve the office that God and the general public entrusted in him:

> Certainly a man who enjoys a life of luxury while everyone else is moaning and groaning round him can hardly be called a king – he's more like a gaoler. (More, 1965, p 62)

In these circumstances, it is folly to believe that critical social scientists can have any meaningful influence on government policies – 'there's no room at Court for philosophy' (More, 1965, p 63). It may well be that some minor policy improvements can be achieved through the involvement of philosophers in government, but there is a high penalty to pay for this – co-optation and corruption:

> You'll never reform them – they're far more likely to corrupt you, however admirable a character you are. By associating with them you'll either lose your own integrity, or else have it used to conceal their folly and wickedness (More, 1965, p 65).

Crime in 16th-century England

More attacked with particular venom government policies on crime. The gist of his criticism was that government policies, on one hand, created crime and, on the other, did nothing to prevent it or to reform offenders – they were just executed in droves for mostly petty larceny offences. In his words, 'you create thieves, and then punish them for stealing' (More, 1965, p 49). This was, to him, both inhumane and ineffective.

More positive measures were needed, to deal effectively with both the roots of crime and the reformation of offenders. On the preventive side, More stressed, above all, employment and a decent livelihood for all. He saw the causes of crime as lying primarily in the social environment rather than, as Hobbes did a century later, in the attitudes of the individual:

> Instead of inflicting these horrible punishments, it would be far more to the point to provide everyone with some means of livelihood, so that nobody's under the frightful necessity of becoming first a thief and then a corpse. (More, 1965, p 44)

He singled out three policies that increased unemployment and poverty, which led to increased crime. First, the demobilisation of soldiers from the army at the end of wars without any means for subsistence or a job in sight meant that many had no real option but to simply roam the land in search of work and food and almost inevitably be involved in petty thieving; the second policy was the unemployment of servants and others when their lord died or when he did not need them; and the third reason he gave for the rise in poverty, unemployment and crime was simply 'sheep':

> These placid creatures, which used to require so little food, have now apparently developed a raging appetite, and turned into man-eaters. Fields, houses, towns, everything goes down their throats (More, 1965, p 46).

More was, of course, referring to the enclosure of arable land for sheep pastures for purely profit reasons – the sale of wool became very profitable at the time. More attributed it all to the greed of rich landowners who were quite prepared to ruin the lives of thousands of families of small farmers in order to increase their profits. Greed, however, has always been a feature of business life. What gave greed its cutting edge at this time was the demographic disaster following the Black Death that made labour scarce and expensive. As a result, sheep farming became far cheaper and more profitable than crop farming:

> In such circumstances, the enclosure of the open fields and their conversion to pasture provided an answer to the landlord's problems. Pastoral farming was more extensive in its nature, and fewer tenants were required. (Wrightson, 2000, p 102)

Whatever the causes of the enclosure movement, the result was the same: whole villages were destroyed, many people became homeless, roamed the countryside and eventually some had no option 'but steal – and be very properly hanged' (More, 1965, p 47). The solution, for More, was obvious: put a halt to the eviction of small farmers, revive agriculture and stop the rich from establishing monopolies in farming.

As for the punishment of offenders, More argued that execution of petty thieves should cease. Punishment should fit the crime. Apart from the very serious offenders, the rest should be sentenced to forced labour and should be made to pay back to their victims what they stole. The underlying principle would be that they should be treated in such a way that 'they are forced to become good citizens, and spend the rest of their lives making up for the harm they've done in the past' (More, 1965, p 53).

Poverty in 16th-century England

Poverty was endemic in all early capitalist societies and the evidence shows that it was increasing during the 16th century for a variety of structural reasons. Bearing in mind the rise in population during this time, poverty was numerically an even greater problem. Not unexpectedly, the poor came to be increasingly seen by the authorities as 'the "thriftless poore", and conventionally associated with filth, disease, crime and sedition' (Wrightson, 2000, p 148). Poor relief given to the 'thriftless poore' was usually accompanied by various forms of punishment.

More was careful to distinguish between the various types of poverty and their causes. He did not dwell on the 'thriftless poore' as many had done but commented at length on the working poor. He was scathing of the principles that underlay the distribution of wages and income. People like 'aristocrats, goldsmiths or moneylenders, who either do no work at all, or do work that's really not essential', are so highly rewarded and live in luxury, while those who do all the essential jobs 'get so little to eat, and have such a wretched time' (More, 1965, p 129).

He was one of the first to draw attention to the fact that poverty during working life usually means poverty during old age. This was inevitable: 'since their daily wages aren't enough to support them for one day, let alone leave anything over to be saved when they are old' (More, 1965, p 129). For all their hard work during their working years, an ungrateful social system allowed them to die in misery, he argued. Poverty during working life inevitably meant poverty in retirement.

Private property

More was absolutely certain that no progress was possible in solving these social problems so long as private property remained the central institution in society. This is because, he argued, vested interests and the ideology of private property stand in the way of reforms that have the communal interest at heart. Private property is successfully defended through the ideology that it serves the public interest. He also rejected the claim that work incentives would suffer as a result of the abolition of private property:

> I'm quite convinced that you'll never get a fair distribution of goods, or a satisfactory organization of human life, until you abolish private property altogether. So long as it exists, the vast majority of the human race, and the vastly superior part of it, will inevitably go on labouring under a burden of poverty, hardship, and worry. (More, 1965, p 66)

He conceded that certain improvements can be made but they cannot change the central feature of an unequal stratified society. He concluded that 'equality of distribution of goods', the essential condition for the solution of the various social problems, 'is impossible under capitalism' (More, 1965, p 66). This line of thinking put him in a paradoxical position for, as a deeply religious man, he could not advocate rebellion in order to change the established social order. How then is his Utopia to be achieved if reform is ineffective and revolt is unacceptable? Most writers of utopias do not deal with this thorny problem while those who do, like Marx, provide answers that are not totally convincing. More adopted a Marxist position on the distribution of resources and power in society but, as a deeply religious man, he could not countenance violence or revolution. Instead, he put forth how such problems could be solved in an ideal society – in a Utopia.

Life in Utopia

More's Utopia is an island, 500 miles long and 200 miles wide at its broadest section; it has 40 cities, each of which is surrounded by agricultural land; farms are distributed evenly in the countryside; all cities are obviously small and they are similarly planned, with the capital resembling London. The life of citizens is based on a series of clear principles or regulations covering all aspects of life designed to meet the basic needs of all.

Work

Every adult, man and woman, must work for six hours a day only – which is long enough to produce all the basic and other necessities for the whole population. This is unlike 'the slavery', More argued, that existed in other societies where people worked 'from early morning till late at night, like cart-horses' (More, 1965, p 76). Farming is the staple trade for all, and everyone must learn farming as well as another trade, 'though the weaker sex are given the lightest of jobs, like spinning and weaving, while the men do the heaviest jobs' (More, 1965, p 75). More rejects the argument that such a short working day cannot produce enough for all – on the contrary he thought that there was abundant labour since all adults would be employed, unlike other societies where many sections of the population remained idle for part or the whole of their life:

> First you have practically all the women – that gives you nearly fifty per cent for a start. Then there are all the priests, and members of the so-called religious bodies – how much work do they do? And all the rich, especially the landowners, popularly known as nobles and gentlemen. Include their domestic staffs. Finally throw in all the beggars who are perfectly hale and hearty, but pretend to be ill as an excuse for being lazy. (More, 1965, p 77)

In their anxiety to ensure that everyone works and no one shirks their responsibilities, the inhabitants of Utopia decreed that people need permission before they can travel to other towns. Moreover, once they reach their destination, they are expected to work at their trade if they stay for more than 24 hours. Anyone who breaks this rule twice is punished very severely – he or she becomes a slave.

Influenced by what he saw as the vice-spots of London, More argues that there should be no wine-taverns, alehouses or brothels in Utopia. All must not only work but they must also lead Christian lives. In words that were used later by George Orwell's Big Brother:

> Everyone has his eye on you, so you're practically forced to get on with your job, and make some proper use of your spare time. (More, 1965, p 84)

Leisure

In view of the shorter hours of work, people would have more leisure time and they should use it constructively in order to improve their physical and mental abilities as well as improve their personalities. Most Utopians, More believed, would choose to attend lectures during their spare time, some might work extra time on their trade, or they could play chess and suchlike games, practise music, or exceptionally just talk in the communal halls. What is not acceptable is for people to be idle, to be gambling or to pursue such 'stupid pleasures' as hunting and hawking, which result in the mutilation of animals and birds purely for public amusement. Strangely, hunting was not totally banned but, being such a cruel pastime, it was left to unfree citizens:

> So the Utopians consider hunting below the dignity of free men, and leave it entirely to butchers, who are slaves. (More, 1965, p 95)

A socialist welfare state

Private property and private services are abolished in Utopia. This is reflected in many aspects of life. Land is communally owned, communally worked and the produce is shared out to all. All adults are trained in farming and they work in it either full time or part time or for a few years in their life.

Good-quality houses with gardens are provided to all by the state. More understood the connection between bad housing and ill-health from his life in London and hence his insistence that housing, sanitation and streets should be of the highest standard. To emphasise their public nature, houses were not to be locked. Working clothes and other clothing are also provided by the state but, in order to reduce class distinctions, clothing is utilitarian rather than fashionable; it is the same for all, only distinguishing between men and women, married and single; it is made to last rather than for fashion; and it is made at home by each household.

Free health care is provided to all in generously equipped and well-staffed large hospitals situated just outside the town. In the towns, meals are taken at the communal halls, while in the countryside, out of necessity, meals are taken at home. Whether at home or at the hall, food is provided free to all. People can also visit the general stores and ask for other things needed in the household. These are provided free without too much fuss, for not only is there abundance but also people are not that greedy to ask for more than they need, a reflection of More's humanistic belief in the goodness of human beings.

Primary education is free and compulsory to all, boys and girls. It is the responsibility of priests to run the educational system and to ensure that 'as much stress is laid on moral as on academic training' (More, 1965, p 123). Adults educate themselves in their spare time with the exception of a small number of very talented individuals who receive full-time education.

In view of all these state provisions, 'there obviously can't be any poor people or beggars' (More, 1965, p 84). Every effort is also made to discourage the belief in relative affluence, that is, the belief that possessing non-essential goods makes you a better person than others. In this way, the possibility that state services may be overused or otherwise abused is minimised:

> No living creature is naturally greedy, except from fear of want – or in the case of human beings, from vanity, the notion that you're better

than people if you can display more superfluous property than they can. But there's no scope for that sort of thing in Utopia. (More, 1965, p 80)

Representative government

A representative form of government is used in Utopia. At the local level people elect their controllers, who in turn elect the mayor by secret ballot. The main duty of the local controller is to ensure that people work and they do their job properly. Each town also sends representatives to the island's senate in the capital where mostly general issues pertaining to the whole island are discussed. Most of the decision-making is done at the local level. All public appointments, including priests, are made through secret ballot to ensure that the best candidates get the jobs, 'for the welfare of a state depends entirely on the quality of its administrators' (More, 1965, p 107) – a slight exaggeration but a useful reminder that even the best plans can founder because of faulty implementation.

Implicit in More's plans on government is the notion of commonality of interests so that political parties are not necessary. Utopia was based on consent, it met everyone's needs, and conflict of interest was not on the agenda.

Marriage, family and divorce

Unlike Plato's Republic, More's Utopia uses the family as its basic social unit. Girls may marry at 18 and boys at 22. Premarital and extramarital sexual relationships are severely punished not only on moral grounds but also in order to protect the institution of marriage. More's stress on marriage and marital fidelity are unsurprising and it may reflect his life experience. As a young man, he thought of becoming a priest but, according to his friend Erasmus, 'as he found he could not overcome his desire for a wife, he decided to be a faithful husband rather than an unfaithful priest' (Erasmus, quoted in Kenny, 1983, p 11).

A rather unusual habit among the Utopians is the 'pre-nuptial inspection': before marriage, the prospective bride is exhibited 'stark naked to the prospective bridegroom' and vice versa in the company of chaperons so as to ensure that both parties have as good an idea as possible of what they are getting themselves into. Marriage, however, for the Utopians is based not simply on physical attraction but on moral qualities as well. As More puts it (on behalf of men!):

A pretty face may be enough to catch a man, but it takes character and good nature to hold him. (More, 1965, p 105)

This emphasis on 'pre-nuptial inspection' may be the result of Plato's influence who considered nudity acceptable. Or, 'it may have been a device to detect whether the prospective partner had syphilis, the new and spreading disease of More's time' (Bronowski and Mazlish, 1960, p 74).

Divorce can be granted to the innocent party in cases of adultery; and, in very rare cases, on grounds of incompatibility but by mutual consent only and under special permission. Adulterers are sentenced to penal servitude and while remorse may lead to pardon, 'a second conviction means capital punishment' (More, 1965, p 104) – one of two reasons for capital punishment, the other being rebellion by slaves.

The authority structure of the Utopian family is no different from that of the then prevailing family elsewhere. It is simply patriarchal in nature, for neither Erasmus nor More, as exemplars of humanism, championed the equality of women in society. Thus, in Utopia:

> Husbands are responsible for punishing their wives, and parents for punishing their children, unless the offence is so serious that it has to be dealt with by the authorities, in the interests of public morality. (More, 1965, p 104)

Crime in Utopia is not a serious problem in view of all the preventive steps taken by the state in education, employment, housing, food and other aspects of life. When it does occur, it is the responsibility of the mayor, the priest and other public officials, who can use both punitive and reformatory measures.

Despite all the emphasis on equality, freedom and participation in government, slavery is still accepted in Utopia. It is, however, not an essential part of the economy of society. The number of slaves is small and they are 'either Utopian convicts or, much more often, condemned criminals from other countries' who voluntarily chose work in Utopia to death in their country (More, 1965, p 101). They perform either menial or morally repugnant jobs, such as butchering. There is no condemnation of slavery in Utopia – simply an acceptance of it and a plea for the humane treatment of slaves.

War is a last resort to the Utopians and only in self-defence, for they loathe violence. Both men and women, however, receive military training at regular intervals just in case they are needed although fighting is left, mostly, to mercenaries. Like Erasmus, More argued for peaceful resolution of national conflicts.

An assessment of *Utopia*

The first part of *Utopia* is, by general agreement, one of the major early attempts to discuss seriously the social problems of unemployment, poverty and crime in a capitalist society. Many, however, have found the second part of *Utopia*, with its stress on equality of condition, oppressive and dehumanising. Allen speaks for many when he points at 'those houses all alike, those people so much alike that they are content hardly to differ in dress, that monotony of grave entertainment and garnishing of the mind' (Allen, 1928, p 156). Similarly, Gray finds the stagnation of thought, the grey uniformity of life and the absence of change depressing and concludes:

> No utopia has ever been described in which any sane man would
> on any conditions consent to live, if he could possibly escape. (Gray,
> 1946, p 62)

One can understand and sympathise with some of these views from a 20th-century
perspective. But we will never know whether the impoverished masses of the
16th century would have objected to exchanging their starvation, poverty and
slums for the compulsory employment, adequate food and the uniformly built
houses of Utopia. More's was not the only utopia of the period. The 17th century
spawned several utopias, perhaps as a reaction to the rising inequalities produced
by an increasingly commercial economic system: Campanella's *The City of the
Sun* and Fénelon's *Les Aventures de Télémaque* are the two best-known (Gray, 1946,
pp 70–5). Despite their many flaws, utopias will continue to be written of, for
they hold out the promise of a better world. In Oscar Wilde's classic comment:

> A map of the world that does not include utopia is not even worth
> glancing at, for it leaves out the one country at which humanity is
> always landing. Progress is the realisation of utopias. (Wilde, 1954,
> p 340)

Martin Luther (1483–1545)

The Reformation can be said to have formally begun with the publication of
Luther's Ninety-Five Theses and his consequent excommunication by the Pope
in 1520. Luther's theses attacked, in essence, 'the entire theology and church
structure that stood behind them' (Bronowski and Mazlish, 1960, p 108). Luther's
views on welfare are the main focus of this section, though we begin with his
two central religious values – faith and obedience – for they have both political
and welfare implications.

Luther's religious values: faith and obedience

Individual faith is the cornerstone of Luther's theology. It is only through this
private communion with God that the individual can hope to achieve salvation
from Original Sin. It is a private relationship with God in the sense that it does
not have to be mediated through priest, monk, friar or pope. The individual can
pray to God directly, he can ask God's guidance and forgiveness directly, and he
can receive God's blessing directly. It is also the cornerstone in another sense:
without faith there is no hope of God's salvation however many good works the
individual may do in his life. In Luther's words: 'Works can justify no man before
God without faith' (Luther, 1520a, p 31).

Luther's emphasis on the liberty of the individual was confined to the religious
field. In the political and social field, it is obedience that rules the day. Children
should honour and obey their parents; wives their husbands; citizens their rulers;

workers their bosses; and servants their masters and mistresses. Obedience should be reciprocated by consideration on behalf of those in authority. Obedience, however, is still due even if those in authority behave unreasonably or tyrannically. As Mackinnon puts it: 'To commit injustice in the attempt to obtain justice is to wrong God's Word' (Mackinnon, 1929, p 201).

Disobedience for Luther 'is a sin worse than murder, unchastity, theft, dishonesty, and all that goes with them' (Luther, 1520a, p 81). Only in cases where the ruler acts against God may his subjects disobey him and even then only through passive resistance. Rulers, however, are entitled to use force in order to preserve peace and security in society. In political terms, what Luther's value system managed to achieve, albeit unintentionally, was to substitute the tyranny of the monarchy with that of the papacy; and to encourage that process which saw the gradual replacement of Church welfare with parish welfare.

Poverty relief

The incidence of poverty in Western Europe in the early 16th century could not have been too dissimilar from that in England. It is estimated that 15 to 30 per cent of the population of the towns in Western Europe may have been paupers and vagrants (Smith, 1920, pp 558-9), although, as in England, the spotlight was on the 'thriftless poore' – 'the gangs of sturdy vagrants, led by and partly composed of old soldiers, who wandered through Europe' (Smith, 1920, p 558).

The abolition of monasteries and suchlike Church institutions in Protestant countries added to the numbers of the poor, though it is difficult to be certain about the extent of this simply because Church property was to be used partly for poor relief.

Luther's ideas on poor relief appear mainly in two of his publications in 1520 and 1523. They make the following proposals. First, the responsibility for poor relief should lie with the lay authorities of the local commune or parish. An overseer with special responsibility for the poor should be appointed 'who knows all the poor and informs the city council or clergy what they needed' (Luther, 1520b, p 190). Local communes, however, were not as eager as Luther was to undertake such a major responsibility because of the cost implications, if nothing else.

Second, neither poverty nor begging should be seen as being in line with God's wishes. Luther clearly moved away from the Catholic tradition of the Middle Ages which venerated apostolic poverty and the mendicant friars. Begging by friars, students and others should be made an offence. He felt that there were so many beggars, mendicant friars and others that it sapped the will of the people as well as their finances.

Third, and related to the second proposal, a distinction should be made between the deserving and the undeserving poor – relief to the first, punishment to the second. On this, Luther followed a long line of previous writers from Plato and Aristotle onwards. Moreover, punishment of the undeserving poor was already common practice. In the Netherlands, as far back as 1506, an edict was issued ordering that tramps 'be whipped, have their heads shaved, and to be further punished with stocks' (Smith, 1920, p 559). Even relief to the deserving, however, was to be made only if there were no relatives who could help:

> No men or women beggars shall be tolerated in our parish, since anyone not incapacitated by reason of age or illness shall work or, with the aid of the authorities, be expelled from the parish. But those among us who are impoverished by force of circumstances, or are unable to work because of old age or illness, shall be supported in suitable fashion out of our common chest. (Luther, 1523, p 186)

Fourth, the responsibility of the parish was limited to its own parishioners. People coming in from outside the parish had no right to poor relief and they should be expelled. Again this was an age-old idea going back to Classical Athens and was rigorously enforced by the parishes in many European countries.

Fifth, Luther envisaged that the common chest funds for poor relief would have many resources: charitable donations, income from the monasteries and other Church properties as well as any income from the parish. If these funds proved inadequate, then every member of the parish should 'according to his ability, and means, remit in taxes for himself, his wife, and his children a certain sum of money to the chest each year' (Luther, 1523, p 192). The income of the chest funds, however, was used not only for poor relief but also for the salaries of teachers and the maintenance of school buildings.

Sixth, Luther did not see private property as the cause of poverty, as More had argued in his *Utopia*. Indeed, private property to him was the bedrock of a Christian society – without it, society degenerates to the level of the animal kingdom. This was a major reason for his condemnation of the Peasants' Revolt – some of its members were arguing for the abolition of private property (Pascal, 1933, p 193).

These specific proposals on poverty should be considered within the wider religious value system of Protestantism. The emphasis on individual faith, individual responsibility and obedience created an ideological environment that was not supportive of collective responsibility for the poor. As Troeltsch puts it, Lutheran ideas on poor relief did not succeed because Lutheranism as a creed 'was too much engrossed with the personal interior life, too much imbued with the idea that everyone ought to work, and too much alienated from the old ideal of charity' (Troeltsch, 1931, p 566).

The 16th century witnessed the beginning of the gradual transfer of the responsibility for poor relief from Church to the local state together with some degree of rationalisation – what Kingdon has called: 'laicisation and rationalisation' (Kingdon, 1971, p 51). Laymen began to take over responsibility for the administration of poor relief and they tried to coordinate and rationalise the various poor relief institutions. This trend took place at the same time as the growth of Protestantism but it would be wrong to see them as causally related.

For one thing, this process started just before Luther's break with Rome and, for another, Catholic as well as Protestant countries followed the same pattern. It was, however, a trend encouraged by Protestant and resisted by Catholic counties since the latter persisted in considering the Church as the main provider.

Education

At the beginning of the 16th century, a variety of schools – monastic, cathedral, chantry, guild and burgher schools – were in existence, catering for a minority of the child population. Teachers were mainly clergy and the subject matter was mainly Catholic education, although the teaching of the classics was beginning to play a greater part. The abolition of monasteries, the confiscation of Church property by kings in Protestant countries, the decline in employment prospects in religious occupations, and the new spirit of commercialism created a climate where education was being seen as not so important. Money and wealth now came from business and trade where education did not seem to be that important.

It is to Luther's credit that he vigorously rebuffed this attitude and put forward clear ideas for the education of all children, boys and girls. His ideas on education 'represent a great advance on those of the great majority of contemporary churchmen' (Pascal, 1933, p 223). He defended the provision of education on social, religious and economic grounds. On the religious side, he argued that unless people were literate, they would not be able to read the scriptures themselves, as Protestantism advocated. Socially, literate people make better parents and better citizens than illiterate people. Economically, both society and the individual would benefit, for the country needed educated people in all occupations, not just in the Church. It is true, he argued, that monastic education was useless – it made students 'asses, blockheads, and numbskulls', but that need not be so (Luther, 1524a, pp 352–3). A new curriculum was necessary that would be useful not only to the intelligent but to the ordinary children, for they are all important to society. In Luther's down-to-earth language:

> For a good building we need not only hewn facings but also backing stone. (Luther, 1530, p 231)

He strongly disagreed with those who argued that the state could not afford to provide universal and free education to all children. If the municipal authorities could afford to spend money on buildings and fortifications in the town, they should not begrudge expenditure on education, which was more important for the welfare of the individual and society:

> A city's best and greatest welfare, safety and strength consist rather in its having able, learned, wise, honourable, and well-educated citizens. (Luther, 1524a, p 356)

Resistance to compulsory education came not only from the authorities but also from many of the parents who felt they could not afford to lose their children's labour. He, therefore, proposed that boys should attend school for one or two hours a day and spend the rest either working or learning a trade; and girls should attend school for only one hour a day in order to leave them with ample time for their duties at home. If these measures proved insufficient, then elementary education should be made compulsory. Parents had no right to keep their children away from school. If the state could compel people to do military service, 'how much more can it and should it compel its subjects to keep their children at school' (Luther, 1530a, p 257).

Education beyond the elementary stage was for the exceptionally gifted who would eventually become teachers or hold ecclesiastical positions or go on to further study at the universities. In addition, libraries should be established in the main towns, which people could use freely, provided only certain types of books were kept – those that fitted in with Luther's views on Christianity.

As for the curriculum, Luther was in favour of teaching the classic languages because they enabled the individual to read the scriptures in the original language; he was in favour of the teaching of history for he believed that this could show us 'what to seek and what to avoid in this outward life' (Luther, 1524a, p 369); and he was supportive of the teaching of mathematics and medicine. Above all, however, the curriculum should cover fully the teaching of the Holy Scripture. He was against the teaching of those aspects of classical education that emphasised the importance of reason over faith in life. For this reason, he wanted a root-and-branch reform of university curricula because they gave more emphasis to Aristotle than to Christ, to secular than religious subjects, to intellectual questioning than to obedience:

> Nothing could be more devilish or disastrous than unreformed universities. (Luther, 1520b, p 202)

Women, marriage and divorce

It is a moot point whether Luther's views on women represent an advance over the Catholic position. Basically, they both followed the traditional Christian view that women are, by nature, inferior to men and that this inferiority should be reflected in the various institutions of society – family, school, Church, work and so on. Any differences between them are of marginal significance.

Beginning with single women, it can be argued that the Protestant abolition of convents closed one avenue whereby single women could function without the close supervision of men. On the other hand, however, we do not know 'whether women loathed or cherished the cloistered regime' (Cameron, 1991, p 403). Luther's emphasis on marriage, his rejection of celibacy and virginity, may be said to have improved the status of married women. The debit side of this, however, was that Luther's views on family discipline increased further the husband's domination over his wife.

As we saw earlier, Luther stressed more strongly than the Catholic creed the importance of the education of girls though he made it clear that boys should spend longer at school than girls. Both creeds saw women's role primarily as wives and mothers in the home, where the husband's authority was unquestioned. In the work situation, they both envisaged different, and inferior, occupations for women. Luther was more forthright in his condemnation of prostitution than many Catholic writers were; he asked for the closure of brothels but for the punishment of the prostitutes only – not of their male clientele.

Crawford's conclusion on the gender issue sums up the situation well:

> For all their talk of individualism and equality, priests and ministers of both the Protestant and Catholic churches believed in female inferiority and subordination. (Crawford, 1993, p 41)

Luther not only emphasised the importance of marriage but he also insisted that it was a religious duty for people to marry – marriage was 'a divine ordinance which is not our prerogative to hinder or ignore' (Luther, 1522, p 18). Men should marry by the age of 28 at the latest and women between the ages of 15 and 18, always taking into account the advice of their parents on the choice of their spouse.

God exempted only two categories of persons from this duty – the sexually impotent by birth or by accident; and those very few whom God called to spread His Gospel. Priests also should be married for both theological and practical reasons while the number of monks and nuns should be limited. These views are in slight conflict with those of St Paul, St Augustine and the Church Fathers who stressed celibacy and by implication downgraded the significance of marriage.

Luther outlined four functions of marriage: sexual satisfaction, the prevention of wicked lust, companionship and, above all, procreation. Having children within marriage 'is the end and chief purpose of marriage' (Luther, 1519, p 12). He praised parents' work in rearing children – it is 'the shortest road to heaven' (Luther, 1519, p 12). He wanted parents to have as many children as possible without worrying about the financial implications for he was sure God would take care of that.

> Let God worry about how they and their children are to be fed. God makes children, he will surely also feed them. (Luther, 1522, p 48)

Marriage is for life, and divorce should be a rare thing, granted always after attempts at reconciliation failed. He put forward four grounds for divorce: first, when either of the spouses was not physically able to fulfil the conjugal duty of marriage; second, when one of the spouses, usually the wife, refused to fulfil the conjugal rights even though physically she was able to do so; third, on grounds of deliberate and prolonged desertion; and, fourth, because of adultery. Interestingly enough, he did not include cruelty, for husbands had the right to be cruel to their wives without any fear of retaliation by either Church or state.

Luther was particularly angry at deserters, for they neglected not only their wives but their children too, and he had this full-blooded message for them:

> There is no villain whom I would rather have hanged or beheaded than this scoundrel. (Luther, 1530b, p 313)

He considered adultery worse than bigamy because some of the figures of the Old Testament had been bigamously married but no one was said to have committed adultery. In cases of adultery, the innocent party should be allowed to remarry after the divorce, provided attempts at reconciliation were first made, and provided that at least six months elapsed from the date of the divorce. Of all the grounds of divorce, it was adultery that was the most common and on which Luther dwelt at length. He blamed the new commercialism with the import of silk clothes and gold jewellery from India as well as the relatively freer spirit spawned by the Renaissance – they both encouraged unbecoming conduct in both men and women but particularly in the latter who had often been portrayed throughout the long Medieval period 'as merely seducers and temptresses' (Labarge, 2001, p 29).

Economic issues

Two points must be borne in mind in trying to understand Luther's economic views. First, as a theologian, he was more at ease with the Medieval view on wealth creation; and, second, he was writing at a time when trade, banking and investment were on the rise. This placed him in a dilemma of disapproving wealth accumulation on one hand but having to accept it on the other. On balance, he was more of a conservative on economic issues in contrast with his radicalism in religious affairs.

As a theologian, his views on wealth stemmed from St Paul whom he quotes often, particularly the well-known cliché that 'The love of money is the root of all evils' (St Paul, epistle, I, Timothy, 6:10). He accepted that trade was necessary but he insisted it should be practised in a Christian way. He was critical of the free market rule of trade that 'I may sell my goods as dear as I can in order to make as much profit as I can' (Luther, 1524b, p 247) because it showed a total disregard of other people. Instead, he proposed that trade should be conducted on the Christian principle 'I may sell my wares as dear as I ought, or as is right and fair' (Luther, 1524b, p 248). This allowed for some profit to be made, the amount of which should be calculated on the amount of time and labour invested at the wage rates of day labourers. His formula was not likely to warm the hearts of the rising generation of entrepreneurs.

He was even more critical of interest earned from the lending of money which he referred to as usury in much the same way that previous ecclesiastical writers had done. Basically, he would have preferred interest-free lending of money but he accepted that in the new commercial world where money was made out of money borrowed, a case could be made for some interest payment but the rates should be as low as possible – between four and six per cent and certainly not as high as the 10 per cent moneylenders often charged. His guiding principle was: 'The smaller the percentage the more godly and Christian the contract' (Luther, 1524b, p 305).

Charging above the recommended rates put moneylenders in conflict with God and it was no surprise that such 'robbers and usurers' often, and deservedly, died unnatural deaths, according to Luther. These were strong views at a time when usury was on the increase because of the rise in trade and banking. Luther's views on economic issues straddled rather uncomfortably the medieval condemnation of wealth and usury at one end and the new spirit of capitalism at the other. Not unexpectedly, they proved inadequate in holding back the free market drive for increased profitability, untrammelled by ethical considerations.

Jean Calvin (1509–64)

Although Calvinism grew out of Lutheranism, it developed its own unique religious, economic and social philosophy of life. At the centre of its religious creed is the notion of predestination – a notion that distinguishes it from all other Christian creeds and which also has important socio-economic implications.

Calvin defined predestination as 'the eternal decree of God, by which he determined what he wished to make of every person. For he does not create everyone in the same condition, but ordains eternal life for some and eternal damnation for others' (Calvin, quoted in McGrath, 1988, p 126). Whether a person goes to Paradise or to Hell is, according to Calvin, predetermined by God and there is nothing the individual can do to alter this. It is neither good works nor faith that decides salvation – it is simply God's will. This may appear arbitrary and harsh but God has His reasons, Calvin argued. The fact that human beings cannot understand God's way of thinking does not make His decisions arbitrary or harsh, if one accepts the fundamental premise that God is always just.

This might suggest that predestination takes the heart out of human endeavour – but far from it. In fact, it has the opposite effect because the only way an individual will discover whether he or she may be one of God's elect is through work. Those individuals who become successful in their work or business through Christian methods may be the elect, chosen by God both for success in this world and salvation in the next. It follows that work for Calvinism is even more important than for Lutheranism, let alone for Catholicism.

Work had always been valued in Christian thought but under Calvin it became divinely ordained. God created human beings in order to work and glorify His name – He did not intend them to be lazy. A person who does not work is like 'a block of useless wood'; and 'there is nothing more disgraceful than a lazy good-for-nothing who is no use either to himself or to others but seems to have been born only to eat and drink' (Calvin, quoted in Bouwsma, 1988, p 199). Calvin not only stressed work but also praised efficiency at work, specialisation and retraining. Like Luther, he emphasised the importance of education for boys and girls and one of his followers, Knox, drew up a system of national education for Scotland.

It was partly for reasons of economic efficiency that Calvin was against slavery. He felt that it was more efficient to employ servants than slaves and he was glad that slavery had disappeared from Europe, with the exception of Spain where it survived because of the influence of the Moslem religion. Nevertheless, he did not condemn slavery outright, because it had been practised by the patriarchs of the Old Testament and had been accepted by the apostles.

Calvin also departed from the long Christian tradition that saw wealth as an impediment to salvation. He rejected the traditional interpretation of Christ's advice to the wealthy young man to sell his property and help the poor. In his opinion, people have a duty to hold on to their property in order to support their family and to help the poor as well. He turned down both the apostolic notion of poverty and the communal ownership of property.

Wealth, however, should not be squandered on frivolities. It should be put to good use – saved, invested and increased in accordance with fair trading principles. Frugality, restraint and modesty were at the centre of Calvin's prescriptions for a Christian life. Extravagant living, expensive food, ostentatious clothing, dazzling ornaments, sensual, let alone sexy, types of amusement, and suchlike, were contrary to God's will. Calvinism encouraged production but strongly discouraged consumption. The rich should remember, he wrote, that they 'must one day give a reckoning of their vast wealth, that they may carefully and faithfully apply their abundance to good uses approved by God' (Calvin, quoted in Bouwsma, 1988, p 202).

In brief, Calvin's views on work, wealth, saving and investment were much in line with the emerging needs of a capitalist economy. Tawney rightly observes that Calvinism 'is perhaps the first systematic body of religious teaching which can be said to recognize and applaud economic virtues', with the result that its ideal society supports both the accumulation of wealth through hard labour and the strict observance of traditional Christian values (Tawney, 1990, p 114).

Calvin's ideas on poor relief were not original. He argued that the poor deserve help, they have a right not to go hungry, but they must live moral lives and they must work when they can. He played a central role in the reorganisation of poor relief in Geneva along the two lines discussed earlier – laicisation and rationalisation. As the acknowledged political and religious leader of Geneva, he gave his full backing to these changes but he was not their philosophical architect. In fact the opposite may be the case:

> When it came to deciding how the Christian community should institutionalise its obligation to help the poor, it was not Calvin who influenced Geneva, but rather Geneva that influenced Calvin. (Kingdon, 1971, p 61)

What was striking, and abhorrent to many, was his philosophy of social control. He attempted to control through edicts and the work of the magistrates and the ministers of religion all aspects of life in Geneva – education, courting, marriage, dress, theatre, sex life, and so on. He went into such details that nothing was immune from his social police – 'not even the choice of Christian names, hair styles, personal ornamentation or the number of courses at banquets. For Calvin there were only private persons, not private matters' (Hopfl, 1990, p 93). If all failed, people could be excommunicated and could be banished. His Geneva was not to be a place of wanton pleasure and gay amusement. His social control approach to life stemmed from his strong views on obedience. Like Luther, he believed that the ruler must be obeyed even in cases where he is wrong because 'God does nothing without a purpose; evil rulers are placed over us by God for punishment for our sins' (Harmon, 1964, p 188).

Women were one of the major groups in society that bore the brunt of his social control policies (Bouwsma, 1988, chs 3 and 4). He had very little positive to say about women except as wives and mothers – in this role they performed divine work. In other aspects of life, however, they were seen in a very negative light. To begin with, women are, Calvin argued, inferior to men by divine rule and by nature; they are born to obey; and their place is in the home. Women, to him, seemed over-concerned with sex: hence their preoccupation with fine clothes, jewellery and provocative hairstyles; their tendency to act as temptresses; to be full of gossip; and for not breast-feeding their babies. His views on women are some of the most misogynist found in the Christian literature.

Calvinism and capitalism

Both Luther and Calvin emphasised the importance of certain 'puritan' values to the life of their followers: hard work, thrift, restraint, saving, investment and the creation of wealth through acceptable Christian methods. This was particularly true of Calvinism because of its core value of predestination that considered success at the workplace as a possible sign of salvation. Tawney likens Calvin's concept of predestination with Marx's thesis of historical materialism in the sense that both notions assured their believers that the future belonged to them – salvation for the middle-class Calvinists and communism for the working-class Marxists (Tawney, 1990, p 120).

Max Weber, in his celebrated *The Protestant Ethic and the Spirit of Capitalism*, written in 1904, sought to show that these puritan values of Calvinism influenced the conduct of those who held them and, as a result, they were one of the causes for the emergence of the new ascetic type of capitalism:

> He sought to show that the inherent logic of these doctrines and of the advice based upon them both directly and indirectly encouraged planning and self-denial in the pursuit of economic gain. (Bendix, 1966, p 63)

Weber accepted that capitalism existed before the Reformation. The great cities of Europe were banking and trading centres dominated by a few families – the Medicis, the Fuggers and so on – but it was a different type of capitalism. He called it 'adventure capitalism' because it was hedonistic and tended to consume its profits, in contrast to the new type of 'ascetic capitalism', which discouraged flamboyant consumption and encouraged long-term investment of profits. He also acknowledged that 'the Protestant ethic' was one of the many factors – material, intellectual and ideological – that contributed to the rise of capitalism and that by itself it would not have been sufficient. Nevertheless, it was an important influence. In brief, he was arguing for a pluralist explanation of the rise of capitalism, even though he stressed the importance of puritan values more than the others. He pointed out that though the material conditions for the rise of capitalism existed in many countries in Europe, it thrived most in those countries with a puritan religious ideology. His thesis has been interpreted as a corrective to Marx's materialistic interpretation of history that is examined in Chapter 10.

Critics of Weber's thesis argue that the Calvinist ethos was not the cause but the result of capitalist development. Material factors are more important than idealistic factors. Others point out that both Luther and Calvin preached state provision of services, state subsidies of industry, the use of taxation as well as state control of prices and of interest rates – none of which are necessarily conducive to the growth of capitalism. Neither Luther nor Calvin was an advocate of laissez-faire capitalism (Lindberg, 1996, pp 371–2). While this second criticism is true, there is no doubt that the balance of power in Calvin's creed was in favour of wealth accumulation for investment and further profits. Additionally, his followers stressed wealth creation even more than he did and they ignored the social use of wealth in much the same way that Medieval monks made more use of the secular enjoyments offered by monastic life than the opportunities it provided for solitude and prayer.

It is the first criticism that has been at the heart of the debates over the years. As we shall see in Chapter 10, Marx gave pride of place in the causation of major changes in history to the material factors in society – how people work, what tools they use, how they are organised at work, how they earn their living. He never claimed that ideas and beliefs are not important but he did insist that they must be seen within the socio-economic environment in which they emerge. The position taken in Chapter 10 is that in complex historical events both sets of factors play their part and even detailed research may find it impossible to unravel and estimate their relative strength.

Weber oversimplified the Calvinist view of the world but his thesis that some of the religious ideas of Calvinism were factors that encouraged the growth of early European capitalism appears correct, bearing in mind all the qualifications made in the previous paragraph.

Conclusion

The Renaissance and the Reformation mark the beginning of the long process that witnessed the decline of the Church in political, economic, social and even religious affairs. They were not the major causes of this decline – indeed their explicit aim was to strengthen Christian beliefs. Indirectly, however, they both encouraged a more individualistic approach to religion that may have contributed to the decline of religious beliefs as well as of the Church as an institution. The major forces, however, for this decline were the social and economic changes that were taking place in production, trade, banking, investment, consumption, urban living, travel – the very same changes that encouraged both the Renaissance and the Reformation.

One of the major political effects of the Reformation was to strengthen the territorial state ruled by hereditary monarchs with absolute powers. Having broken with the Catholic Church, Luther made alliances with those princes who were anxious to assert their independence from the power of the Pope in non-ecclesiastical matters. It was no accident that many princes openly supported the Lutheran break with Rome.

Both the Renaissance and the Reformation provided some new ideas on the provision of welfare services and poor relief. Above all they encouraged the view of state responsibility for social welfare at the local level even though the local state was not always ready to assume such a responsibility. All four thinkers supported strongly a better provision for the poor.

There is no doubt either that all four thinkers emphasised the significance of education for both boys and girls, even though they gave priority to the education of boys. Luther's criticism of those parents who did not send their children to school, even when this was free of charge, was particularly significant for it signalled his determination for a universal system of education.

In the long-standing debate on the position of women in society, all four thinkers remained fixated on the traditional Christian view of female inferiority. Even More's *Utopia*, so radical in all other aspects of life, remained true to the doctrine of patriarchy. Calvin's misogynist views were among the strongest stigmatisation of women and they were the most unacceptable face of his creed.

More's *Utopia* is by far the most interesting book produced by the four thinkers discussed in this chapter. It is a passionate critique of the ill-effects of unregulated early capitalism on the social conditions of the general public despite rising economic affluence. It avoids committing the error of seeing the solution to these problems either through the reform of individuals or by a return to the feudal past; it looks forward to the day when capitalism can be regulated and adequate social provisions be made for all on a communal basis.

FIVE

Absolutism
Thomas Hobbes (1588–1679)
Liberalism
John Locke (1632–1704)

This chapter examines the two main political ideologies that were spawned by the civil war and its aftermath in mid-17th-century England: the absolutism of Hobbes; and the liberalism of Locke. The central issues that divided them were the nature of government, the issue of private property, the nature of law, civil rights, social policy issues and religious tolerance (Peters, 1956, pp 33–5). The chapter will concentrate on the social policy issues far more than other discussions on these two thinkers.

The main preoccupation of Hobbes and Locke was to devise a secular political theory that safeguarded individual security either side by side with individual liberty, as in Locke's work, or at the expense of individual liberty, as in the case of Hobbes.

The political upheavals and debates of this period took place at a time of rising economic growth, widening income inequality and increasing relative poverty – an economic climate that was hardly conducive to social stability. In England and Wales, the national income doubled between the 1560s and the 1640s while 'the distribution of that income was markedly and increasingly uneven. This was an expanding economy, but one with a growing problem of structural poverty' (Wrightson, 2000, p 198).

Thomas Hobbes (1588–1679)

Just as Plato's utopia was a reaction to the constant political upheavals in Athens, Hobbes' theory of the absolute monarch was a reflection of what he saw as the ravages and anarchy caused by the civil war in England – it was, as he put it, 'occasioned by the disorders of the present time', which he attributed to the mistaken ideas that stressed individual judgement, private conscience, equality, rights and limited sovereign power. Such ideas encouraged people to question the existing social order and gradually lead to anarchical behaviour. He had in mind the radical egalitarian ideas of the Levellers and the Diggers, who openly challenged the existing political and economic system in favour of a democratic welfare-minded form of government where the legal rights of every citizen were protected.

Hobbes' theories aimed at providing a cure for political unrest and revolution not only in England but everywhere; and at creating a stable, orderly society ruled with the iron fist of a hereditary monarch. Although the physical security of the individual was the overarching element of his ideas on human welfare, he found time to write about human nature, crime and punishment, wealth and poverty, and the position of women in society – the issues that are a major concern of this book.

Human nature and absolutism

Hobbes rejected the Aristotelian view of human beings as sociable political animals and, hence, of society emerging out of human desire to live together peacefully so as to fulfil common needs. We seek society, he wrote, 'not so much for love of our fellows, as for love of ourselves' – in order that 'we may receive some honour or profit from it' (Hobbes, 1651, i, 2).

For Hobbes, most people, on most occasions in their life, are egoistic creatures pursuing their self-interest; they are generally ruled by passions rather than by reason; and they are, broadly speaking, equal in physical and mental strength so that no one can impose their will on others. Altruism and love of others are in such short supply that it is not possible to construct a state based on such sentiments. The state can only function well if it is based on the values of human self-interest and individualism.

In the state of nature, that is, in a society without a sovereign ruler, individuals will pursue their own interests and will inevitably be in constant conflict with one another. It is an anarchical society where only power counts: notions of right and wrong, justice and injustice, are non-existent because there are no government laws to guide human conduct. Even if people make agreements among themselves to behave peacefully towards each other, such agreements are empty promises because they lack the backing of the law. As he put it, 'covenants, without the sword, are but words, and of no strength to secure a man at all' (Hobbes, 1668, xvii, 2). Unlike many others before and after him who considered the unwritten laws in societies without organised governments as binding on individuals, Hobbes insisted that only laws passed by governments can guarantee security and justice in society for only they have the power of the state behind them necessary for their enforcement. In his words: 'Where there is no common power, there is no law. Where no law, no injustice' (Hobbes, 1668, xiii, 13).

For this reason, life in the state of nature is not of the idyllic communitarian type painted by many previous writers; rather it is a bed of nails: a tangled web of real, and potentially deadly, disputes where every man is at war with every other man. As he put it, 'every man is enemy to every man' with the result that life in the state of nature is 'solitary, poor, nasty, brutish, and short' (Hobbes, 1668, xiii, 9). This is inevitably so because human beings 'at the same time have an appetite for the same thing', which cannot be divided or shared between them (Hobbes, 1651, i, 6).

Despite the fact that human beings are motivated primarily by acquisitive passions, they possess enough reason to realise that such a society is against their real interests and may also see the death of many of them. While Hobbes was predominantly a relativist, maintaining that there are no agreed values or concepts in any society let alone universally, he argued that there is one thing after all that all human beings are agreed upon – fear of death. It is, primarily, this fear that will unite people in the state of nature in a common effort to find a solution to the problem of anarchy that threatens their life. Fear of death and the consequent search for security are the major driving forces behind the formation of governments. The origin of a lasting society, he wrote, 'consisted not in the mutual good will men had towards each other, but in the mutual fear they had of each other' (Hobbes, 1651, i, 2).

Hobbes adopts the well-used notion of a social contract to develop his ideas. But while all others used the notion of the social contract to restrict the ruler's powers on the grounds that 'individuals were presumed to be born free and equal' (Peters, 1956, p 195), Hobbes used it to show how human beings come to agree among themselves to give up their individual right to self-defence in favour of a sovereign assembly or a sovereign individual that will provide security for each and every one of them. They agree, he wrote, 'to confer all their power and strength upon one man, or upon one assembly of men, that may reduce all their wills unto one will' and abide by his decisions in most things in life (Hobbes, 1668, xvii, 13). Rulers have many duties but they 'are contained in this one sentence, the safety of the people is the supreme law' (Hobbes, 1651, xiii, 2).

Although Hobbes offers the choice between an assembly and one man, he prefers the individual sovereign ruler because he is freer to act decisively on issues of security and peace – he is not constrained by committees and meetings. Obedience to the sovereign ruler is total and revolutions are not part of Hobbes' political theory, however tyrannical the regime may be. Indeed the sovereign by definition can do no wrong for he has been empowered to act by the very will of the citizenry. In contrast to the Christian tradition, which argued that God above empowered the monarch with absolute power, Hobbes claims that it is the people below who created their sovereign ruler – their Leviathan, their mortal god.

Both the Christian writers and Hobbes seem to be unaware of the problems of corruption, nepotism and ossification that are inherent in regimes whose actions are not open to any scrutiny or challenge. Their assumption that the interests of the ruler and the ruled coincide does not stand up to the mildest of scrutinies, logically or historically.

Hobbes has also been criticised for sacrificing individual liberty to individual security. This is a charge he rejects for, in his eyes, absolutism is not the suppression but the guarantee of individual liberty in a world of imperfect, self-seeking human beings. Anarchy rather than absolutism is the enemy of individual liberty. He sees liberty in one-dimensional terms, as the absence of political impediments that enable an individual to pursue his life within the bounds of law:

> A Free-man is he that in those things which by his strength and wit
> he is able to do is not hindered to do what he has a will to. (Hobbes,
> 1668, xxi, 2)

Hobbes commits the same error on the issue of liberty versus security as all other
thinkers who are committed to monocausal explanations of complex problems and
who see their solution in absolute and simplistic ways. As a result, he is unwilling
to concede the common-sense point that neither absolute security nor absolute
liberty can create a tolerable society; it is the balance between these two social
values that is the issue rather than their individual worth. He committed this
error because of his over-cynical view of human nature. Jones rightly observes
that whether Hobbes' political theory 'stands or falls depends on whether the
account he gives of human nature is correct' (Jones, 1947, p 147).

Crime and punishment

Law-breaking is inevitable in any society but particularly in the Hobbesian state
which is inhabited by restless, egoistic human beings in constant pursuit of the
interests of themselves and their families. Hobbes acknowledged that despite
the despotic rule that he envisaged, crime would be a problem and went on to
attribute it not to any adverse socio-economic conditions but to individual fault
or shortcoming:

> The source of every crime is some defect of the understanding, or
> some error in reasoning, or some sudden force of the passions. (Hobbes,
> 1668, xxvii, 4)

Indeed, the only time he accepts a socio-economic motive behind an offence, he
is prepared to excuse it. Following the Christian tradition, he argues that when a
human being is so destitute of the basic needs of life that he risks dying, stealing
of food is excused. The potential damage to the offender – death – is greater
than the damage to society caused by the offence. It is in line with his argument
that people have every right to protect their life and they are entitled to do all in
their power to avoid death. Thus a person condemned to death has every right
to resist because no human being renounces the right to life.

He provides four scales by which to assess the severity of crimes: 'first by the
malignity of the source or cause; secondly, by the contagion of the example; thirdly,
by the mischief of the effect; and fourthly, by the concurrence of times, places,
and persons' (Hobbes, 1668, xxvii, 29). Thus offences committed unwittingly
are less serious than those committed in full knowledge of their illegal nature;
similarly offences committed on the spur of the moment are less serious than
those committed with premeditation. Offences that affect many are more serious
than those affecting only a few; it follows that crimes against the state are more
serious than crimes against individuals. Murders are more serious than stealing;

and 'to kill with torment greater than simply to kill' (Hobbes, 1668, xxvii, 43). The person, the time and the place are also important dimensions: 'to kill one's parent is more serious than to kill another; to rob a poor man is a greater crime than to rob a rich man' (Hobbes, 1668, xxvii, 51); and so on.

He similarly categorises the various punishments into various types: corporal, capital, pecuniary, ignominy, imprisonment, exile or a mixture of these. There is nothing unusual in this categorisation for all these punishments were in common use at the time. It is his views on the aims of punishment that are more interesting for they were well ahead of his time. In deciding the form or the severity of punishment, he said, 'we must have our eye not at the evil past, but the future good' (Hobbes, 1651, iii, 11). This means that 'the end of punishment is not revenge and discharge of choler, but correction, either of the offender or of others by his example' (Hobbes, 1668, xxx, 23). Bearing in mind his concern with public order and civil disobedience, it is not surprising that the severest punishments are to be inflicted on those who commit crimes against the state or their masters, for they can encourage others to follow their example. The leaders of such crimes are to be more severely punished than those who simply follow them.

Hobbes was clear throughout his writings that human beings are equal in physical and mental strength; existing inequality was the result of social and political practice rather than of inherent abilities. He was at odds on this with both Plato and Aristotle who believed that the elite of society is inherently superior to the rest. Following from this premise of basic equality of ability, Hobbes argued that justice should be administered without any social favours or biases towards the rich and the mighty. Public peace demands, he writes, that justice be administered equally so that 'as well as the rich and mighty as poor and obscure persons may be righted of injuries done to them, so as the great may have no greater hope of impunity when they do violence, dishonour, or any injury to the meaner sort, than when one of these does the like to one of them' (Hobbes, 1668, xxx, 15).

Bearing in mind Hobbes' belief that the causes of crime are to be found in individual failings, it is not surprising that the only measure he offers for the prevention of crime, apart from punishment, is public education. People are to be taught to be law-abiding – to avoid physical violence, to steer away from sexual offences and not to commit fraud or theft. He is on rather weak ground on this not only because of his neglect of social causal factors but also because of his perception of human beings as rapacious individualists.

Wealth and poverty

By the middle of the 17th century, England was a commercial nation where the majority of men were in either full-time or part-time paid employment. English society was beginning to be dominated by the capitalist ethos of 'possessive individualism' where 'man's labour is a commodity' (Macpherson, 1962, p 48) that could be sold freely in the marketplace and where society consisted 'of a series of market relations' (Macpherson, 1962, p 263). Traditional Christian ideas on the undesirability of wealth and usury, on the apostolic nature of poverty and on charity had little place in either the theories or the policies of such a society.

Hobbes' views reflect this new approach to these issues. He defines the safety of the people broadly to include not only 'the preservation of life in what condition soever, but in order to its happiness'. This means that rulers should do what they can 'to furnish their subjects abundantly, not only with the good things belonging to life, but also with those which advance to delectation' (Hobbes, 1651, xiii, 3).

His writings on wealth and poverty, however, are scattered and incidental, compared to his writings on the virtues of absolutism. He begins by pointing out that God provided human beings with enough land, animals, vegetables and minerals to satisfy their needs provided that they were all willing to be industrious. Part of the land should be kept for common use – 'wells, ways, rivers, sacred things, etc; for else men could not live' (Hobbes, 1651, iv, 14); another portion of land should be allocated to the state 'to sustain the whole expense to the common peace, and defence necessarily required' (Hobbes, 1668, xxiv, 8). The rest of the land should be privately owned. In the state of nature, men should not possess more land than they needed for their survival, if this meant that others could not have enough for their necessities. In the commonwealth, the initial distribution of land was the responsibility of the sovereign, whose decisions could not be questioned.

Wealth is not only accepted but it is praised, especially if it is the result of one's industry rather than the benefit of inheritance. It helps to acquire friendships and to provide protection and security to its owner. Unlike the Stoics, who argued that wisdom is superior to wealth, Hobbes reverses the relationship between the two – 'he who is rich is wise'. Poverty in the sense of lacking basic necessities is 'evil', while poverty in the sense of being satisfied with just the basic needs of life is commendable for 'it delivers its owner from envy, calumny, and plots' (Hobbes, 1658, xi, 7 and 8).

Hobbes' views on poor relief are unspectacular – they follow closely on the then prevailing thought and practice. As we pointed out in Chapter 4, poor relief was beginning to be taken over by the local communes in Western Europe. In England, The Elizabethan Act of 1601 required local parishes to levy taxes on their wealthier members so as to pay for the cost of poor relief. Hobbes follows this trend and argues that the relief of poverty cannot be left to the whims of charity – it has to be the responsibility of the state, of the commonwealth, as he prefers to call it. This is despite his view that, generally speaking, the poor are themselves to blame for their poverty. Everyone knows, he claims, that 'riches are gotten with industry, and kept by frugality, yet all the poor commonly lay blame on the evil government, excusing their own sloth and luxury' (Hobbes, 1651, xii, 9).

Although the state has the responsibility of providing for its poor, it must distinguish between the deserving and the undeserving poor – a view held from Plato onwards by most thinkers discussed in this book so far. Work rates very highly in his value system: 'it is truly a motive for life. Idleness is torture' (Hobbes, 1658, xi, 11). He accepts the general assumption of the times that the able-bodied unemployed are themselves to blame. They are not, therefore, entitled to poor relief from the state: instead, 'they are to be forced to work' and, where that proves not possible, 'they are to be transplanted into countries not sufficiently inhabited' (Hobbes, 1668, xxx, 19). He does, however, concede that the government ought to encourage the creation of jobs in 'navigation, agriculture, fishing, and all manner of manufacture' so that there would be no excuse for anyone of not finding employment (Hobbes, 1668, xxx, 19).

The deserving poor, that is, those who, as a result of an accident that could not be foreseen, become unable to maintain themselves, 'ought not to be left to the charity of private persons, but to be provided for by the laws of the commonwealth' (Hobbes, 1668, xxx, 18). He felt, however, that the deserving were a declining minority compared to the undeserving poor whose numbers were still increasing.

Hobbes was quite prepared to argue the case for government taxation to finance its services and was very critical of those who expected the state to protect them but who were unwilling to support government taxation. He maintained that on grounds of prudence, taxation should not be levied on incomes but on expenditure – not according to the ability to pay but according to the propensity to spend. Although he thought that the rich ought to pay more than the others because they received more in government protection services, he still felt that it is best that they should do so through taxes on expenditure so as not to undermine incentives to work and to save:

> For what reason is there that he which laboureth much, and sparing the fruits of his labour, consumeth little, should be more charged than he that living idly, getteth little, and spendeth all he gets, seeing the one hath no more protection from the commonwealth than the other? (Hobbes, 1668, xxx, 17)

Clearly, Hobbes was concerned with the provision of basic needs and even then to the deserving poor only. The satisfaction of non-basic needs was not of any concern to him. This is not surprising bearing in mind his views on absolute government, his concern over social stability, and the fact that physical survival only was the responsibility of government. As Tuck points out, famines were common in Europe and it was only in Hobbes' time that 'Western Europeans became more or less the first people in the history of our planet who could reasonably expect not to face devastating famine at some point in their lives' (Tuck, 1989, p 73). The issue of relative needs had to wait for a couple of centuries before coming onto the political agenda – it had to wait until human beings were certain of their daily basic needs.

Women in society

Hobbes' views on the position of women in society are brief and incoherent, if not conflicting. He begins by pointing out that in the state of nature, that is, in a society without any government, men and women are broadly speaking equal in the same way that there is broad equality among men or among women – a view contrary to that of most writers before him. As he put it:

> There is not always the difference of strength or prudence between the man and the woman as that the right can be determined without war. (Hobbes, 1668, xx, 4)

This means that mothers and fathers have, theoretically speaking, the same right to be equal parents to their children. But this is impossible, 'for no man can obey two masters' (Hobbes, 1668, xx, 4). Hobbes shows the absolutist nature of his views here for he does not believe that authority can be shared between parents and order maintained too. In such a situation, the mother assumes dominion over the children: the father of the child may not be known; and it is the mother who first feeds and cares for the child. In his colourful phrase, 'the birth follows the belly' (Hobbes, 1651, ix, 3).

Having pronounced this broad equality between men and women, he proceeds to confuse the issue with other references that see men as superior to women. In his discussion of the debates surrounding succession in monarchy, he writes that males should have precedence over females because 'men are naturally fitter than women for actions of labour and danger' (Hobbes, 1668, xix, 22); in cases where there are no children, the eldest brother is to be given preference (Hobbes, 1651, ix, 18); and in the various references to the family he tends to describe the father rather than the mother as 'the sovereign' whose command must be obeyed (Hobbes, 1668, xx, 15).

He tries to explain some of these differences in a 'commonwealth' as the result of male dominance in the framing of legislation. The civil law is in favour of the father, he says, 'because for the most part commonwealths have been erected by the fathers, not by the mothers of families' (Hobbes, 1668, xx, 4). At a superficial level, this may be a satisfactory explanation, but it is unsatisfactory at a higher level, for it does not say how men came to dominate legislatures. As Okin observes, Hobbes' explanation 'does not answer the problematical question of *how* just half of a race of people, all of whom are equal in what is for Hobbes the most important sense, could come to be in a position to found a commonwealth in which they had dominion over all the members of the other half' (Okin, 1979, p 198).

Conclusion

The centrepiece of Hobbes' political philosophy is that the main function of the state is, first, to provide physical security to its citizens and, second, that this is best done by an authoritarian, hereditary monarchy. Many commentators have always agreed with the first part of his thesis. As recently as the mid-1990s, Lady Thatcher, prime minister of the UK throughout the 1980s, wrote in her memoirs that 'the primary purpose of the state is to maintain order', for unless the state does this resolutely, 'not only bad but eventually good people will flout its authority' (Thatcher, 1995, p 542).

It is the second part of Hobbes' thesis – which is, in fact, the distinctive part – that has not received the support that he may have hoped for. To begin with, many disagreed with his views of human nature – the acquisitive, self-interested, aggressive individual – and hence rejected the whole theory built on them. But even those who may have had some sympathy with his views of human nature, parted company with his conclusion that hereditary, absolute power can best deal with the problems of security in society. They fall into two overlapping groups: first, those who rightly point out that to expect human beings to give up their life in the state of nature for life in a dictatorship is like encouraging them to leap 'from the frying-pan into the fire' (Raphael, 1977, p 71). Second, there are those who believe that some form of public involvement in society and in government is, in the long run, a better guarantee to security than blind obedience, even for people of Hobbesian character. Individuals need more than punishment and fear – they 'need civilizing traditions and institutions, a settled way of living and a social atmosphere which, while helping them to train their ambivalent dispositions into kindly habits of behaviour, will allow them to indulge their peculiarly human capacities for conversation, for laughter, for curiosity, for invention and for criticism' (Watkins, 1973, p 132).

Hobbes' contribution to debates on material welfare lies not in the little that he wrote on the subject but on his basic theoretical argument that there is no such thing as 'society' with a collective interest but rather a number of egoistic individuals pursuing their own interests. This became part of the laissez-faire doctrine that was used by right-wing politicians, first, to obstruct the introduction of state welfare measures; second, and more recently, to reduce the scope and generosity of comprehensive state welfare provision; and, third, to stress the significance of individual over social factors in the causation and treatment of social problems.

John Locke (1632–1704)

Locke merits a fulsome discussion as a welfare thinker because he wrote so much on education, poor relief, work, slavery and gender issues. He is often described as the father of liberalism – that diffuse body of ideas and policies that ranges from laissez-faire democracy to the comprehensive welfare state. It is a sign of the vagueness of Locke's philosophy that it can be interpreted so differently. Some of Locke's ideas were certainly a departure from the ideas and practices of his era but others were mere reflections of it.

Human nature and government by consent

Locke's political theory stems from a certain conception of human nature that differed substantially from that of Hobbes. In the state of nature, argues Locke, human beings were free and equal: free in the sense that there was no ruler to direct their actions; and equal in the sense that they all possessed human reason to guide their activities according to the law of nature. Locke's human beings in the state of nature are not as aggressive and destructive as those of Hobbes because their nature is different and also because they are guided by the law of nature. They are free to pursue their interests but the law of nature guides them to observe the interests of others, too – liberty does not degenerate into licence:

> The state of nature has a law of nature to govern it, which obliges everyone. And reason, which is that law, teaches all mankind who will but consult it that, being all equal and independent, no one ought to harm another in his life, health, liberty, or possessions. (Locke, 1689b, ii, sec 6)

Human beings in the state of nature are reminded that they have to answer for their actions to God one day, an argument similar to that of Augustine or Aquinas (Gough, 1950); and aggressors know that they can be forcibly resisted from their actions by the rest of society. Despite all this, a state of war exists in the state of nature, though it is not as violent and constant as that portrayed by Hobbes. It is for this reason that human beings decided to invest some of their rights – not all – into a civil authority that would represent the whole society and arbitrate on disputes:

> To avoid this state of war is one great reason of men's putting themselves into society, and quitting the state of nature. (Locke, 1689b, iii, sec 21)

Unlike Hobbes, however, Locke maintains that the civil authority created is not given absolute powers – it is given limited and conditional powers and it is answerable to the public. In the same way that the majority put the government in power, it can also remove it from power, including by revolution in extreme cases, if it is found that it does not govern according to the agreed laws. It is government by public consent as compared to the absolutist form of government envisaged by Hobbes. Thus, the absolute government envisaged by Hobbes is unacceptable to Locke for it lacks public consent, it involves the concentration of power – legislative, executive and judicial – into the same hands, and it is not answerable to the people (Locke, 1689b, vi, sec 90). Hobbes and Locke agree, however, that the establishment of government was not through divine will, as the Christian writers maintained, but through human action.

Locke, however, is no democrat in either the contemporary sense or in the Classical Greek sense. When he talks of the majority, he means the majority of the land-owning men in society – he excludes all the rest of the male population as well as all women. Nor does he support the widespread and direct involvement of freemen in government, as it was practised in Athens. The propertyless could expect to be ruled fairly, but they could not expect to have any say in the election of the government.

Locke was no egalitarian either, in the strong sense of that term. When he talked of equality, he simply meant potential equality of reason and equality of rights in some aspects of life – not equality of rights in all aspects of life, or equality of opportunity or of outcome. It is these contradictions that make Locke difficult to classify in political theory with the result that he has been described both as an individualist and as a collectivist.

One of the rights that he championed was religious freedom for most people in society – something that was in conflict with the ideas and the practices of his time, as shown by the number of religious wars at that time. He was not the first to put this forward but he was certainly the most influential. Religious freedom was justified, he argued, on both ethical and intellectual grounds. On ethical grounds, 'a church has no right to prosecute anyone'; and on intellectual grounds 'we can never know for certain that our religious opinions are correct and all others are false and heretical' (O'Connor, 1952, pp 211–12). He excluded, however, three groups from religious freedom: the atheists; those who show allegiance to a foreign power; and those who would not grant religious freedom to others, had they been in power – probably the Roman Catholics, as the Levellers had argued.

Private property

If the primary aim of the state in Hobbes' theory was the maintenance of social order, in Locke's theory it was the preservation of private property because it is property that provides security and liberty to the individual:

> The great and chief end of men's uniting into commonwealths, and putting themselves under government, is the preservation of their property. (Locke, 1689b, ix, sec 124)

Being the primary aim of government, it was not unexpected that he supported the use of draconian sanctions in order to protect private property. It is these views on property together with many other parts of his theory that lend support to the charge that his whole political theory was a justification of the rule of the propertied classes. Prior to Locke, the general view was that in the state of nature property was held in common and was used in common. Private property developed through conquest, usurpation, the Fall of Man from God's grace and such other ways. Locke changed all this by insisting that private property existed in the state of nature itself and was the result of human labour. It is, therefore, proper that when governments are installed by public consent they should make the protection of property their primary concern.

Locke began with a theory that stressed the social purpose of limited private property and ended with a view that freed private property from almost all restrictions and of almost all obligations for the public interest. In the state of nature, he argued, the amount of land that any one person could own depended on three criteria: how much he could cultivate himself, whether he could consume all the produce without waste and whether enough land was left for others. Private property was created through a person's labour – a process that was in accordance with God's wishes. He gave land to all in common, but He did not intend it to remain fallow and neglected:

> He gave it to the use of the industrious and rational; not to the fancy or covetousness of the quarrelsome and contentious. (Locke, 1689b, v, sec 34)

The net effect of the three criteria was that the amount of land that could be possessed by any one person was limited and hence there was enough land for all. Locke, however, proceeds from this to expand his theory in a way that justifies unlimited possession of land and any other property. With the invention of money, he argued, the profit motive enters the formula to the benefit of all: money made it possible for an industrious man to buy land from the others without breaking the three rules of property. He could now pay others to cultivate the land so that it did not remain uncared for; it was also possible to sell the produce so that none was wasted; and those without land could be gainfully employed – and all this change came about by voluntary agreement and proved mutually beneficial to all:

> It is plain that men have agreed to disproportionate and unequal possession of the earth, they having by a tacit and voluntary consent found out a way how a man may fairly possess more land than he himself can use of the product, by receiving in exchange for the overplus gold and silver, which may be hoarded up without injury to anyone. (Locke, 1689b, v, sec 50)

Bearing in mind the fact that land in his time was heavily concentrated in the hands of the nobility, Locke is suggesting that this was fair since it came about through voluntary agreement, that those without land could find employment elsewhere and that all sections of the community benefited from this concentration – propositions that fly in the face of the then existing reality. What Locke's theory of property succeeded in doing was to 'provide a moral basis for capitalist society' (Macpherson, 1962, p 221).

There is another aspect of Locke's theory that has long been questioned. Essentially he believed that property and freedom are interrelated: thus he placed government in the hands of the propertied classes – what he called 'the industrious and rational' – without showing any concern for the disenfranchisement of the rest of the population. He argued that the labouring classes, apart from their mental inadequacies, are so preoccupied with the problems of earning a living that they have no time or inclination for the political issues of their society – a view similar to that of Aristotle and Plato. Since then, there has been a greater appreciation of the fact that the freedom that human beings have 'must depend, in any society, largely on how property is distributed' (Plamenatz, 1963, p 337), and this belief has contributed to the political forces that have led to the introduction of progressive taxation, wealth taxes and other aspects of welfare state provision.

Locke's views on property fitted in well with an expanding economy, an unregulated labour market and the political dominance of the men of property. In many ways, they reflected the dominant views of society and had long been coming. In Tawney's words:

> Locke merely poured into a philosophical mould ideas which had been hammered out in the stress of political struggles, and which were already the commonplace of landowner and merchant. (Tawney, 1990, p 256)

Work

Locke's views on work were not central to his political theory. They appeared in a short note late on in his life and were probably prompted by his ill-health. He begins by claiming that work is a God-given obligation that benefits individuals and societies not only in economic but in medical, political, social and moral ways:

> We ought to look on it as a mark of goodness in God that he has put us in this life under a necessity of labour: not only to keep mankind from the mischiefs that ill men at leisure are very apt to do; but it is a benefit even to the good and the virtuous, which are thereby preserved from the ills of idleness or the diseases that attend constant study in a sedentary life (Locke, 1693a, p 440)

The basic necessities of life for all could be secured by half the working day if people were employed in useful labour. The desire, however, for luxury goods means both that people have to work harder, in occupations not necessary for the welfare of humankind, and an inability to satisfy public demands. He is particularly concerned that the sedentary lifestyles of the studious, like himself, and the voluptuousness of the rich damage their health – they are the cause of 'the spleen and the gout and of those other decays of health' (Locke, 1693a, p 440). It also prevents the studious from reaching ripe old age or makes their old age so rife with ill-health that they cannot be productive, while 'the sober and working artisan and the frugal laborious countryman performs his part well, and cheerfully goes on in his business to a vigorous old age' (Locke, 1693a, p 441). It is difficult to know whether this was true in Locke's time, though epidemiological statistics from the 19th century onwards do not support such a conclusion – middle- and upper-class people suffer less from disease and they live longer than working-class, let alone poor, people.

Locke thus proposes that the working day should be reorganised so that the studious and the wealthy spend a minimum of three out of the 12 hours a day on some labouring job, while the working men spend three hours daily on learning. The physical health of the first group will benefit, the educational standards of the working class will improve, and the populace will 'be delivered from that horrid ignorance and brutality to which the bulk of them is now everywhere given up' (Locke, 1693a, p 442). Such a programme of work will also have political effects, for the general public will be less likely 'to be blown into tumults and popular commotions' (Locke, 1693a, p 442) by agitators.

Locke ends his note on the optimistic conclusion that 'if the labour of the world were rightly directed and distributed there would be more knowledge, peace, health, and plenty in it than now there is. And mankind be much more happy than now it is' (Locke, 1693a, p 442). He says nothing about the level of wages that were woefully low in his time with the result that many families of working men lived in poverty. On the whole, however, it is true to say that Locke's views on the issue of labour were ahead of his time, just as More's ideas in *Utopia* were. His proposals that the rich and the studious should do physical work while the labouring men should have time to read show that he did not believe that the then existing social conditions were inevitable. These views, however, are in stark contrast to his harsh views on both the causes and the remedies of poverty, which are discussed in the next section.

Poverty: causes and remedies

Locke's views on poverty and poor relief are contained in a 1697 memorandum to the Board of Trade, of which he was a member,, that was examining ways of improving the 'Employment of the Poor'. He begins by pointing out that both the number of the poor and the expenditure on poor relief had risen consistently and sharply over the years. The cause of this rise, he argues, was not adverse structural factors because there was an expanding economy and a rise in job creation. It was the result of individual character and behavioural failings:

> If the causes of this evil be looked into, it will be found to have proceeded neither from the scarcity of provisions, nor from want of employment for the poor. The growth of the poor must therefore have some other cause; and it can be nothing else but the relaxation of discipline, and corruption of manners: virtue and industry being as constant companions on the one side as vice and idleness on the other. (Locke, 1697, p 447)

If the causes of poverty were personal failings, then the remedies of the problem of poverty should naturally concentrate on the correction of the individual's failings. Locke's diagnosis of the causes and the remedies of the problem of poverty merely reflected the then generally held view that the poor were to blame for their misfortune. The purpose of any poor relief system, he argued, was not simply to give out monetary benefits but to put the poor to work. In the same way that the rich earned their wealth through hard work, the poor, too, should earn their living through an honest day's work.

Locke classifies those receiving poor relief from the parishes into three groups and puts forward different reform proposals for each one of them. He also distinguishes between men and women as well as between adults and children. His three categories are: the deserving poor, the semi-deserving and the undeserving. This is how he describes the three groups:

> First, those who can do nothing at all towards their support.
>
> Second, those who, though they cannot maintain themselves wholly, yet are able to do something towards it.
>
> Third, those who are able to maintain themselves by their own labour. (Locke, 1697, p 447)

He makes two general reform proposals for all those on poor relief: first, 'the suppressing of superfluous brandy shops and unnecessary alehouses' (Locke, 1697, p 447); and, second, the strict enforcement of poor relief legislation. He had some harsh words for those of the overseers of the poor who did not take their duties of setting the poor to work seriously. These two measures would, he thought, make some contribution towards restraining the 'debauchery' of the poor and thus make it easier to set them to work (Locke, 1697, p 447). It was a general assumption of the period that the poor spent most of their time and money drinking and thus not working but relying on poor relief.

Beginning with the third group, the wholly undeserving male poor, 'the begging drones', as he calls them, aged 14 to 50 years, he advances a series of complex measures, over and above the existing poor relief regulations. If found begging in maritime counties, away from their own parish, and without a pass, they should be arrested and brought before a justice of the peace who should sentence them not to a house of correction because of the lenient regime prevailing there, nor send them back to their parish because of the expenses involved, but to one of His Majesty's ships for a period of three years 'under strict discipline, at soldier's pay (subsistence money being deducted for their victuals on board), and be punished as deserters if they go on shore without leave' (Locke, 1697, p 449). As for those in this group found begging without a pass in inland counties, they should be sent to a house of correction, provided discipline was made stricter and life more difficult in these institutions, for a period of three years' hard labour.

He is particularly harsh, to the point of cruelty, on those of the 'undeserving' males who forge passes in order to beg: a first offender 'shall lose his ears' while a second offence should mean that 'he shall be transported to the plantations, as in the case of felony' (Locke, 1697, p 449).

Women found begging outside their parish without a pass are to be treated less severely than men. Broadly speaking, they should either be sent back home and charged for the costs involved or they should be sent to a house of correction for a period of three months before being returned to their parish (Locke, 1697, p 449).

Locke's prescription for children, those under the age of 14, found begging outside their parish appears harsh, particularly in view of the humane methods of education that he proposes for other children, as we shall see later in this chapter. Those found begging near their parish 'shall be sent to the next working-school, there to be soundly whipped, and kept at work till evening' before being allowed to go home; those found begging a long way from home should 'be sent to the next house of correction, there to remain for six weeks' (Locke, 1697, p 450).

Locke hoped that these additional measures would reduce substantially the number of the 'undeserving' male poor, the 'idle vagabonds'. If, after all these measures, any one of them complained that he could not find work, the guardian of the poor should find him employment; and if that failed, the guardian should allocate him for work to one or more of the local parishioners at wages lower than the going rate. If the individual refused to accept such employment, he should be sent either to an HM ship or to a house of correction for three years and his wages be used to support his family.

Locke had far less to say for the second group that he considered as the largest of the three groups. The composition of the group was very wide: it included the disabled, married women on poor relief and all the children whose parents received poor relief. The adults in this group should be helped to find part-time or full-time work but with few, if any, sanctions. It is the children that receive most of his attention.

He proposes that parishes should set up working-schools, 'to which the children of all such as demand relief of the parish should be obliged to come' in order to learn some useful occupation such as spinning or knitting (Locke, 1697, p 453). The curriculum of such schools and the discipline is in marked contrast to what he proposes for the education of the children of the rich, as it will become clear in a subsequent section. There is no discussion of any curriculum, teaching methods, pupil–staff relationships and so on for the working-schools. These schools were meant as places of work, of learning a trade and of social discipline.

Despite all this, he sees a number of advantages from the provision of such schools: mothers will have more free time to enable them to find employment; the burden of poor relief will be reduced; children will learn work habits in addition to a trade; the children will be better fed than at their home; boys will be apprenticed till the age of 23 to local handicraftsmen, or found employment with local gentlemen or farmers; and the children will be obliged to go to church and thus freed from 'their idle and loose way of breeding up' (Locke, 1697, p 454).

That Locke's proposals were harsh to the extreme is shown by the fact that they were rejected by the Board of Trade. The consensus view of the Board was that 'the poor were unemployed because there was a shortage of jobs, and that the solution was not new punitive measures, but new schemes for state investment in order to create gainful employment' (Wootton, 1993, p 116). His views on labour discussed in the previous section and on education to be discussed below; his belief in Christian values including 'love your neighbour as yourself'; his willingness to be generous to the deserving poor who should have 'meat, drink, clothing and firing' (Locke, 1697, p 452); and his persistent argument that human beings must think coherently, make his views on poverty draconian to the extreme. Perhaps, the importance that he placed on work and on supporting oneself through work overrode his other beliefs. This may help also to explain the fact that during his life, he 'visited the poor who were sick, dispersing charity'; and the fact that in his will he stipulated that some of his money should go 'to various "deserving" poor of his parish' (Marshall, 1994, p 325).

Slavery

No sooner had slavery been abolished in Europe than it reappeared in the form of the African slave trade – the forced transportation and sale of millions of Africans as slaves to the plantations in the Americas. About two million African slaves were transported during the 15th and 16th centuries across the Atlantic, with many more to follow in the 18th and early 19th centuries.

A great deal of controversy surrounds Locke's position on the issue of slavery: his writings appear to both reject and endorse slavery; but the major charge against him concerns his personal involvement in the slave trade.

Most of his references make it clear that slavery is unacceptable though some of them do the exact opposite. In all the theoretical discussion, he was not concerned with the African slave trade as such but rather with the condition of slavery in general. Very early in the *First Treatise*, he makes it abundantly clear that slavery is contrary to the kind of society he has in mind where individuals are free to decide their destiny so long as they do this within the law and they acknowledge the right of others to do likewise:

> Slavery is so vile and miserable an estate of man, and so directly opposed to the generous temper and courage of our nation, that it is hardly to be conceived that an Englishman, much less a Gentleman, should plead for it. (Locke, 1689a, p 1)

In several parts of the *Second Treatise*, too, he takes up the same position: men are born to be free and are not suited to slavery. In one instance, however, he seems to support slavery when he says that prisoners captured in a just war may be killed or kept as slaves by their conquerors:

> This is the perfect condition of slavery, which is nothing else but the state of war continued between a lawful conqueror and a captive. (Locke, 1689b, iv, sec 24)

But this type of slavery does not support the classical practice or the plantation practice of slavery where the children of the slaves were also slaves. In addition, a just war is defined narrowly to refer to wars fought in the defence of one's property against an aggressor.

There is, however, general agreement that Locke was directly and indirectly involved in the African slave trade in three ways: he bought shares in slave trading companies; he acted as secretary and policy advisor to groups involved in the slave trade; and he owned land in Carolina where slaves were employed. Moreover, in the *Constitution of Carolina*, which he drafted, he makes it abundantly clear that though slaves must be allowed religious freedom, this does not mean that they are exempted from slavery or that it reduces the power of master over slave.

> Every freeman of Carolina shall have absolute power and authority over his Negro slaves, of what opinion or religion soever. (Locke, 1669, 110)

A good deal of debate has taken place of how one can reconcile Locke's views on slavery with his actions. Three different positions have emerged: those who see this contradiction 'as an embarrassing but insignificant lapse' in Locke's philosophy; those who feel that Locke 'tortured his basic theories in order to accommodate American slavery'; and the third group that sees 'the justification of slavery as an integral part of Lockean theory' (Glausser, 1990, pp 205, 206, 210).

All that can be said with certainty is that Locke's writings are conflicting enough to place him in both the anti- and the pro-slavery lobby. His practice, however, is clearly supportive of slavery. His failure to condemn the inhumanities of the slave trade and of slave work in America, of which he had ample knowledge, coupled with his failure to explain the conflict between his theory and his practice, leave him open to the charge that he helped to strengthen the institution of slavery (Spellman, 1997, p 120).

The position of women

Locke is far more concerned with the family, with the husband–wife relationship and with parent–child relationships than about men and women as individuals. What he has to say about the former, however, has implications for the latter.

He begins by criticising the then current Christian belief that God held Eve, rather than Adam, responsible for the Original Sin and that, as a result, God gave men powers over women. Bearing in mind that Adam was 'a helper in the temptation, as well as a partner in the transgression', it was not rational that 'Adam could expect any favours, any grant of privileges, from his offended maker' (Locke, 1689a, pp 44, 45). Nevertheless, he proceeds to argue that though God's words were not intended to subjugate women to men, they referred to the marital situation – the obedience that 'every wife owes her husband' (Locke, 1689a, p 48).

The obedience that the wife owes to her husband, however, must not be interpreted to mean that the power that parents have over their children rests wholly with the father – the mother has 'an equal title' to this and it is, therefore, clearer if we refer to such power not as 'paternal' but rather as 'parental' (Locke,

1689b, vi, sec 52). But if the children owe obedience to both their parents, they are entitled to receive adequate parental care. The power that parents have over their children stems not from the biological factors of birth but from the social factors of caring – the fact that parents are the carers and guardians. Thus it is the foster-parents, and not the natural parents, that have the duty of caring for the children and, in return, have the right to expect children's obedience and honour (Locke, 1689b, vi, sec 65).

He sees the family as the beginning of civil society. Marriage is 'a voluntary contract between man and woman' with many aims – sexual satisfaction, mutual support, companionship, but above all procreation and the care of children (Locke, 1689b, vii, sec 78). It is, however, inevitable that there will be disagreements in any family and it is important that one of the parents must have the final say. In such situations, the final word rests with the father 'as the abler and stronger' of the two. Like Hobbes, he begins with the equality of the sexes and ends with the superiority of the male. Despite this, he refutes the claim that this makes the husband superior to the wife: 'it gives the husband no more power over her life than she has over his'. In the last resort, she has the 'liberty to separate from him' if the laws and the customs of the country allow; and 'the children upon such separation fall to the father or mother's lot, as such contract does determine' (Locke, 1689b, vii, sec 82).

It is difficult not to draw the conclusion that despite Locke's many caveats, his theories did not advance the cause of women and may, in fact, have reinforced women's subordination particularly in view of his theories of property and inheritance where the male takes precedence over the female; and his view that since the husband represents the family in the world, women's political rights are implicitly ignored.

Education and childhood

Locke's *Some Thoughts Concerning Education* was meant for the education of the sons of the gentry, though parts of it could be said to apply to the daughters of the gentry as well as to other children. This emphasis on the education of the sons of the nobility was not unique to Locke, for all the educational works of the period bore the same bias. It was believed that the education of the gentleman's son was crucial because he would become 'the future public person whose example would presumably set the moral tone for the nation' (Spellman, 1997, p 82).

Until the 17th century, there was no recognition of childhood as a stage of development or of children as individual beings with rights, ideas or personalities. Children were seen mainly in economic terms: as a form of labour in most cases and as part of the chain of inheritance, in the case of the propertied classes. Locke was one of the first to stress the individuality of children, even though he referred to a minority of children. Life for most children was extremely hard and they were subjected to the most brutal physical punishments. The few who were lucky enough to go to school endured a curriculum that was divorced from their everyday life; rote learning was the norm, and teachers were often hard taskmasters. These and other aspects of childhood and education help to explain the progressive nature of Locke's ideas on education for the elite.

Like the Classical Greeks, Locke believed that education was vital for both the child and society. It was particularly important for the top classes in society, for they would then provide the right leadership for the country. It was an elitist educational theory in a rigidly stratified society. Yet, Locke departed from the Platonian view that ideas are inherent in human beings and they are passed on in abstract terms. He was clear of the value of learning by experience; of the importance of the environment in the child's education without rejecting the significance of hereditary factors. In the following quotation he stresses the environment but in other places he emphasises heredity. This is not unusual because 'like ourselves, he was unable to make up his mind between them' (Garforth, 1964, p 52):

> Of all men that we meet with, nine parts of ten are what they are, good or evil, useful or not, by their education. It is that which makes the great difference in mankind. (Locke, 1693b, p 1)

Again borrowing from the Classical Greeks, he also emphasised the importance of both physical and mental education. He has a long list of comments concerning the proper diet of children, the amount of sleep they need and even the kind of bed that they must use. In all this advice, it is clear that he writes for the children of the rich, for most people could not possibly afford to follow his advice:

> A sound mind in a sound body is a short but useful description of a happy state in this world. (Locke, 1693b, p 1)

What was important for the education of children was not merely the amassing of knowledge but the acquisition of the proper values for the development of their character. This process must begin from infancy at home and the parents have as much a part to play as the teachers. The fundamental principle for moral development was the denial of one's pleasures, and neither parents nor teachers should give in to the children's vanity. Children should learn that they are not to have anything because they want it but because their parents or teachers think it is good for them:

> The great principle and foundation of all virtue and worth is placed in this: that a man is able to deny himself his own desires, cross his own inclinations and purely follow what reason directs as best, though the appetite lean the other way. (Locke, 1693b, p 3)

Locke's view on the relationship between parents and children is a mixture of realism and idealism where both discipline and love play their part. He is critical of the excessive use of physical punishment but he is also prepared to sanction it in certain circumstances – for 'obstinacy and rebellion', for persistent lying and for obstinate crying. Any physical punishment of children, however, should be administered by a trusted servant, in the presence of the parents. The earlier the process of disciplining started, the less the need for physical punishment would be.

The most difficult part of child rearing and of education, he argues, is to find the right balance between encouraging and disciplining a child; how to allow self-expression and how to set limits to questioning, how to praise and how to criticise, how to reward and how to sanction, how to allow children to play and how to prevent them from annoying others. Whoever finds the right answers to these apparent contradictions 'has, in my opinion, got the secret of education' (Locke, 1693b, p 64).

Locke wanted parents and teachers to discourage children from being cruel to birds, butterflies and animals not only because this is reprehensible in itself but also because it would adversely affect the child's character: 'they who delight in the suffering and destruction of inferior creatures will not be apt to be very compassionate or benign to those of their own kind' (Locke, 1693b, p 116).

Bearing in mind the state of schools, their teaching methods, their curriculum and the educational standards of the teachers, it is not surprising that Locke elected for the education of the sons of the gentry at their own home. He wanted children to be taught not by rules but by example, not by rote learning but by experience, not by fear but by respect, and always in accordance with the child's ability because 'in many cases all that we can do or should aim at is to make the best of what nature has given' (Locke, 1693b, p 66). Since the greatest skill of a teacher is how to make his subject interesting in order 'to get and keep the attention of his scholar', it is obviously important that teachers should not be so harsh that they make themselves 'such scarecrows that their scholars should always tremble in their sight' (Locke, 1693b, p 167).

Locke's curriculum was wide-ranging: 'it was a typical gentleman's education' (Yolton, 1971, p 75). It included the three R's and several other subjects including languages – Latin as it was the language of learning, French for travels abroad and Greek for the best scholars. Drawing, too, was important, for it would prove useful to a gentleman on his travels. He was also keen that all young gentlemen should learn some practical trades – gardening so that they would be able to advise their gardeners, and carpentry so that they could make useful things in the house including their children's toys (Locke, 1693b, p 201). In this he went against Aristotle's view that practical subjects are unbecoming to the intelligent and the liberally minded.

Locke's educational programme contains many proposals that continue to have validity today while many other proposals, including those on physical punishment, would be rejected by most educationists today. Its elitism inevitably offends, and rightly so, contemporary democratic ideals despite the fact that Locke's ideas were considered radical at the time. Bearing in mind the social and political structure of his society, it is not surprising that Locke's educational theory was elitist. 'Egalitarian democracy in education', writes Gay, 'would have seemed the wildest of utopian dreams to men of Locke's time' (Gay, 1964, p 15). Most educational theories reflect in varying degrees their society, however radical they may appear to contemporaries.

Conclusion

An assessment of Locke's ideas from a social welfare perspective has to be mixed. His views on human liberty, the rejection of absolutism, his support of the rule of law, religious toleration, government by consent, the right of resistance to an unjust regime, and the core of his educational ideas are major contributions to human welfare. As Dunn points out, 'there is a real justice in seeing the European Enlightenment as Locke's legacy' (Dunn, 1984, p 21).

Some of his ideas, however, were so dominated by the ideas of his era that they have failed to pass the test of time. His exclusion of most people from the right to vote, his theory of property, his ambivalent theory of the slave trade, his views on women, and above all his ideas on poor relief reflected and reinforced the prejudices of his time as well as the interests of the propertied classes. His harsh treatment of the children of the poor was in marked contrast to his broad-minded approach to the education of the children of the rich.

SIX

Early feminism
Mary Astell (1668–1731), Sophia and Mary Wollstonecraft (1759–97)

The same socio-economic forces that propelled the debates over men's rights at such high speed during the 17th and 18th centuries also ushered in, haltingly and grudgingly, the debates over women's rights – the 'woman question', as it was then known.

The rising economic affluence, the growth of secular debates, the spread of education among the middle classes, increased urbanisation and the widening of geographical horizons provided the social environment for a few bold female spirits to speak out against their oppression. Of particular significance was the growth of the professional middle classes – lawyers, doctors, clerics – some of whose wives and daughters found it difficult to accept the dominant ideology of female inferiority.

It was then universally believed that women were not only different from men but inferior, too, physically and mentally; their place was not in the public domain but in the private sphere as wives, mothers and daughters destined to serve and obey their menfolk; education was not necessary and, in fact, it could be counter to their welfare, for their main aim in life was to find a husband and raise a family. It was a deeply ingrained view that was backed by religion, custom, law and, often, economic necessity; and was accepted not only by men as a group who benefited from it but also by most women who suffered as a result.

A number of themes run through the early feminist writings: women were not inferior to men by nature; any inferiorities were due to socio-economic reasons; a great deal of attention was focused on the absence of adequate educational facilities for women; the absence of occupational opportunities for educated women was always criticised; the oppressive nature of marriage was a central concern; it was not so much the institution of marriage per se that was being criticised but rather the male cruelty within the married home; and, finally, the overall concern was primarily with the condition of middle-class, professional women. The condition of working-class women was either ignored or was seen as part and parcel of the condition of middle-class women. Concern for the condition of working-class women came later, at the close of the 18th century and throughout the 19th century (Offen, 2000).

In this chapter we consider briefly the views of Mary Astell and Sophia, before we concentrate on the work of Mary Wollstonecraft – the first theoretical feminist writer, 'the founder or foremother of Western feminism' (Yeo, 1997, p 1), who had a lot to say on many of the issues discussed in this volume – wealth and poverty, education and family relationships – in addition to her main concern on the position of women in society.

Mary Astell (1668–1731)

Astell's major book, *A Serious Proposal to the Ladies, for the Advancement of their True and Greatest Interests* (1694) is a blend of radicalism and conservatism, more prescriptive than conceptual. She accepts the fact that women's achievements in society have been meagre; that the behaviour of middle- and upper-class ladies is often 'frivolous'; but rejects the claim that this is the result of their innate inferiorities to men. Rather the behaviour of women is the product of custom and a lack of proper education:

> Ignorance and a narrow education lay the foundation of vice, and imitation and custom rear it up. (Astell, 1694, p 27)

She is particularly critical of the established norm that the ladies' most cherished aim in life is to dress, look and behave in such a way as 'to attract the eyes of the men', particularly men 'whose foreheads are better than their brains'– and they are the majority in society (Astell, 1694, pp 10, 25). She beseeches women to abandon the fashion of 'pursuing butter-flies and trifles', of 'imitating the impertinencies of our neighbours' and, instead, to aim at higher things – education, modesty and self-pride – for it is only in that way that they can become independently minded persons, and better wives and mothers. If women were rightly educated, they would 'see through and scorn those little silly artifices which are used to ensnare and deceive them' (Astell, 1694, p 23). They would then hold their own better in a man's world.

She holds men responsible for initiating, fostering and enforcing the social system of women's subjugation even though women are also to blame for so easily acquiescing to such a system. Men should not be too critical of women's conduct because 'it is the product of their own [men's] folly, in denying them the benefits of an ingenuous and liberal education' that would have opened the door to a virtuous life (Astell, 1694, p 23). It is a wonder that, despite all the handicaps, there are so many women who are wise and good. Had men faced the same disadvantages, 'perhaps they would be so far from surpassing those whom now they despise, that they themselves would sink into the greatest stupidity and brutality' (Astell, 1694, p 13). She, therefore, rejects the argument by 'men of more wit than wisdom' that 'women are naturally incapable of acting prudently' (Astell, 1694, p 15).

Despite her criticisms of men and the social system, she does not argue for women's rightful place in public life. All she asks for is for women to be educated in a way that would develop their personalities so that they could become wise wives and mothers. She argues against the loveless marriages based on economic considerations and supports the institution of marriage, based on freedom and rationality. Women, have an important role to play as mothers but they can only fulfil this properly if they receive the right kind of education. Parents who neglect their children commit a crime that is 'beneath brutality'; while mothers who 'through pride and delicacy remit their little one to the care of a foster parent' are in all intents and purposes abandoning their responsibilities (Astell, 1694, p 18).

Despite her strong plea to women to abandon their frivolous and aimless way of life, she was aware that this would prove impossible for most women because of the heavy hand of tradition – 'that merciless torrent that carries all before it' (Astell, 1694, p 27). What was needed to deal with the 'woman problem' was a comprehensive set of solutions because 'single medicines are too weak to cure it' (Astell, 1694, p 35). Her solution was the establishment of a residential community cum university, a religious ladies college, where women with financial means could go to educate and improve themselves.

Astell had high hopes for the good effects of such a college: it would provide a retreat from the world for those women who felt the need for it; it would raise women's understanding of the true goals of Christianity; it would demonstrate that, contrary to common belief, unmarried status can be socially acceptable for women; it would improve the educational standards of women, particularly in philosophy; emphasise the attributes of an independent, socially responsible woman, contrary to the dominant model of courtly behaviour; encourage the development of personal friendship based on love and trust; provide a simple life in terms of lifestyle, food and clothing; and provide a base from which women could go out into the world and carry out charitable work of a varied kind – 'relieving the poor, healing the sick, instructing the ignorant, counselling the doubtful, comforting the afflicted, and correcting those who err and do amiss' (Astell, 1694, pp 53–4).

Apart from the immediate, direct good effects, there were also the less immediate advantages: it would set an example to other women of how best to live their lives; it would show to the world that women can live useful and independent lives; and it would encourage the growth of a value system that was different from the prevailing one. Superficially, the whole idea bore some resemblance to earlier notions of convent life though it was essentially different: women could leave the college whenever they wanted to, they went out to the community for charitable work, they could get married when they left, and their stay in the college was considered temporary as a preparation for life outside. Indeed, Astell argues that the college experience will make them better wives and mothers – a reason good enough for men to support the project, she argued. She was hopeful that her scheme would receive strong support for only 'the beaux perhaps, and topping sparks of the town will ridicule and laugh at it' (Astell, 1694, p 103).

Although the scheme never materialised, the ideas involved in it added to the volume of feminist writing demanding an improvement of women's condition in society. Astell wrote from a religious and conservative perspective and it is tempting to discount her contribution to feminist thinking. This would be a mistake, for Astell's demands were radical for her period: the education of women, companionate marriage, independent minds for women, dedication to the common good and the abandonment of 'social frivolity' (Kinnaird, 1983, p 38).

There is no extensive discussion in Astell's work of the impoverished living conditions of working-class women and how this affected other aspects of their lives. As expected, there is very detailed debate of the futility of the 'frivolous' lifestyle of the lady, and the middle-class attempt to copy it. As mentioned earlier, middle- and upper-class concerns dominated the debate of feminist writings.

Sophia, an anonymous author

There is no agreement on the identity of Sophia, whose book, *Woman Not Inferior to Man* (1739), was the most spirited rebuttal of the prejudicial belief that women were inferior to men. Some attribute it to Lady Montague (Blease, 1910, p 44) while others believe that it was written by the Cartesian thinker François Poullain de la Barre, best known for his strong advocacy of the equality of the sexes in his book *De l'egalite des deux sexes* (1673) (Roberts and Mizuta, 1995, p xii).

Sophia begins by raising for discussion a question to which the social sciences have not yet been able to provide a satisfying answer: how do we prove or disprove a prejudicial belief? What kind of evidence is needed, who is going to provide it and, above all, who is going to assess the evidence in order to reach a conclusion on the validity of the prejudice in question. She suggests that the only impartial way to assess the claim of male superiority is through the use of reason and proceeds to do this in ways that she considers impartial.

She states the issue as follows: men are unanimous in their belief that women 'are made only for their use, that we are fit only to breed and nurse children in their tender years, to mind household affairs, and to obey, serve, and please our masters' (Sophia, 1739, p 11). The only evidence they provide for this is that God made men before women and other creatures. But this very same claim can be used to argue that 'men were made for our use rather than we for theirs' (Sophia, 1739, p 11). It is also worth remembering, she adds, that religion had been promulgated from the very start by men.

Events from everyday life do not provide any evidence of the inferiority of women. Beginning with procreation, she notes that both sexes are needed, for 'either without the other would be entirely useless' (Sophia, 1739, p 11). In terms of jobs, she stresses that the most important job in life is 'the nursing of children' – the future generation of society – and on this issue women deserve 'the first place in civil society' despite the fact that men have managed over the years to depict child rearing as something low and degrading.

Although men occupy all the important positions in society, this has nothing to do with innate ability – it is the result of education, interest and custom:

> All the diversity must come from *education, exercise, and the impressions* of those external objects which surround us in different circumstances (Sophia, 1739, p 23; author's emphasis)

She derides men's circular argument about women's potential for learning and their ability to hold important jobs in society. As she puts it: 'Why is learning useless to us? Because we have no share in public offices. And why have we no share in public offices? Because we have no learning' (Sophia, 1739, p 27). It is a circular argument that stands up to no rational examination and, as such, must be rejected. Reason, after all, is the yardstick by which arguments must be assessed. She, therefore, concludes that had women had the same advantages of studying as men, there is no doubt that they would have been just as good in the sciences and other forms of knowledge.

Turning to ability to govern, she feels certain that women would have been better at it than men had proved to be so far because of certain feminine values: reserve, meekness and tenderness. Her evidence for this is that women are often made the governesses of families long before the male members of the family mature to take over; young wild men are often married so that they can be tamed by their wives; and queens have proved better rulers than kings in England:

> England has learned by repeated experience, how much happier a
> kingdom is, when under the protection and rule of a woman, than it
> can hope to be under the government of a man. (Sophia, 1739, p 38)

As for teaching, she has no doubt that since women possess greater talent for public speaking than men, they would make better teachers and holders of other offices where public speaking is necessary. Moreover, even with the best of training, men cannot attain the same level as women:

> All the oratory of the schools is not able to give men that eloquence and
> ease of speech, which costs us (women) nothing. (Sophia, 1739, p 39)

Despite this superior feminine talent, women are absent from university chairs and other similar public offices – evidence of the fact that it is not absence of talent but prejudice that keeps women out of such positions. Sophia believes that women are capable of filling any public office but one – the priesthood. God forbade women to enter the priesthood and 'therefore we know better than to lay claim to what we could not practise without sacrilegious intrusion. But why God forbad us, it would be presumptuous to enquire' (Sophia, 1739, p 45).

As for army service, Sophia insisted that women were as good as men in the planning of war and in the leadership qualities required to carry out the plan. She downplays the significance of physical strength as a prerequisite to planning and leading a war because if physical strength was vital then the strongest men would have been the leaders – which is far from being the case. Women also possess as much courage as men, if not more, shown by the fact that they 'often behave more courageously than the men under pains, sickness, want, and the terrors of death itself' (Sophia, 1739, p 52).

Finally, women exhibit more trust and loyalty in marriage than men – a sign of strength and fortitude under testing conditions as well as of the oppressive nature of marriage:

> Where is there a woman, who having generously trusted her liberty with a husband, does not immediately find the spaniel metamorphosed into a tiger, or has not reason to envy the lesser misery of a bond-slave to a merciless tyrant? (Sophia, 1739, p 19)

Despite her strong views on gender equality, she is clear that she does not intend 'to stir up any of my own sex to revolt against men, or to invert the present order of things, with regard to government and authority' (Sophia, 1739, p 56). She wanted to establish through 'reasoned' argument that women are not inferior to men and that 'it would be to the joint interest of both to think so' (Sophia, 1739, p 56); to encourage women to improve their minds so that they could act with dignity rather than frivolity; and to pressurise men 'to confess their own baseness to us, and that the worst of us deserve much better treatment than the best of us receive' (Sophia, 1739, p 62).

In conclusion, Sophia rightly assessed that to fight prejudice one needs not only reasoned argument but a counter-ideology, too – one that exalts the strengths of those at whom prejudice is directed. Although her book is a mixture of reasoning and polemic, the approach she adopted on women's emancipation was well ahead of its time.

Mary Wollstonecraft (1759–97)

Wollstonecraft's work is concerned with the emancipation of women – both from the domination of men and from their own subservient beliefs and conduct. She treats women's issues as part of the wider political environment – the country's system of government, its social structure and its ideological climate. She wrote so much in such a short period of time and always to meet deadlines that her work is inevitably repetitive and not as cogent or lucid as it might otherwise have been. Nevertheless, her work is the most theoretical account of women's issues during this period and her major book, *A Vindication of the Rights of Woman* (1792), remains a classic in feminist literature. It is only in recent years that her work has been accepted not only for its contribution to feminist thinking but also to political theory (Pateman, 2003).

Private property and society

Wollstonecraft follows a long line of thinkers who believed in the idea of natural rights – rights given to human beings either by God or by nature that were inalienable. Her major contribution was her insistence that these rights were given to both men and women in equal ways and to equal degrees. This inevitably meant that the oppression of any human being was contrary to their natural right of freedom – hence poverty, slavery and women's bondage are contrary to natural rights, they are against God's wishes. Wollstonecraft put it as follows:

> It is necessary to emphatically repeat, that there are rights which men inherit at their birth, as rational creatures; and that, in receiving these, not from their forefathers, but, from God, prescription can never undermine natural rights. (Wollstonecraft, 1790, p 13)

She, therefore, rejected the Lockean principle that the security of private property is the core of liberty and of stability in the family and society. Indeed, she reverses the argument to claim that 'the demon of property' is 'a selfish principle' that sacrifices 'nobler' human principles. The hereditary concentration of property, particularly by the landed classes, undermines the natural rights of many in society in various ways and thus weakens human welfare:

> From the respect paid to property, flow most of the evils and vices which render this world such a dreary place to the contemplative mind. (Wollstonecraft, 1792, p 154)

To begin with, the hereditary principle of property with its inevitable stratification system debases both the rich and the poor. It creates, on one hand, 'the polished vices of the rich, their insincerity, want of natural affections, with all the specious train that luxury introduces'; and, on the other, 'a broken spirit, worn out body, and all those gross vices which the example of the rich, rudely copied, could produce' (Wollstonecraft, 1790, p 620). But it does more than that – it polarises society into two warring camps, the rich and the poor, with mistrust and hate between them:

> Envy built a wall of separation, that made the poor hate, whilst they bend to their superiors; who, on their part, stepped aside to avoid the loathsome sight of human misery. (Wollstonecraft, 1790, p 62)

The gross inequalities of property inevitably mean that society has no social cohesion, for individuals and groups behave towards each other with suspicion, mistrust and enmity, with the result that the national character is degraded. Inequality of rank inevitably degrades the minds of both the oppressors and the oppressed:

> Among unequals there can be no society; from such intimacies, friendship can never grow. (Wollstonecraft, 1790, p 39)

The inheritance of private property, as it then functioned among the landed classes, not only debased relations within society but it also degraded relationships within the family. Not only did it not enhance family stability, it divided family loyalties because of the inheritance laws: the eldest son received almost all and the other sons received little. Many of the younger sons found their way into the clergy, where they may have had neither talent nor interest. Moreover, anxious to gain promotion in the priesthood, they served the dominant interests with servility to the detriment of their self-esteem as well as of the public good:

> Few Bishops, though they have been learned and good Bishops, have gained the mitre without submitting to a servility of dependence that degrades the man. (Wollstonecraft, 1790, p 21)

The disinheritance of daughters had 'a pernicious effect on female morals', worse than the effect it had on sons because most professional jobs were closed to them (Wollstonecraft, 1790, p 22). Girls were brought up in ways so that they would sexually appeal to men, often married off to men of property for whom they had no affection thus creating many loveless marriages. It would have been better, Wollstonecraft argued, if property 'were more equally divided among all the children of the family' (Wollstonecraft, 1790, p 23). This would make it easier for talented younger children to thrive.

The inheritance principle also meant the creation of a permanent landed aristocracy and a court culture that the middle classes tried to imitate in servile ways with the result that other and better values were neglected. Men of ability among the professional classes also played on the follies of the aristocratic rich in order to make a good living. In these ways, aristocratic power corrupted society.

Wollstonecraft was also critical of the effects of property on democracy. Sordid interest, she thought, dominated most elections with the result that it may be true that the House of Commons in England 'is filled with everything illustrious in rank, in descent, in hereditary, and acquired opulence – but that it contains everything respectable in talents is very problematical' (Wollstonecraft, 1790, p 43).

Wollstonecraft is not an advocate of the abolition of private property. Although, she argued for inheritance laws that distributed property more equally among the children of the family, she was a greater advocate of self-made persons – men and women who worked hard to make their way in the world. She favoured a property system based on 'talents' and 'virtues', on what we may call today 'social capital'.

Kelly observes that the 'critique of landed property is the core of Wollstonecraft's political economy', for she draws connections between private property on one hand and government, family, marriage, women's position and education on the other (Kelly, 1992, p 95). While this is true, it has to be seen within the context of her own moral views because these enter into her discussion at all times.

Wealth and poverty

Wollstonecraft's writings on poverty are not very extensive but they are clear in their condemnation of poverty, which she defines in fairly generous terms

– people should 'not be obliged to weigh the consequence of every farthing they spend', they should have sufficient 'to prevent their attending to a frigid system of economy which narrows both heart and mind' (Wollstonecraft, 1792, pp 156–7). She also perceives poverty in structural terms: as the result of the conduct of avaricious landlords and the rising commercialism backed up by a discriminatory legal system. She refers to the enclosure system that increased poverty and to many of the practices of rich landlords that impoverished and criminalised the common man.

She condemned the game laws that restricted the right to hunt to substantial landowners or long leaseholders, and which allowed landlords to use decoy fields to attract game next to the property of a smallholder. This increased the richness of the game for hunting but reduced the yield of the crops of the poor smallholders:

> Game devour the fruit of his labour; but fines and imprisonment await
> him if he dares to kill any – or lift his hand to interrupt the pleasures
> of his lord. (Wollstonecraft, 1790, p 16)

She is equally critical of the penal laws that could send men to prison or to the colonies or to the scaffold for the most minor of offences but allow the rich to inflict all sort of injustices on the poor – a complaint voiced and made famous in More's *Utopia*, discussed in Chapter 4.

In her books for children, she describes with empathy the living conditions of the poor in the country and in London and occasionally puts explicitly the responsibility for poverty on the shoulders of the rich. Although she comments on the moral vices of the beggars and of other groups of the poor, she sees them as the result rather than the cause of their poverty.

What Wollstonecraft does not do is to discuss the poverty of women, as such. It is true that poverty was endemic during this period among both men and women. It may also be true that poverty was more of a problem among some groups of women – widows, single women and abandoned wives (Hill, 1984, p 156) than among men in general. Women found it more difficult than men to obtain employment, their wages were lower and often they were left to care for their children on their own. On the other hand, the severest of punishments were meted out to the young male unemployed who were seen as a threat to society. The guiding principle for setting the level of wages and, hence, of poor relief was expressed by Arthur Young as follows:

> Everyone but an idiot knows that the lower classes must be kept poor as
> they will never be industrious. (Young, quoted in Tawney, 1990, p 268)

Wollstonecraft's solution to poverty bypassed wages and poor relief levels and honed in on the provision of employment in order to make people independent, self-employed farmers or traders. Her particular proposal was for the division of large estates into smaller farms; the use of some land from the commons for the poor; and the use of forest land for cultivation by the poor. To those who might object that such a project was tantamount to misappropriation of common property, she asks rhetorically: 'Why might not the industrious peasant be allowed to steal a farm from the heath' (Wollstonecraft, 1790, p 61), when the rich have been doing it for years? The poor had a right to a better life than the one they were having in the expanding economy of England.

She held an ambivalent position concerning commercialism: she welcomed the economic wealth and independence it brought to some sections of society but she decried its overwhelming concern with profit maximisation, its neglect of the common good and the dehumanisation of factory work where men are 'turned into machines' and they pass their lives by 'stretching wire, pointing a pin, or spreading a sheet of paper on a plain surface' (Wollstonecraft, 1794, p 386).

She argued that the changes needed to abolish poverty could not take place until the dominant ideology of the nation changed – when self-interest and commercialism gave way to a concern for the public good of all citizens:

> 'How can we expect to see men live together like brothers, when we only see master and servant in society? For till men learn mutually to assist without governing each other, little can be done by political associations towards perfecting the condition of mankind' (Wollstonecraft, 1794, p 332)

Using the example of the French Revolution, she warns the rich that poor people 'are rendered ferocious by misery' and they will take their merciless revenge on their exploiters (Wollstonecraft, 1794, p 332). Although she started as a firm supporter of the French Revolution, she became horrified at the brutality of the revolutionaries and their rejection of the rights of women, and eventually came to accept that, perhaps, reform is the only way to make improvements in society. She faced the same dilemma of reform versus revolution that many advocates of fundamental social change have faced over the years. Gradual reform often runs out of steam, and revolution tends to repeat the errors of the past under new slogans.

She accepted, for example, that inequality of talent is normal among human beings, but that does not mean that 'men of every class are not equally susceptible of common improvement' (Wollstonecraft, 1794, 370). It is, therefore, the moral responsibility of governments to reduce such inequalities. Yet experience shows that this rarely happens and that the interests of the majority are ignored in favour of the interests of the few – a trend that she considers 'a monstrous tyranny, a barbarous oppression, equally injurious to the two parties, though in different ways' (Wollstonecraft, 1794, p 371). Jones quite correctly argues that her explanation and solution to poverty reflect her feelings 'rather than the arguments of political theory' (Jones, 2002, p 45).

Contemporary historians are agreed that government measures to relieve poverty during this period were driven more by fear of political unrest than by charitable or moral motives. In a comparative study of several European countries, for example, Rimlinger concludes as follows:

> In England, France and other European countries, governments became initially concerned with the lot of the poor not for purposes of relieving suffering, but for the maintenance of law and order. (Rimlinger, 1971, p 190)

Wollstonecraft's condemnation of slavery is equally forthright. She rejects all the arguments from traditionalists and from the plantation owners, for she sees slavery in moral, rather than in any other, terms as the destruction of human rights. She sees no merit in the economic argument that slavery has economic advantages for the country or in the legalistic claim that the plantation owners bought their land with the slaves as part of it. For her, 'the infernal slave trade' is morally unacceptable and she asks, in her usual rhetorical way, 'But is it not consonant with justice, with the common principles of humanity, not to mention Christianity, to abolish this abominable mischief?' (Wollstonecraft, 1790, p 53).

As with poverty, she argues that slavery debases the whole society. It degrades both the slaves and the slave owners, for 'while it gave the air of arrogance to one class, the other acquired that servile mien that fear always impresses on the relaxed countenance' (Wollstonecraft, 1790, p 346).

In several parts of her work, she likened the slavery of the plantation with what she called women's slavery in the married home and drew oblique analogies between the revolt of the slaves and women's efforts for freedom from men's domination (Ferguson, 1996). It was a comparison, however, that some feminist writers have criticised for giving the impression that African slavery was not as harsh and inhuman as it really was (Bannerji, 1997), particularly in view of the inconsistency with which Wollstonecraft used the notion of slavery in relation to women. In one case, for example, she explains that when she calls women slaves, 'I mean in a political and civil sense' (Wollstonecraft, 1792, p 185) – a definition that belittles the harshness of the African slave trade and subsequent slavery. It is a criticism that is based largely on personal judgements, for it is impossible to weigh the oppressive nature of the two situations and reach a dispassionate conclusion.

Women's emancipation

Male domination was so pervasive and women's grievances so widespread in all aspects of life that Wollstonecraft's criticisms inevitably overlapped with those made by other feminist writers, notably Sophia. What distinguishes her work, which is also the heart of her vision, is her stress on women's independence based on rationality. Her retort to Rousseau's argument that if women were educated like men, they would lose their power over men was characteristic of her vision for women's future:

> This is the very point I aim at. I do not wish them to have power over men; but over themselves. (Wollstonecraft, 1792, p 69)

She disposes of the traditional Christian argument that women were responsible for the Original Sin and hence they had to suffer more than men. Such traditional beliefs are false and they stood in the way of progress of all humankind:

> We must get entirely clear of all the notions drawn from the wild traditions of original sin on which priests have erected their tremendous structures of imposition, to persuade us, that we are naturally inclined to evil. (Wollstonecraft, 1794, p 306)

Reason was the powerful medium for women's independence; and reason could only be achieved through the right kind of education, she argued. The implied formula is that reason is knowledge, and knowledge is mental power, which spills over to other forms of power. To challenge men's dominance at work, at home and in politics, women had to be properly educated in order to develop their reasoning powers, which would guide their actions in different aspects of their lives. Ignorance is the worst recipe for women's emancipation:

> Reason is the simple power of improvement; or, more properly speaking, of discerning truth. (Wollstonecraft, 1792, p 59)

Elsewhere she adds 'it is the right use of reason alone which makes us independent of everything' (Wollstonecraft, 1792, p 132).

She compared reason with sensibility, which women were encouraged by men to have and to cherish; and found sensibility wanting in all respects, for it rendered women unable to compete with men on an equal footing as well as unfit to be good mothers. Possession of reason meant behaviour based on rationality while sensibility resulted in behaviour based on feelings – a poor substitute in everyday life. She offers numerous illustrations of the power of reason and the weakness of sensibility. Women of sensibility, she thought, 'are the most unfit' for caring for children because:

> they will infallibly, carried away by their feelings, spoil a child's temper. The management of the temper, the first, and most important branch of education, requires the sober steady eye of reason; a plan of conduct equally distant from tyranny and indulgence: yet these are the extremes that people of sensibility alternately fall into. (Wollstonecraft, 1792, p 75)

Reason was the basis, too, for women's employment in the professions – in law, medicine, management and others. Her plea for extending women's employment in the professions was based on the assumption that there were enough educated women who could do this as things stood then and that there would be many more when women's education was improved. She was a firm believer that men and women possessed the same innate abilities even though custom and tradition may have indicated differently. She decried the fact that 'the few employments open to women are menial', and as a result 'the most respectable women are the most oppressed' (Wollstonecraft, 1792, p 163). While working-class women could find some employment, menial though it was, middle-class educated women were excluded from professional occupations. Her conclusion that 'respectable' women were more oppressed than working-class women is clearly an indication of her excessive concern with middle-class women rather than an objective assessment of the situation.

Men justified women's exclusion from politics largely on the grounds that women could not make sound impartial decisions that were based on reason. It is no surprise that Wollstonecraft would argue that many women were fit to enter politics because they were educated and possessed reason, apart from the fact that it was their fundamental right to do so, as it was for men, most of whom were not educated. She argued that women should have representatives in Parliament even though she understood that such a suggestion would seem strange to many:

> I may excite laughter for I really think that women ought to have representatives, instead of being arbitrarily governed without having any direct share allowed them in the deliberations of government. (Wollstonecraft, 1792, p 161)

All the above demands for improving women's position in society were accepted by other feminist writers of her time and after. It is her views on femininity and her attacks on 'courtly ladies' that have caused some debate in feminist circles. The following quotation epitomises the dominant view of a 'woman' in Wollstonecraft's time and reflects also everything that she most abhorred:

> Women are told from their infancy, and taught by the example of their mothers, that little knowledge of human weakness, justly termed cunning, softens the temper, outward obedience, and a scrupulous attention to a puerile kind of propriety, will obtain them the protection of man; and should they be beautiful, everything, everything else is needless, for at least twenty years of their life. (Wollstonecraft, 1792, p 23)

The cultivation of such 'feminine' values made women look weak, artificial characters and useless members of society. More than that, men had taken advantage of that, both as lovers and as husbands. What is worse, women had internalised those values, they behaved accordingly and they colluded with other societal agencies – education, literature, law, music, poetry, gallantry – in transmitting them to the next generation.

The upshot of these values has been a 'courtly' image of woman as a sex object capable of nothing more than idle prattle, sex and bearing and rearing children at man's pleasure. In her own words, such a view implied that woman 'was created to be the toy of man, his rattle, and it must jingle in his ears whenever, dismissing reason, he chooses to be amused' (Wollstonecraft, 1792, p 38).

Such values and attitudes must change. What is needed, Wollstonecraft boldly said, was a 'revolution in female manners', a rejection by women themselves of the current values of femininity and their implied conduct. She somehow believed that if she could do it, other women could as well. She asked, of course, for changes in education, as we shall see below; and she pleaded with men to accept women as their equals in reason, rights and responsibilities in life. But women must take the initiative by changing themselves though she acknowledged that they would not be easily convinced of the desirability and urgency of this course of action.

> It is time to effect a revolution in female manners – time to restore to them their lost dignity – and make them, as part of the human species, labour by reforming themselves to reform the world. It is time to separate unchangeable morals from local manners. (Wollstonecraft, 1792, p 51)

She could not accept that such 'feminine' forms of conduct could be used as forms of resistance, as women's cunning ways of exerting some influence over men and gaining some power for themselves. For her, it was reason and not feminine sensuality that was the catalyst for women's emancipation. 'Men', she said, 'have too much occupied the thoughts of women' and it was high time that women freed themselves from this state of affairs (Wollstonecraft, 1792, p 130). They could only do this by the use of their reason. Sensuality was a poor substitute and it was only acceptable to her when it was governed by reason.

Not unexpectedly, her view that women's major problem was their preoccupation with their looks, dress, their sexuality or their socialisation into a 'weak' culture of femininity has not gone unchallenged. Certainly, such a view bore little relationship to the everyday lives of working-class women:

> The women working in factories, the women who tended the farms, the female slaves labouring in the fields all suffered more from other causes than the problems presented by reason, moral responsibility, and the image of woman as irrational and frivolous. (Korsmeyer, 1976, p 108)

Marriage and family

Wollstonecraft's views on reason and sensuality have clear implications for marriage and family affairs. She is not against the institution of marriage as such but she wants marriage to be based on reason and friendship rather than simply physical love and sensuality – an egalitarian partnership rather than a tyrannical sexual experience. She, therefore, finds much fault in the way marriages were contracted and in the way wives lost their identities as separate persons once they got married.

Marriage based on physical love will not last because, sooner rather than later, husbands will turn their sexual attentions to other women. Similarly marriage based on economic considerations will degenerate into male oppression. On both accounts, such marriages result in the exploitation and repression of women – and such marriages were the norm rather than the exception. It is for this reason that she often refers to the slavery of women in marriage or, as the heroine in her unfinished novel, *Maria*, observes, 'marriage has bastilled me for life', like many other women (Wollstonecraft, quoted in Sapiro, 1996, p 40).

Her advice is for marriage to be based on equality of the partners from the start so that when the sexual passion declines, friendship can take over to cement family relationships. Without virtue or reason, ' sexual attachment must expire, like a tallow candle in the socket, creating intolerable disgust' (Wollstonecraft, 1792, p 213). Indeed, she goes further to encourage young married couples to check their passion from the outset for the benefit of friendship:

> Friendship is a serious affection; the most sublime of all affections, because it is founded on principle, and cemented by time. The very reverse may be said of love. In a great degree love and friendship cannot subsist in the same bosom. (Wollstonecraft, 1792, p 81)

It is a position that has been criticised by some feminists on the grounds that it amounts to a denial of women's sexuality. Wollstonecraft's life, however, was the exact opposite – an affirmation of women's sexuality. Moreover, she did insist that sexual appetites apply to both men and women and they only become vicious when their satisfaction is not governed by reason. Such passions must be checked and, interestingly enough, the responsibility does not lie solely with women: 'the obligation to check them is the duty of mankind, not a sexual duty' (Wollstonecraft, 1792, p 143), an argument in line with one of her basic principles that: 'The two sexes mutually corrupt and improve each other' (Wollstonecraft, 1792, p 153).

It is true, however, that her views on sensuality and sexuality are not always clear or consistent but the gist of her argument is that women should not, either as single or as married, construct their life around the culture of 'courtly' sensuality for they will be disappointed. Perhaps this was an overreaction to the then prevailing double standard of morality whereby women were expected to be chaste and men were allowed to be sexually free. In the 18th century, as one feminist writer put it, 'marriage and parentage were incidents in the one sex, and essentials in the other' (Blease, 1910, p 7). Although men and women, by nature, have the same sexual desires, they become unacceptable when they are uncontrolled by reason. Sexual relationships, for Wollstonecraft, had to be based on reason, on the equality of the sexes and on responsibility.

No doubt Wollstonecraft's view on sexuality appears prudish to some today when sexual freedom is commonly accepted for both men and women, but her view must be seen within its historical context and as part of her wider plan for the emancipation of women during her time.

Parent–child relationships

Wollstonecraft saw ideal parent–child relationships in the form of a social contract with duties and obligations on both sides. She was very critical of the existing parent–child relationships for they were based on fear and self-interest, primarily designed to reproduce property relationships for the next generation. They were basically authoritarian, particularly for the girls who were expected to show unquestioned obedience to their parents, a preparation for marriage:

> Thus taught slavishly to submit to their parents, they are prepared for the slavery of marriage. (Wollstonecraft, 1792, p 170)

In a democratic, egalitarian family, parents have no absolute right to unconditional obedience by their children. Such obedience must be voluntary and it must be in the form of reciprocity for good parental care. Slavish obedience to parents does not allow for the fulfilment of a child's abilities. Children, however, who have been well cared for by their parents have, in return, a duty to look after their parents when they are old. Children who have been neglected cannot be expected to show obedience to their parents:

> A right always includes a duty, and it may be likewise inferred that they forfeit the right who do not fulfil the duty. (Wollstonecraft, 1792, p 171)

Wollstonecraft saw a connection between the family and society. Democratic families can only exist in societies with a democratic government, in the same way that, in her time, tyrannical families were a reflection of tyrannical government. This was so because of her assumption that education and reason for both men and women were integral parts of a democratic society. Thus, she expresses the fear that family relationships will not change until society changes:

> But, till society is very differently constituted, parents, I fear, will still insist on being obeyed, because they will be obeyed, and constantly endeavour to settle that power on a Divine right which will not bear the investigation of reason. (Wollstonecraft, 1792, p 173)

Such a change of society demands a revolution and this depends, to a large extent, on a radical transformation of the educational system. Elsewhere, however, she points out that the educational system of a society is much influenced by the society in which it operates – thus creating not so much an impasse but a realisation of the problems involved in education acting as a force for societal change.

Education, women's emancipation and social progress

Most writers on education during the 17th and 18th centuries took the view that women were either intellectually inferior to men or that their intellect was different from that of men – the corollary to both being that a different type of education was needed for women, if indeed any was necessary. Upper- and middle-class girls were not expected to either work or to be too well educated; the "learned lady" was an object for ridicule, and learning was seen as unwomanly and masculine' (Hill, 1984, p 45). Education for middle- and upper-class girls should be confined to reading, writing, arithmetic and those subjects – drawing, dancing, music or painting – that would improve a girl's sexual attraction and marriage prospects. As for girls of the working class, education was considered even less necessary and, not surprisingly, school provision was quite inadequate in both quantity and quality. It was also feared that education for such girls would 'make the female poor less willing to offer themselves for servile work' (Hill, 1984, p 47).

It is within this educational climate that Wollstonecraft's writings on education should be seen. Her first three books or manuals on education – *Thoughts on the Education of Daughters* (1787); *Original Stories From Real Life* (1788); and *The Female Reader* (1789) – contain very little that can be called radical. They were books written for the popular market and fitted in with most of the prevalent ideas of the time. There are flashes of radicalism – adults should set good examples for children, their questions should be answered, children should be taught to think, girls should not pay too much attention to dresses, and so on – but these are the exception and many of them fit in with the Lockean views of education, discussed in Chapter 5.

It was not until after the publication of Catherine Macaulay's *Letters on Education* (1790) that Wollstonecraft seems to have adopted the very radical programme on education as set out in her *Vindication of the Rights of Woman*. Macaulay argued for co-education, since she believed that men and women possess similar intellectual abilities, despite the men's greater physical strength. Wollstonecraft wrote to Macaulay saying that 'you are the only female writer who I coincide in opinion with respecting the rank our sex ought to endeavour to attain in the world' (letter quoted in Cracium, 2002, p 24).

Enough citations have already been made in this chapter indicating the importance of education in Wollstonecraft's political theory and to her vision of the good society. From Plato onwards, education was used by philosophers as one of the major media, if not the major, medium for the creation of their ideal society. This was as true of the conservative thinkers wishing 'to shore up the status quo' as of the radicals 'wishing to overturn it' (Richardson, 2002, p 24).

Wollstonecraft's proposals must be seen in relation to her overall aim: the contribution of education to the emancipation of women and to general social progress – the creation of a democratic, broadly egalitarian, society. She was certain that such an aim could not be achieved with simply minor changes to the existing system of education – the whole system had to be radically overhauled. A new structure, a new curriculum and a new administrative authority were needed to carry her programme through.

During her time, schooling for the middle and upper classes was provided either by parents or tutors at home; or in boarding schools. For the working classes, there was a patchy system of charity schools and parish schools. In her earlier work, in line with Locke's ideas, Wollstonecraft was sympathetic to the provision of schooling at home by either parents or by tutors. Now, she turned against it on the grounds that the child relied excessively on one person; that they had no other children to mix with and exchange ideas; and, as a result, they were forced into adulthood too early in its life.

She had always been opposed to boarding schools because she considered them 'the hot-beds of vice and folly':

> At boarding-schools of every description, the relaxation of the junior boy is mischief, and of the senior, vice. Besides, in great schools, what can be more prejudicial to the moral character than the system of tyranny and abject slavery which is established among the boys, to say nothing of the slavery to forms, which makes religion worse than farce? (Wollstonecraft, 1792, p 176)

What was needed was a comprehensive system of day schools for all children – boys and girls, rich and poor – funded by the government adequately. This would avoid the weaknesses of both private education at home as well as boarding schools:

> Thus to make men citizens, two natural steps might be taken, which seem directly to lead to the desired point; for the domestic affections that first open the heart to the various modifications of humanity, would be cultivated whilst the children were nevertheless allowed to spend great part of their time, on terms of equality, with other children. (Wollstonecraft, 1792, pp 175–6)

Wollstonecraft argued for co-education because single-sex schools destroyed modesty as well as understanding between the two sexes. She rejected fears that co-education might undermine morality and discipline; indeed, she argued that the opposite was the case – co-education might be a good preparation for marriage by enabling young people to understand and respect each other without all the male gallantry and female coquetry that was so abhorrent to her. Nevertheless, her proposal was ridiculed and parodied at the time that 'it would be better to bring up boys and girls promiscuously together' (quoted in Cracium, 2002, p 153).

Since schools would be for the children of all classes, they stood a better chance of being well funded in contrast to the existing day schools, which were overcrowded and where the teachers were grossly underpaid and had to rely on the assistance of 'ushers' who were despised by both teachers and pupils because of their lowly status. Moreover, being establishments for all the classes, schools would cease the blatant promulgation of courtly culture in favour of a more civic one.

A parish committee would be responsible for appointing a sufficient number of teachers and it would also be responsible for hearing any complaints of negligence 'if signed by six of the children's parents'. Clearly, this was meant to deal with some of the problems of neglect, unaccountability and lack of parental involvement in schools. She extends the idea of participation to the pupils: they, rather than their teachers, should be responsible for trying and meting out punishments to errant pupils – a practice that would prove 'an admirable method of fixing sound principles of justice in the mind' (Wollstonecraft, 1792, p 188).

Children aged five to nine years should go to the same school and, to prevent class distinctions from dominating the school, 'they should be dressed alike, and all obliged to submit to the same discipline, or leave the school' (Wollstonecraft, 1792, p 186). All children should attend the same lessons – reading, writing, arithmetic, history, religion, natural history and philosophy – some subjects should be taught in the Socratic form of dialogue; but 'these pursuits should never encroach on gymnastic plays in the open air' (Wollstonecraft, 1792, p 186).

Every school should be surrounded by a large playground and garden because children should not be taught for more than an hour at a time and they should all take exercises together. She was a firm believer in the Classical idea of body and mind interacting to produce the best results for the individual. Wollstonecraft was particularly emphatic about the value of exercise to girls, for she wanted to demonstrate that had they the same freedom as boys for exercise, the gulf in physical power between the sexes may not have been that wide. The way she brought up her own daughter also demonstrated this same belief: she dressed her in loose clothing without swaddling her, breast-fed her and took her out in the fresh air – a way of child rearing that was considered unnatural and unhealthy at the time.

After the age of nine, children are divided into two groups – the vocational and the academic. Boys and girls 'intended for domestic employments, or mechanical trades' are educated together during the morning but, in the afternoon, they attend different classes according to the trade they are to follow – an inevitable separation of boys and girls. Those with 'superior abilities, or fortune' go to another school with a more academic programme – languages, science, history, politics, philosophy, and so on. It is not clear from her proposals how long the secondary education lasts: 'young people of fortune' can stay till 'they are of age'; while others should stay, at least on a part-time basis, until they are ready for their professions (Wollstonecraft, 1792, p 188).

She makes the specific point that girls, too, should be taught 'the elements of anatomy and medicine' – something that was considered risqué at the time – not only to make them able to look after their own health but also 'to make them rational nurses of their infants, parents, and husbands' (Wollstonecraft, 1792, p 196). She also repeats the advice of others before her that children should be taught to be humane to animals – for such humanity 'is not at present one of our national virtues' (Wollstonecraft, 1792, p 190). In her usual way of connecting the individual to the general, she felt that cruelty to animals was but the first step on the ladder leading ultimately to the cruelty of the patriarchal home over children and wives.

Her emphasis on education for women did not mean for her that women should abandon their traditional duties of mothers, wives and housewives. Indeed, she felt that education would enable them to carry out these duties, along with other professional duties, better. Women had enough stamina to do both. As she put it:

> An active mind embraces the whole circle of duties, and finds time enough for all. (Wollstonecraft, 1792, p 187)

Her general conclusion from her educational proposals is conditionally optimistic. If and when women become 'rational creatures and free citizens, they will quickly become good wives and mothers – that is, if men do not neglect the duties of husbands and fathers' (Wollstonecraft, 1792, p 197), thus reiterating one of her constant themes: men and women prosper or degenerate together, despite her firm belief that the debasement of women was due to men's oppression.

Conclusion

Wollstonecraft's contribution to feminist theory and the feminist cause has been immense. She is primarily a moralist – 'her political criticism is couched predominantly in terms of morality' (Jones, 2002, p 43). When she writes about the need for poverty alleviation, for the improvement of the condition of women or for the abolition of slavery, her arguments are presented in terms of morality. It is not so much from an economic, a political or a religious but from a moral imperative that these social evils should be erased. Her writings carry a strong moral appeal but often go against the self-evident principle that complex problems require complex explanations.

Wollstonecraft's overwhelming stress on reason and the downgrading of sexuality in people's lives may well be faulted in post-Freudian societies but it was a necessary way of making her case in the society in which she found herself (Todd, 1994, p xxx). Reason was the accepted force for human progress used by all the major social theorists of her time and she used it brilliantly to make her arguments for the advancement of women. Her frowning upon sexual freedom for both men and women may seem prudish but she saw it as instrumental to egalitarian marriage.

Although Wollstonecraft borrowed from both Locke and Rousseau on education, her proposals went beyond them both. They were path-breaking not only in relation to women, but also in relation to public education in general. However, she may have overemphasised the power of knowledge and rationality at the expense of the power of wealth and property even though she may have been aware of this.

Her analysis of the causes and solutions of one of the major issues of her day – poverty – was limited because she saw it primarily in moral terms. There is no adequate discussion of the economic forces behind the widespread prevalence of poverty or of the political forces that militated against its amelioration. Despite this, her whole perception of the issue was far superior to that of either Locke or Hobbes, who saw poverty mainly in individualistic terms. Being overcritical of her on this point, therefore, may be doing her an injustice, bearing also in mind that the major cause that she championed was not poverty but the emancipation of women.

Not only her ideas, but her lifestyle, too, were way beyond her time: she had love affairs, she lived happily in cohabitation for a while, had a child born out of wedlock whom she adored, and got married in the end. Not unexpectedly, her name 'was unmentionable, and her works unreadable for anyone who laid claim to responsibility' during the rest of the 18th and most of the 19th centuries (Moore, 1999, p 5). It was not until the last decades of the 19th century that she began to be read and her radicalism to be appreciated. In more recent times, as mentioned earlier in the chapter, her work has also begun to be seen from the broader political theory perspective – not a mean achievement in a field traditionally dominated by men.

Feminist writings during the 18th century, those discussed in this chapter and others, laid the foundations for 19th- and 20th-century debates. They had little, if any, immediate practical effects, however, for they were way ahead of their times. Interestingly enough, slavery was abolished long before women obtained their rights. Reform for women had to wait until they had enough economic and social power to give force to their demands. Material and ideological factors must normally combine in order to bring about important reforms in society through the political process. Nevertheless, the feminist writings of the 18th and 19th centuries constituted one of the many factors that pushed forward the gender reforms of the 20th century as well as the idea of a democratic welfare state.

SEVEN

A welfare society
Jean-Jacques Rousseau (1712–78)

Rousseau's educational theories would, by themselves, guarantee him a place in a volume of welfare thinkers. His position is strengthened further by his work on poverty and inequality, the role of government in public affairs, his stress on citizen participation and his views on gender issues. We begin, however, with his views on human nature for they are fundamental to his theories elsewhere.

Although there is a tension between some of his major theses (O'Hagan, 2004), on balance, he is essentially a strong advocate of a community of equals where all participate in government decision-making; where they have some property but none too much; and where the satisfaction of basic needs takes precedence over the consumption of luxuries. In such a community of equals, the individual is part of the whole, willing to accept that the interests of the community often take precedence over his interests, knowing that others accept the same condition, too. Rousseau was an advocate of a welfare society rather than of a welfare state.

Human nature

Rousseau rejected Hobbes' view that human beings are by nature aggressive and egoistic for three main reasons. First, in the state of nature there was enough for everyone to satisfy basic needs; hence any quarrels that may have arisen were not of such significance as Hobbes maintained. Second, he is critical of Hobbes' concentration on the destructive human passions to the detriment of communitarian passions – compassion, pity, concern for others and for the common good. Third, the strong egoistic human passions that Hobbes referred to were not the result of nature but, like all other social ills, they were the product of civilisation.

He was sympathetic to Aristotle's view that human beings in the state of nature were sociable and prepared to work together for their mutual benefit. He parted company, however, with Aristotle's view that some human beings are by nature superior to others, some destined to rule and others to obey. He felt that Aristotle 'took the effect for the cause' (Rousseau, 1762a, p 183). It was the social situation that people found themselves in that made them behave either as leaders or as slaves. Slavery was not the result of natural differences between masters and slaves, according to Rousseau, but a social evil imposed by the strong on the weak.

Human beings in the state of nature, he argued, were socially equal to one another, prepared to look after themselves, as well as have some feeling for the welfare of others. They were motivated by two desires – self-love and compassion

– that complemented each other. Self-love was tantamount to individualism while compassion was 'an innate repugnance at seeing a fellow-creature suffer' (Rousseau, 1755, p 73). He was not an out-and-out advocate of altruism, as some have claimed:

> Compassion is a natural feeling, which, by moderating the activity of love of self in each individual, contributes to the preservation of the species. It is this compassion that hurries us without reflection to the relief of those who are in distress. (Rousseau, 1755, p 76)

This compassion for others did not amount to the Christian social value of 'love your neighbour' and doing good to others, including your enemies. He felt that that was too demanding and that a more appropriate social expectation would be: 'Do good to yourself with as little evil as possible to others' (Rousseau, 1755, p 76). In pursuing your own interest, beware of the interest of others.

Equality and liberty

> Man is born free; and everywhere he is in chains.
> (Rousseau, 1762a, p 181)

> God makes all things good; man meddles with them and they
> become evil. (Rousseau, 1762b, p 5)

The fundamental historical premise in Rousseau's major works is that the march of civilisation had reduced both equality and liberty. His ideal society was not the very early primitive stage when men and women roamed the land as individuals but the subsequent stage when men and women lived in households where the man secured the food through fishing and hunting while the wife looked after the household. All households were self-sufficient, there were no social inequalities between them, and they came to each other's help when need arose.

The discovery of metals, the invention of tools, the arrival of settled agriculture, the division of labour and the onset of private property changed all that. From that moment on, social change gained momentum – inequalities increased, individual liberties were suppressed and compassion was extinguished by the rising tide of self-love and vanity. Despite man's natural goodness, argues Rousseau, society as it was then organised 'necessarily leads men to hate each other in proportion as their interests clash, and to do one another services, while they are really doing every imaginable mischief' (Rousseau, 1755, p 118).

Rousseau was not an advocate of either numerical equality or proportional equality, or of equality according to need. He simply argued that the distribution of income in society should not be so unequal that it became a major root cause of many social problems:

By equality, we should understand, not that the degree of power and riches are to be absolutely identical for everybody; but that power shall never be great enough for violence, and shall always be exercised by virtue of rank and law; and that, in respect of riches, no citizen shall ever be wealthy enough to buy another, and none poor enough to be forced to sell himself. (Rousseau, 1762, p 225)

He identified two main sources of inequality: nature and society:

I conceive that there are two kinds of inequality among the human species; one, which I call natural or physical, because it is established by nature, and consists in a difference of age, health, bodily strength, and the qualities of the mind or of the soul; and another, which may be called moral or political inequality, because it depends on convention, and is established, or at least authorised, by the consent of men (Rousseau, 1755, p 49)

Inequalities of the first kind are inevitable and they existed in the state of nature as well as in all other subsequent periods in history. Moral inequality, however, has been the product of the type of social institutions existing in particular countries. For this reason social inequalities had increased over the years that he examined. Moreover, an increasing number of inequalities, he claimed, had been attributed to nature in order to exonerate social institutions from any responsibility and in order to argue that nothing could be done about them. This was a point that has been used against his views concerning the position of women in society, as we shall see later in the chapter.

Rousseau fails to bring out sufficiently the dynamic relationship between the two sources of inequality. Today, there is enough evidence to show that social inequalities can affect natural inequalities: diets and housing, for example, can affect many of people's physical and mental attributes. Vice versa, natural inequalities can influence social inequalities. The relationship between nature and nurture is far more complex and potent than he allowed for.

He divided moral or social inequalities into four kinds – 'riches, nobility or rank, power and personal merit' (Rousseau, 1755, p 111). Riches are the most important type of inequality because they can be used to purchase every other form of distinction. Social inequality had been legitimised through legislation and tradition so that it became acceptable in society and widened with the march of civilisation.

Rousseau was clearly troubled by the wide inequalities of his time and condemned them outright. He was horrified that 'the privileged few should gorge themselves in superfluities, while the starving multitude are in want of the bare necessities of life' (Rousseau, 1755, p 117). Government action was necessary not merely as an afterthought but as preventative action to ensure that wide inequalities in society did not arise in the first place:

> It is therefore one of the most important functions of government
> to prevent extreme inequality of fortunes; not by taking away wealth
> from its possessors, but by depriving all men of means to accumulate
> it; not by building hospitals for the poor, but by securing the citizens
> from becoming poor. (Rousseau, 1758, p 147)

Rousseau belonged to that school of thought that considered government action as not only compatible with liberty but as an essential measure for its achievement. He viewed liberty as 'the noblest faculty of man' (Rousseau, 1755, p 104) but insisted that it could not be achieved without government action in the society of his time.

In the same way that the march of civilisation had reduced the fundamental equality among human beings, it had also reduced their individual liberty. He rejected Hobbes' view that human beings surrendered their liberty willingly to the sovereign in return for protection. He had more sympathy with Locke's position that government was established in order to protect property or rather the property of the rich. For Rousseau, the public were duped into gradually accepting the suppression of their freedom – a process that he considered both immoral and void, for individuals have no authority to surrender their own liberty to others:

> To say that a man gives himself freely, is to say what is absurd and
> inconceivable; such an act is null and illegitimate, from the mere fact
> that he who does it is out of his mind. To say the same of a whole
> people is to suppose a people of madmen; and madness creates no
> right. (Rousseau, 1762a, p 186)

The central message of Rousseau's writings on liberty was that the existing authoritarian monarchies of Europe were illegitimate for they disenfranchised people – they robbed them of their individual freedom and their livelihood. It was a message that endeared him to the French revolutionaries and has given him the dubious accolade of being described as the 'the inspiration and the prophet' of the French Revolution (Jones, 1947, p 249). He, himself, was against revolutions because he believed that gradual change is the best way forward.

His strong support of liberty and equality as two interrelated beneficial values to society meant that he saw slavery as totally unacceptable. Slavery, he said, 'is contrary to nature, and cannot be authorised by any right or law' (Rousseau, 1758, p 130). He rejected the two then prevalent justifications of slavery, that is, that individuals willingly trade their freedom for protection and subsistence; and that as prisoners of war, men exchange their life for slavery. As for the first, he argued that men have no right to trade their own freedom, let alone the freedom of their children, for anything. Any such transactions are, therefore, null and void. As for the second, he considered war as a confrontation between states and not between men, with the result that 'individuals are enemies accidentally, not as men, not even as citizens, but as soldiers' (Rousseau, 1762a, p 187). For this reason, conquerors have no right either to massacre or to enslave the people they conquer and the war prisoners they capture:

> So, from whatever aspect we regard the question, the right of slavery is null and void, not only as being illegitimate, but also because it is absurd and meaningless. The words *slave* and *right* contradict each other, and are mutually exclusive. (Rousseau, 1762a, p 189)

From compassion to vanity

Rousseau never claimed that individuals are by nature, or should be encouraged by society to become, altruistic. He simply argued that in pursuing their own interests, individuals should not lose sight of the interests of others, of the common good. He feared that as societies became more affluent, they became increasingly individualistic, concentrating more on self-love or vanity and ignoring compassionate conduct. The result of this was that the resources of the country were being used to satisfy the demands for luxury by the few at the cost of the basic needs of the people.

Such a process was both unethical and detrimental to the stability of society. He was, therefore, very critical of it all and came to consider luxury as 'the greatest of all evils, for every State, great or small: for in order to maintain all the servants and vagabonds it creates, it brings oppression and ruin on the citizen and the labourer' (Rousseau, 1755, p 123).

He had no time for the argument that luxury items are just as important to the rich as basic needs are to the poor; that the rich may feel just as deprived, for example, without their carriages as the ordinary people may feel without adequate footwear. It was a false argument, he argued, because:

> a grandee has two legs just like a cowherd, and, like him again, but one belly. (Rousseau, 1758, p 160)

His advice to the rich and powerful was that if they wanted to gain more public respect, they should live and behave in ways that were closer to ordinary people's lives:

> The populace would be ready to adore a minister who went to council on foot, because he had sold off his carriages to supply a pressing need of the State. (Rousseau, 1758, p 160)

Rousseau never gave even a passing thought to the argument that the satisfaction of relative needs for the few could encourage higher rates of economic growth so that eventually many of the luxury needs of the few could become the basic needs of the many. This was contrary to his philosophy as an egalitarian and a lover of nature and of the simple life – an attitude that was not too dissimilar to that of many of the Stoics discussed in Chapter 2. It is a strong stream in his thought for it runs not only through his political writings but through his educational psychology, as we shall see later.

Private property and poverty

Private property and poverty were inextricably linked, according to Rousseau. To begin with, the establishment of private property signalled the arrival of both wealth and poverty in society. Over the centuries, as private property became increasingly concentrated, the extent and depth of poverty increased too. Poverty, for him, was primarily the result of the structure of society. It had nothing to do with God's wishes and little to do with the personal characteristics of the poor – the latter were the result rather than the cause of poverty.

He agreed with Locke's three criteria for the justification of private property in land, even though he maintained that in the last resort the individual's title to property 'is always subordinate to the right which the community has over all' (Rousseau, 1762a, p 199). The three criteria for individual entitlement to property were these:

> First, the land must not be inhabited; secondly, a man must occupy only the amount he needs for his subsistence; and, in the third place, possession must be taken, not by an empty ceremony, but by labour and cultivation, the only sign of proprietorship that should be respected by others, in default of a legal title. (Rousseau, 1762a, p 197)

He disagreed with Locke, however, that the introduction of a money economy made these three criteria redundant and thus justified the accumulation of private property. Although he considered the right of property as 'the most sacred of all rights of citizenship' (Rousseau, 1758), he also felt that property should be distributed in a way that 'all have something and none too much' (Rousseau, 1762a, p 199). He remained steadfast to his belief that excessive concentration of wealth is detrimental both to the welfare of the individual and to the social cohesion of the whole society. A very unequal society is certain to be conflict-ridden and its level of togetherness will suffer. He tells the following story to make his point concerning the lack of allegiance that the rich show to their country:

> A stranger, splendidly clad, was asked in Athens what country he belonged to: 'I am one of the rich', was his answer; and a very good answer in my opinion. (Rousseau, 1762b, p 313)

Despite his many criticisms of the existing forms of private property, he only once suggested the nationalisation of the means of production and distribution – that was in one of his lesser-known books, *The Constitution of Corsica* (1765). He argued that the state should 'own everything, and that each person should partake of what belongs to the community in proportion to his services' (Rousseau, quoted in Plamenatz, 1963, p 427). His plan for Corsica was based on an agricultural economy that was designed to meet basic needs rather than luxuries. Self-sufficiency was one of his constant themes in the distribution of resources.

On all other occasions, however, he asked for reductions in the concentration of property. He firmly believed that a very unequal distribution of property was undesirable because it made the rich behave arrogantly, the poor were forced to be subservient and resources were misallocated to pay for luxuries in the midst of abject poverty. Politically, it made the creation of a cohesive society impossible.

Although he stressed self-sufficiency, he also supported the role of the state in preventing and relieving poverty. The state, however, should ensure that it did not undermine individuals' willingness to look after themselves and their families:

> Provision for the public wants is an obvious inference from the general will, and the third essential duty of government. The duty is not to fill the granaries of individuals and thereby grant them a dispensation from labour, but to keep plenty so within their reach that labour is always necessary and never useless for its acquisition. (Rousseau, 1758, p 151)

He was emphatic that in the same way that the rich were not justified in claiming a right to luxuries, the poor had no right either to poor relief that took into account relative needs. For him, human needs become infinite and cannot be satisfied once we move beyond the basics of life. In his words:

> The world of reality has its bounds, the world of imagination is boundless. (Rousseau, 1762b, p 45)

He had no doubt that work is an essential part of life for all for both economic and health reasons. He gave preference to work in agriculture and in such trades as carpentry where, he thought, mental as well as physical effort is necessary. People who do not work and rely on others or on the state to support them are thieves:

> The man who eats in idleness what he has not himself earned, is a thief, and in my eyes, the man who lives on an income paid him by the state for doing nothing, differs little from a highwayman who lives on those who travel his way.... Man in society is bound to work; rich or poor, weak or strong, every idler is a thief. (Rousseau, 1762b, p 158)

Although he condemned idleness for both the rich and the poor, and though he was against paying poor relief to those who could work, his condemnation showed none of the ferocity that marked Locke's position on the issue of poor relief. Locke, of course, lived among the rich and was rich enough himself while Rousseau was always poor and saw the rich as a drain on the national economy and social solidarity.

Taxation and government overload

Rousseau fully accepted the role of the state in social affairs. He pointed out that even the three primary aims of government – to carry out the decisions of the people, to reduce factions in society and to provide for people's basic needs – could only be fulfilled if the state had the necessary financial resources and this inevitably meant some form of taxation. He favoured the type of taxes that took into account the person's ability to pay, with luxuries coming in for the heaviest of taxation:

> He who possesses only the common necessaries of life should pay nothing at all, while the tax on him who is in possession of superfluities may justly be extended to everything he has over and above necessaries. (Rousseau, 1758, p 160)

Despite his radicalism, he showed a shrewd understanding of the problems that governments have to face in order to raise the necessary revenues to finance their operations. He pointed out that a government's fiscal problems could be dealt with not only through raising revenues but also through reducing the number of projects that demand public finance. High on his list was the waging of wars that was often used not to defend the nation but 'to increase the authority of the rulers at home' (Rousseau, 1758, p 157).

The importance of reducing the areas of government activity becomes more urgent, he argued, when it is borne in mind that when one problem has been dealt with, another appears. The demand for government expenditure is endless. There was, thus, always the risk of the government overloading itself with duties, being forced to levy higher rates of taxation without, at the same time, necessarily delivering on its promises to solve society's problems. The inevitable result of such overloading would be a crisis in public confidence in government. This was, perhaps, one of the earliest expressions of the 'government overload' thesis that became so popular in the 1980s:

> While a remedy is found for one evil, another is beginning to make itself felt, and even the remedies themselves produce new difficulties: so that at length the nation is involved in debt and the people oppressed, while the government loses its influence and can do very little with a great deal of money. (Rousseau, 1758, p 155)

Although he advocated a constant review of government activity, he always insisted on the satisfaction of basic needs. Moreover, he considered the community – relatives, friends and neighbours – rather than the central government as the first provider of welfare. It is this that justifies the claim that he called for a welfare society rather than a welfare state.

The role of women in society

In Rousseau's original state of nature, men and women roamed freely, had sexual relations as they pleased, and lived as individuals. Inevitably, women became responsible for rearing children since the institution of marriage was then unknown. Although Rousseau does not comment on gender relationships during this stage of social development, it follows from his discussion that women could not have been inferior to men by nature – after all they had to carry out two roles compared to men's one: like men they had to look after themselves, but unlike men they also had to look after young children.

Strangely, he does not use this period as his frame of reference in the same way that he does in relation to social inequality. Instead, he uses the next stage of social development – the hunting and fishing stage – when men and women lived in households and where the man was the undisputed head. This enables him to claim that the patriarchal family is the natural unit of family life; the implication being that any departure from it is unnatural and, therefore, unwise.

He, therefore, concludes that in the family, 'the father ought to command' (Rousseau, 1758, p 129) and gives four reasons for this, none of which is convincing today. To begin with, he argues that it is important that authority in the family should be concentrated in the hands of one person so that decisions could be taken easily. This is in marked contrast to his political views that are discussed later, where decision-making is democratic and it is in the hands of all the citizens. Second, this undivided decision-making should be in the hands of the father because the mother may be occasionally unavailable due to childbirths. Third, children should be obedient to their father because he has the ultimate responsibility for their maintenance and general upbringing. Finally, servants are responsible to the father as their master – a fact that strengthens his case of being the head of the family. All in all, Rousseau sees the mother's role as important, as that of a companion and a helpmate of her husband, but also at his command:

> Nature has decreed that woman, both for herself and the children, should be at the mercy of man's judgement. (Rousseau, 1762b, p 328)

Although the father is the head of the family, the mother is the emotional heart of the family because she is the first to feed, to care for and to love the children. A child owes her more love and respect than they do to the father because she 'bore him and nursed him at her breast'; a child may be excused if, on the odd occasion, they show disrespect to their father, but such behaviour towards their mother is unpardonable – 'such a monstrous wretch should be smothered at once as unworthy to live' (Rousseau, 1762b, p 5).

Interestingly, Rousseau argues that 'the laws give little authority to the mother', despite her immense contribution to the upbringing and education of the children, the fact that 'she is usually fonder of her children', and 'the right ordering of the family depends more upon her' than on the father (Rousseau, 1762b, p 5). Any mistakes that she makes in caring for her children, because of her 'blind affection' for them, is nowhere near as damaging as the harshness of the fathers towards their children.

What Rousseau seems to be saying is that the role of the father and the mother are different and that the family and society benefit when each carries out his or her role satisfactorily. This, however, is a generous interpretation of parental roles because at the end of the line the father has the upper hand over the mother.

Rousseau certainly did not believe in the natural superiority of men over women, for he stressed the point that, apart from their sexual differences, men and women are the same, in terms of biology:

> But for her sex, a woman is a man; she has the same organs, the same needs, the same faculties. The machine is the same in its construction; its parts, its working, and its appearance are similar. (Rousseau, 1762b, p 321)

Mentally, too, the two sexes are different but of equal worth and complementary to each other, according to Rousseau. Women are wittier and more observant than men, while men possess more reason and intelligence than women. During the Enlightenment, however, reason and intelligence were the favoured mental attributes and, as a result, Rousseau has been interpreted as implying that men are mentally superior to women. But this is not necessarily the case because Rousseau, unlike Locke and other Enlightenment figures, stressed the importance of passions over reason in individual and societal affairs. What he seems to be saying is that men and women complement each other:

> Woman has more wit, man more genius; woman observes, man reasons; together they provide the clearest light and the profoundest knowledge which is possible to the unaided human mind. (Rousseau, 1762b, p 350)

In relation to sex, men and women are clearly different. Rousseau admits that it is difficult to know which differences should be attributed to nature and which to cultural factors. The ideal man is 'strong and active'; the ideal woman is 'weak and passive'; his role is to command and protect her; hers is to serve and please him. As he put it, 'woman is specially made for man's delight' (Rousseau, 1762b, p 322).

Rousseau makes a long list of what he considers to be the main female attributes: modesty, dependence, attractiveness, passivity and above all chastity. He fails to recognise that some of them are contradictory and he does not always stress the fact that they are socially derived, rather than being natural. They do not stem from the woman in the original state of nature but from the woman in subsequent society and hence they cannot be, by his definition, innate.

Despite their subservience to men, women, he argues, command a good deal of power, not in a direct, overt way but in an indirect, concealed manner. They possess this power through the influence they exercise over men behind the scenes, by using their feminine characteristics. The best of them can have immense power over men:

> The woman who is both virtuous, wise, and charming, she who, in a word, combines love and esteem, can send them (men) at her bidding to the end of the world, to war, to glory, and to death at her behest' (Rousseau, 1762b, p 356)

He considered it a great error of judgement on behalf of those who argued that women should be educated and encouraged to behave like men – as Wollstonecraft and others argued (see Chapter 6) – for this would prove to their disadvantage. As we shall see later, he envisaged that boys and girls should be educated together up to puberty after which they would receive different forms of education:

> The more women are like men, the less influence they will have over men, and then men will be masters indeed. (Rousseau, 1762b, p 327)

Even though men are imperfect and can be both cruel and unfaithful in marriage, Rousseau counselled that the wife 'should early learn to submit to injustice' for the maintenance of her marriage, for the reform of her husband and for her own sake. Should she behave in bitter or vindictive ways, she may exasperate her husband, who may then respond with greater harshness. As he put it, the wife 'must be gentle for her own sake, not his' (Rousseau, 1962b, p 333).

He adopts, however, an egalitarian position in relation to young people. He advocates that young people should be able to choose their own partners for marriage, as against the then prevailing practice of arranged marriages for property considerations. Parents should, of course, be consulted before the final decision:

> Parents choose a husband for their daughter and she is only consulted as a matter of form; that is the custom. We should do the opposite; you will choose, and we shall be consulted. (Rousseau, 1762b, p 364)

There are numerous contradictions in Rousseau's writings on women: they must be sexually attractive but not aggressively so; they must be sociable but not domineering; they must learn many things but they must not appear learned; they must not be mere housewives but their place is at home; 'women are more responsible for men's follies than men are for theirs' (Rousseau, 1762b, p 328); they must be chaste, but men are allowed to have sexual affairs.

Any freedom that Rousseau allowed for women when they were single disappears once they get married. Although he argues that single women should go out with their mothers to balls, sport, music, plays and they may 'even be allowed a certain amount of coquetry', they should, once they get married, live in retirement. His favourite family life is that of Classical Athens:

> When the Greek women married, they disappeared from public life; within the four walls of their home, they devoted themselves to the care of their household and family. This is the mode of life prescribed for women alike by nature and reason. (Rousseau, 1762b, p 330)

It is a strange paradox that Rousseau attacked social class inequalities and slavery with such gusto and relish, yet he not only accepted gender inequalities but, on occasion, he presented them as so structural that they appeared almost as natural. It was this that so disappointed Wollstonecraft, who was a great admirer of his views on social inequality and of his ideas for a more equal society.

Recent feminists have been divided on how to interpret Rousseau's writings on gender. Many feminist writers are rightly puzzled by his general attitude to women:

> For this generally egalitarian philosopher, sex was the only legitimate ground for the permanent unequal treatment of any person. (Okin, 1979, p 154)

The argument that Rousseau's views simply reflected public opinion is a rather generous assessment and makes it possible 'to get him off the hook' (Strong, 1994, p 135). After all, he rose above the prejudices of his time in the case of class and slavery. Perhaps, the best conclusion to draw is that Rousseau genuinely believed that the fulfilment of sex roles he described was the best way to make possible the creation of his ideal society. Most of these sex roles were in line with existing practice but some were not. He did not believe that gender differences were natural but he thought that sex roles performed a useful function in society. Differential treatment of the sexes was, therefore, justified, he argued. Although contradictory, his views were, on balance, male-dominated.

Education

Rousseau's writings on education fall into two categories: his ideas on how children should ideally be educated; and his plan for a national system of education. The former was most original and was discussed at length in his book *Emile* – 'the book that was to change Western educational thought' (Bowen, 1981, p 183); or the book that came to be seen as 'the charter of childhood's freedom' (Compayre, 1907, p 24). Rousseau was influenced by Montaigne and Locke; in return, he exerted a major influence on such education figures as Pestalozzi, Froebel and Montessori. His plan for a national educational system was brief; it was discussed in one of his lesser-known books – *Considerations on the Government of Poland* (1773); and had no lasting influence.

Ideal education methods

Like Locke, Rousseau set out his views on the ideal way of educating children in the context of a private tutor educating a young man and a young woman. Unlike Locke, however, the young man was not of noble birth and the aim of his education was not to make him a gentleman but a broad-minded individual who is a good person, husband, father and a good citizen. Rousseau was painting a picture of the ideal method and he understood that not all the aspects of his method could be applied to all the children in the country because of many practical difficulties.

Despite their different educational philosophies, both Locke and Rousseau encouraged the acceptance of childhood as a stage in human development. Children were not just young adults but had their own needs, desires and ambitions. They were different in many ways from adults, they were the future of their society and they should be cherished and loved as such.

> Love childhood, indulge its sports, its pleasures, its delightful instincts.
> (Rousseau, 1762b, p 43)

Rousseau divided the educational period for a person into four stages beginning with infancy, that is: from childbirth to the age of two; two stages of childhood up to the age of 13; and adolescence from then on. He also suggested that educational influences come from three major sources: children learn from nature, from their experiences and from people. Each of these sources of education is best suited to one of the three stages of education: nature for infancy, experiences for the two stages of childhood, and people for adolescence.

Several main principles run through his ideas on education. First, the educational experience must be liberating for the individual in order to counteract the fact that throughout his life 'man is imprisoned by our institutions' (Rousseau, 1762b, p 10). In order to find their potentialities, the individual must be able to think freely – this requires a broad rather than a narrow system of education. Yet, at the same time, they must become a good citizen, willing to take into account the common good. There was always a tension between Rousseau's free-thinking man and his loyal citizen.

Second, 'true education consists less in precepts than in practice' (Rousseau, 1762b, p 9). The infant, the child and the adolescent must learn more from experience than from abstract, dry teaching. The child is far more likely to enjoy and to benefit from education by finding out for themself, with the guidance of the tutor, rather than by being rigidly taught in the classroom.

Third, books are, nevertheless, a necessary part of education but they should reflect existing knowledge and contemporary life – they should be relevant to people's lives. This was an understandable reaction against the rigid, and dated, school curriculum that children had to go through, as the following quotation illustrates:

> A boy at the age of twelve or thirteen was being required to read
> the sixteenth century Latin grammar of Lubinus, the seventeenth
> century grammar of Tursellinuss, the *Phaedrus* of Plato, the *History* of
> Flavius Josephus of the first century AD, along with selections from
> the Bible, French literature and history, and French grammar. (Bowen,
> 1981, p 191)

Fourth, mental and physical education must go together, for one reinforces the
other, and vice versa, 'a feeble body makes a feeble mind' (Rousseau, 1762b,
p 21). There is an element of exaggeration in this long-standing belief, for many
a person with a weak physique can be a brilliant pupil; vice versa, many people
with a strong physique do not necessarily excel in academic lessons. Nevertheless,
this had been a widely held belief from Classical Greece onwards. Rousseau was
influenced by the ideas of Classical Greece since he regarded Plato's *Republic* as
'the finest treatise on education ever written' (Rousseau, 1762b, p 8).

Fifth, children must be allowed to proceed at their own speed rather than be
forced to learn according to a fixed schedule. Children's innate abilities vary as
do their interests. Proceeding at their own speed is, therefore, the only way that
accords with their nature. For Rousseau, any practices that were contrary to
nature's ways were to be avoided.

Sixth, like all other educators, he stressed the importance of education in
moulding the character of the individual and the culture of the nation. This
was particularly important to him because of his belief that people and states
get set in their ways and find change very difficult. Gradual change, encouraged
by education, is the best way forward. Revolutions can sometimes be helpful in
bringing about change but 'such events are rare; they are exceptions' (Rousseau,
1762a, p 218).

Infancy is the first stage of development. Rousseau believed that 'Man's education
begins at birth; before he can speak or understand he is learning' (Rousseau, 1762b,
p 29). Throughout life, human beings learn more from experience and everyday
life than from formal education in schools.

During infancy the source of education is primarily nature itself because the
infant learns by themselves to talk, to eat and to walk. The mother is the most
important person in the infant's life because of natural reasons. Had God meant
fathers to be the most important persons, 'he would have given them milk to
feed the child' (Rousseau, 1762b, p 5).

Rousseau criticised the various ways in which cultural norms had come to
make the infant's development unnatural and harmful to their education and
development. He called for the abandonment of the practices of swaddling and
wet nursing because they were unnatural and hence detrimental to the infant's
physical and mental development. Swaddling prevented the child's free movement
while wet-nursing deprived the child of its mother's love: 'there is no substitute
for a mother's love', he declared (Rousseau, 1762b, p 13).

He argued that infants should be allowed to experience more sensations, pleasant and unpleasant, than they were permitted to do by their parents or guardians because this is how they learn. Overprotection was not to their advantage. Play was most important but children's toys should not be bought at great expense but rather should be ordinary things from the child's environment – an argument very similar to Locke's:

> Toys of silver, gold, coral, cut crystal, rattles of every price and kind; what vain and useless appliances. Away with them all!... a small branch of a tree with its leaves and fruit, a stick of liquorice which he may suck and chew, will amuse him as well as these splendid trifles, and ... he will not be brought up to luxury from his birth. (Rousseau 1762a, p 36)

Rousseau stressed the importance of good diet, fresh air, adequate housing and life in the country, away from the overcrowded cities. He realised, of course, that many families could not achieve this, and he knew that the contemporary trend was towards increased urbanisation and factory work. At the same time, however, he felt that cities were the breeding ground for vice and corruption and that they had a very high infant mortality rate – 'one half of the children who are born die before their eighth birthday' (Rousseau, 1762b, p 15). He believed that life in the country would reduce all these problems:

> Men are not made to be crowded together in ant-hills, but scattered over the earth to till it. The more they are amassed together, the more corrupt they become. Disease and vice are the sure results of over-crowded cities. (Rousseau, 1762b, p 26)

He considered the two stages of childhood the most dangerous period because children learn mainly from their life experiences; though they have to be guided, they should also be allowed to do as they wanted, as far as possible. He emphasised learning in two ways: by example and by experience. There is no point in asking children to behave in ways that the tutor himself does not: 'you yourself must set the pattern he shall copy', he advised (Rousseau, 1762b, p 59). Similarly, he believed that abstract lessons in such subjects as history, geography, science and others, were not of much use during the childhood stage because children's reasoning was not up to it.

Children should learn by experience from their immediate environment before moving on to abstract learning. Thus, instead of basing geography lessons on names, numbers, maps, globes and other such aids, the tutor should begin with the real things that are familiar to the child:

> His geography will begin with the town he lives in and his father's country house, then the places between them, the rivers near them, and

then the sun's aspect and how to find one's way by its aid. (Rousseau, 1762b, p 134)

Rousseau does not quite explain how the child will learn to read and write during childhood and one must assume that he hopes that it will be done gradually through example, interest and individual assistance when the child is ready. He is certainly against rushing the education of children; he does not approve of rote learning; and he disapproves of the practice where all children are treated alike irrespective of their abilities and interests.

As for discipline, he is rather relaxed about it. Children, he argued, should never be punished at the whim of adults as was often the case in his time; they should be punished only when they clearly did something wrong. This may sound a trite comment today but it must be seen against the then prevailing cruelty to children when, 'The constant companion of childhood was fear of the rod' (Bowen, 1981, p 186).

Rousseau disapproved of severe punishment more than Locke did. He argued for a balance between lax and harsh punishment: the first spoils the child while the second suppresses their individuality. Certainly, children should not be punished for just being boisterous because boisterousness was part of the child's development:

> Nature provides for the child's growth in her own fashion, and this should never be thwarted. Do not make him sit still when he wants to run about, nor run when he wants to be quiet. Let them run, jump, and shout at their heart's content. (Rousseau, 1762b, p 50)

He advised tutors to allow children to experiment even at the risk of some physical pain, for this was part of nature's lesson to the child. A tutor should be most annoyed with himself if his tutee never experienced pain while learning. 'To bear pain', he claimed, 'is his first and most useful lesson' (Rousseau, 1762b, p 41).

As a lover of nature, he was against cruelty to animals as part of his general principle that one should not hurt anybody. He considered it unnatural for children to eat meat – it was not only unhealthy but also contrary to their moral development. Children, he argued, prefer vegetable foods and they should not be made to change to meat. It could turn them into cruel persons, evidenced by the fact that:

> The great meat-eaters are usually fiercer and more cruel than other men. The English are noted for their cruelty while the Gaures are the gentlest of men. (Rousseau, 1762b, p 118).

It is true, he wrote, that the English feel that they are 'good-natured people', but 'no one else says it of them!' (Rousseau, 1762a, p 118).

Puberty marks the beginning of both reason and sexual awakening. Up till then, Rousseau advised against lessons on any subject for he believed that children's reasoning powers were too weak. Now, however, adolescents can begin to reason and they can be taught by teachers and tutors all the subjects provided that the teaching is conducted in an interesting way; that it is done in a practical way, wherever possible; and that it takes into account the adolescent's interests and abilities.

One of the major criticisms of Rousseau's educational ideas is that he underestimated children's reasoning powers and, as a result, he left formal teaching far too late, until adolescence. If Locke assumed reasoning too early in a child's life, Rousseau left it rather late. One critic complained that Rousseau's approach to education was both too leisurely and too passive – the teacher spent too much time as an interested bystander during childhood education. 'The best educator', according to Rousseau, 'is the one who acts least, intervening only to remove obstacles which would hinder the free play of nature, or to create circumstances favourable to it' (Compayre, 1907, p 25).

Puberty brings with it the first signs of sexual awareness with the two sexes showing an interest in each other. Rousseau was quite willing that sexual matters should be explained to adolescents in circumspect ways. His advice for marriage was that the two partners should be of similar social backgrounds – similar education, wealth and status. If that was not possible, then it is best for the man to marry below rather than above his status because it is the man's social standing that determines the social position of the whole family.:

> When he marries into a lower rank, a man does not lower himself, he raises his wife; if, on the other hand, he marries above his position, he lowers his wife and does not raise himself. (Rousseau, 1762b, p 370)

The dawning of sex awareness at puberty signals also the beginning of the separation of the sexes in education. Up till then, boys and girls could be educated together; now it is best if they are taught separately because they have different social destinations – boys are destined for the outside world of work while girls' destination is in the household as wives and mothers.

Rousseau insisted that it was in women's best interests that the education system should cultivate feminine values for them and that it should present for them subjects that suited their abilities, interests and societal roles. Girls should be taught, apart from reading and writing, such artistic subjects as drawing, embroidery, lacemaking and sewing. Physical education is important for both sexes but the aim is different: the development of strength for boys; the development of grace for girls, even though these two traits are not exclusive of each other. A girl's education should prepare her for her major role in society – to be the 'helpmate' of man. It is this principle that guides the choice of subjects:

> A woman's education must be planned in relation to man. To be pleasing in his sight, to win his respect and love, to train him in

childhood, to counsel and to console, to make his life pleasant and
happy. (Rousseau, 1762b, p 328)

National education system

Rousseau was invited by a member of the Polish nobility to prepare a report for
the improvement of the government of Poland, a country that was at war with
itself and with its neighbours at the time. His proposals were an attempt to bring
some unity to the country – hence the strong emphasis on social solidarity
and patriotism in his proposals. Although our understanding of his views on
national education come mostly from this report, he also made it quite clear
in his other writings that the state had a responsibility for the education of its
children. Education should not be left to the 'intelligence and prejudices of fathers'
(Rousseau, 1758, pp 148–9) for it had national implications. After all, 'Families
dissolve, but the State remains' (Rousseau, 1758, pp 148–9).

Although education should be a state responsibility, parents had the duty of
ensuring that their children were educated by ensuring that they went to school.
Nothing can excuse them from this duty:

> Poverty, pressure of business, mistaken social prejudices, none of these
> can excuse a man from his duty, which is to support and educate his
> own children. (Rousseau, 1762b, p 17)

The main aim of education is not economic but social – to create citizens who
love their country, who acknowledge the importance of the common good, who
value a distinct national solidarity. He feared – clearly very prematurely – that
national identities had disappeared in Europe and were replaced by a Western
European culture:

> Today, there are no longer Frenchmen, Germans, Spaniards, or even
> Englishemen. (Rousseau, 1773, p 96)

Governments in Europe had failed to instil into their citizens a sense of civic pride
that cements national culture. Instead, they made material success their primary
goal with the result that concern for wealth was the primary consideration of
their citizens:

> The one desire of their hearts is luxury; their one passion is for gold.
> (Rousseau, 1773, p 96)

Poland, like all other European countries of the time, was a rigidly stratified society
and its educational system reflected this: colleges for the upper nobility, academies
for the lower nobility, and cathedral or parish schools for the majority of children

– most of whom did not attend school. Rousseau's first recommendation was to replace this class system with a national system of education for all.

Schools would be open to children of all classes and they would be free of charge or, if need be, with such low fees that even the poorest parents could afford them. Rousseau did not go so far as to make private education either at home or in private schools illegal but he argued that a certain number of bursaries should be provided for the very intelligent children of poor parents who qualified for private schooling. A national system of education was a government recognition that all citizens and their children should be equal in the eyes of the state.

Contrary to his view on educational methods, he advocated that, by the age of ten, every child should 'be acquainted with all his country's productions; and at twelve, with all its provinces, highways, and towns. At fifteen, he should know all its history; at sixteen, all its laws' (Rousseau, 1773, p 97).

As if to emphasise again the importance of creating a patriotic culture, he argued that 'only Poles should be allowed to act as teachers'; and they should all be married men who distinguished themselves by their behaviour. Rousseau was against teaching becoming a profession; he preferred teachers to move into other jobs after a while.

Not unexpectedly, he stressed the importance of sports in the national curriculum. He stipulated that all schools must have a gymnasium and that all children, irrespective of whether they went to state or private schools, should play games together and in public so as to reinforce social solidarity. As a public acknowledgement of this, he demanded that prizes for the winners at the games should be conferred not by the decision of the masters but by 'acclamation on the judgement of the spectators' (Rousseau, 1773, p 100).

In brief, Rousseau's views on a national system of education appear ordinary today, but they were radical at the time even though others before him had made similar proposals. A national system of education, for him, was to be for all children; it should aim at reducing class divisions; and at promoting social solidarity and national pride.

Rousseau's ideal society

Rousseau's ideal society is based on four interrelated, but contested, concepts: the goodness of human nature, which has already been discussed; the general will; the small territorial state; and direct citizen participation in decision-making on government affairs.

The goodness of human nature

To recapitulate briefly: Rousseau's view was that human beings have the potential of both individualism and compassion; they have the innate ability and desire to both look after their own interests and, at the same time, to take into account the welfare of others. The nature of social institutions can tip this fine balance either towards individualism or towards compassion. In the past, he argued, the balance had been tipped towards inequality but it was possible, though difficult, to change this so that social institutions, particularly education, could stress compassion and the common good more and the individual self-interest less than they had done in the past.

Rousseau was unclear as to how this could best be done but he seems to have put a good deal of the responsibility on the shoulders of a wise legislator who can advise the government to institute legislation that promotes the common good. This is the role he was invited to play in drafting a constitution for Poland and for Corsica. But, as he himself recognised, governments may not be minded to do this; or, if they are, the public may not be ready to follow. This is the perennial problem of all thinkers who think the impossible.

The general will

Rousseau uses the concept of the general will to refer to the ethical code of the body politic of a country – an ethical code that advocates both equality and liberty. It is the source of its laws that promote and protect the common interest above all individual or sectional interests. It can only exist because of the goodness of human nature that enables individuals to place a high value on the common good. If one adopted a Hobbesian view of human nature, it would not be possible to put forward seriously the notion of the general will, as Rousseau uses it.

The general will comes about as a result of the social compact through which citizens are prepared to merge their individual interest into the common good:

> The body politic is also a corporate being possessed of a will; and this general will, which tends always to the preservation and welfare of the whole and of every part, and is the source of its laws, constitutes for all the members of the State, in their relation to one another and to it, the rule of what is just and unjust. (Rousseau, 1758, p 132)

For the general will to come about citizens have to give their approval – there needs to be a social contract. The idea of a social contract goes back to Classical Greece and was used by many writers, including Hobbes and Locke, as we saw in Chapter 5. Although they all tried to present the notion of the social contract as a scientific concept, the truth is that it is basically ideological, expressed in semi-scientific language. Rousseau uses the concept of the social contract to lend support to his views on the importance of the community to human welfare:

> As an individual everyone of us contributes his goods, his person, his life, to the common stock, under the supreme direction of the general will; while as a body we receive each member as an individual part of the whole. (Rousseau, 1762b, p 424)

Rousseau acknowledged that in any society there are sectional interests but he hoped that these would be either weak or that they would cancel one another out. Every attempt should be made to reconcile them to the demands of the general will. Failing this, the sovereign power has the right to impose the general will over the sectional wills. Rousseau uses some strong language to make his point, for he believes that without the sovereignty of the general will, his scheme of the ideal society collapses:

> Whoever refuses to obey the general will shall be compelled to do so by the whole body. (Rousseau, 1762a, p 195)

Rousseau claims that this is not tantamount to crushing the freedom of the individual; rather, 'he will be forced to be free' (Rousseau, 1762a, p 195), that is, the individual should be forced to recognise that as a member of a community he has responsibilities to others in the same way that they have responsibilities towards him.

In a competitive, acquisitive society the reconciliation of the sectional and the general will is very problematic, and at times impossible. But Rousseau believed that in his scheme of things this was not an insuperable problem because of the goodness of human nature and the emphasis given by all to the satisfaction of the needs of all citizens:

> But when the citizens love their duty, and the guardians of the public authority sincerely apply themselves to the fostering of that love by their own example and assiduity, every difficulty vanishes. (Rousseau, 1758, p 141)

The notion of the general will has been criticised not only on the grounds that it is vague but also that it undermines the basic value of individual liberty. This is certainly true if one perceives individual liberty as a one-dimensional value – as the absence of constraint. It is, however, not a valid criticism if one sees liberty as a two-dimensional value meaning not only the absence of constraint but also the satisfaction of human needs. It is the second definition, as we saw earlier, that Rousseau adopted.

Even as a one-dimensional concept, freedom cannot be absolute in any society. In advanced industrial societies, there are numerous examples where individuals are 'forced to be free': employers are forced to abide by labour codes that, for example, do not allow them to dismiss employees at will; individuals have to observe an array of legislation with which they do not agree; they have to pay taxes even though they may not benefit from them; drivers have to take out several insurance policies before they are allowed to drive their vehicles; children have to go to school and their parents can be prosecuted if they persistently fail to do so; voting in general elections is compulsory in some countries; and so on. Failure to observe such legislation involves sanctions, including imprisonment.

Rousseau applied the notion of the general will in a very perceptive way in the case of crime. Although he believed that in a state that is well-governed under the guidance of the general will 'criminals are rare', he acknowledged that there will always be a few individuals who will violate the law. For most offenders, reform is the first line of approach because human beings are redeemable:

> There is not a single ill-doer who could not be turned to some good.
> (Rousseau, 1762a, p 209)

On the very rare occasions when the state considers it necessary to punish an offender, it must use other means than the death penalty. This was an important departure from the prevalent practice of sending even minor offenders to the guillotine. After exhausting all the possibilities, the state may deem it necessary to use the death penalty. Such cases, however, should be extremely rare; and even then, there should be the possibility of the state pardoning the offender. Rousseau's general principle on the death penalty is this:

> The State has no right to put to death, even for the sake of making an example, any one whom it can leave alive without danger. (Rousseau, 1762a, p 209)

Direct citizen participation

Rousseau made a point of distinguishing between the state body that takes major legislative decisions and the body that implements the laws enacted by the legislative body. Direct citizen participation was necessary in the law-making body, the legislature, but the actual implementation of these laws, the government administration, should be left to paid administrators. He felt that direct involvement in the making of the laws of one's country has two advantages over legislation made by monarchs or even by representative democracy. First, it will result in better legislation in the sense that it will better reflect the views of the general public; and, second, people are more likely to obey the laws when they know that they took part in their making.

Both of these claims have been questioned. It has been argued that legislation based on the views of the general public can, at times, be nothing more than a reflection of public prejudices. This may be true but the argument for democratic participation 'is not that the majority is always right, but that no minority can be trusted not to prefer its own advantage to the good of the whole' (Cole, 1993, p xlvi). The second claim has been criticised on the grounds that people only obey the laws out of either tradition or fear – a rather weak and debatable criticism. Rousseau's support of direct citizen participation has had an enduring impact particularly during the second half of the 20th century with the expansion of the welfare states in advanced industrial societies. Citizen participation came to be seen as empowering service users, as a way of reducing professional power, as well as a useful tool for social planning (Meacher, 1992).

Rousseau acknowledged that, ideally, the more unanimous citizens' opinions were on the framing of laws, the stronger the general will would be. But where this was not possible, 'the vote of the majority always binds all the rest', with one important exception – no one had the authority to deprive a person of his freedom permanently, that is, to make him a slave (Rousseau, 1762a, p 277).

Important positions in the government should be filled either through the normal selection process or by lot, depending on the nature of the position, a practice similar to that used in Classical Athens:

> When choice and lot are combined, positions that require special talents, such as military posts, should be filled by the former; the latter does for cases, such as judicial offices, on which good sense, justice, and integrity are enough, because in a State that is well constructed, these qualities are common to all the citizens. (Rousseau, 1762a, p 280)

This differentiation between the legislature and the government was similar to Locke's view of the separation of powers between the various branches of government. But it had something more to it: Rousseau 'believed that the vigilant exercise of the powers of sovereignty by the people themselves was the only safeguard against despotism' (Wokler, 1995, p 72). While others in the past had used the abstract concept of natural law or divine law to protect the liberty of the individual against despotic governments, Rousseau used the general will – people's joint voice.

The small nation state

Although Rousseau's ideal stage of human development was the patriarchal hunting and fishing era, he rejected outright any suggestion that his ideal society of the future meant going back to 'living in the forests with the bears' (Rousseau, 1755, p 125). The ideal society for the implementation of his ideas on the general will and direct citizen participation was the middle-sized nation state, that is, a state that was 'neither too large for good government, nor too small for self-maintenance' (Rousseau, 1762a, p 219). Corsica, he thought, would be just about the right size.

He gave a number of reasons why the emerging large nation states of his time would not be appropriate for his plans. These objections must be viewed in the light of the then prevailing conditions of communication, which were, obviously, rudimentary compared to modern methods of mass communication.

First, large countries entail long distances and this, in turn, makes good administration more difficult; second, they involve several layers of government – central, regional, local – which increase administrative costs; third, bearing in mind the diversity of cultures in a large country, respect for the law will vary reflecting the appropriateness, or otherwise, of the legislation to regional cultures; fourth, in such big countries, it is difficult to identify either talent and virtue among the population or to detect and punish crime; fifth, 'the State is governed by clerks' (Rousseau, 1762a, p 220), simply because politicians are overwhelmed with other business; and, finally, the state spends so much of its time and energy on simply maintaining its authority among people who do not know each other that it has precious little time 'for the happiness of the people' (Rousseau, 1762a, p 220).

It may well be that modern methods of mass communication have either taken care of, or have softened the force of, many of Rousseau's arguments but the fundamental point of increased citizen alienation in a large state remains as true today as it was then. It is a point repeated by many since then and it is of particular relevance in the contemporary world with the ongoing emergence of regional and global units of government. It is difficult to see how, say, a Hungarian and a Finn, or a Greek and a Scot, will share any feelings of togetherness just because they are citizens of the European Union.

Rousseau's view on the advantages of small units of administration found a strong expression in the second half of the 20th century under the slogan 'small is beautiful'. It was argued that large organisations using advanced technology are inefficient as well as dehumanising for their employees. It would be far better, it was claimed, to plan on a small scale, to employ small organisations and to use intermediate technology (Schumacher, 1974). As in Rousseau's case, this was an argument that went contrary to current trends and had little effect on the continuing expansion of conglomerates. There are advantages in large organisations and large states, which seem to outweigh their disadvantages in an increasingly globalised world.

Theory and practice

Many 'utopian' thinkers show no interest in how practical their proposals are. Rousseau, like Plato before him and Marx after him, was aware of the difficulties involved in the practical implementation of his theoretical ideas. He showed this quite clearly in his report for the reform of Polish society and government (Rousseau, 1773). He acknowledged that radical ideas can only be implemented gradually and some of them have to be amended to fit existing realities. The implementation of radical ideas, he said, was like the problem 'of squaring the circle in geometry' (Rousseau, 1773, p 3) It is, therefore, prudent not to start off 'by hurling ourselves into unrealistic proposals' (Rousseau, 1773, p 25).

Reforms have to be acceptable to the people if they are to succeed – they cannot be implemented by force from above. Education was the key to the preparation of the public for reforms:

> It is education that you must count on to shape the souls of citizens
> in a national pattern and so direct their opinions, likes and dislikes,
> (Rousseau, 1773, p 19)

Sensible though this sounds, it runs the risk of creating a stalemate. For example, Rousseau was a firm opponent of wealth and luxury, so much so that he believed that their existence made the creation of a free and stable society impossible. Thus, he advised that luxury cannot be stamped out 'with sumptuary laws. You must reach deep into men's hearts and uproot it by implanting there healthier and nobler states' (Rousseau, 1773, p 18). It is a moot point, however, whether such a crucial change can be achieved in such a cultural way without any changes in the economic sphere of society.

Similarly, on the issue of the emancipation and enfranchisement of the serfs, he advised that the government should proceed with caution despite his firm belief that 'serfs are men, even as you are; they have in them the capacity to become everything that you are' (Rousseau, 1773, p 30). Caution was necessary to overcome both the opposition of the owners and the slavishness of the serfs. Without this precautionary step, he warned, 'depend on it that the enterprise will turn out badly' (Rousseau, 1773, p 30).

On other occasions, he was willing to modify his ideas in order to make them implementable. As mentioned above, he was a firm believer in the small participatory state – it was the most democratic as well as the most efficient form of government organisation. Yet, he was prepared to accept that this could be achieved in a country of the size of Poland provided that the country was made into 'a confederation of thirty-three tiny states' (Rousseau, 1773, p 76), so as to bring government closer to the people. Furthermore, he suggested two other measures that soften the weakness of representative democracy: frequent election of the deputies in order to reduce the risk of corruption; and direct accountability on behalf of the deputies to their constituents to enable the views of the public to prevail in government. Representative democracy in a large state would thus get closer to the ideal of participatory democracy in a small state.

Despite these and other concessions, Rousseau remained firm in his central belief that a self-sufficient, egalitarian, largely agrarian society was the ideal to aim at. If this were achieved, there would be 'neither beggars nor millionaires; luxury and indigence will disappear simultaneously' (Rousseau, 1773, p 74).

Conclusion

Rousseau believed that human beings are born with the innate tendency both to look after themselves and to help others when necessary. He was not an outright supporter of either possessive individualism or unadulterated altruism. He simply felt that individualism and altruism could coexist and influence human conduct for the better.

His view of human nature meant that he was a supporter of both equality and liberty. He not only saw no necessary conflict between them, but he saw them as compatible and mutually reinforcing. Liberty was not meaningful to him if it was not accompanied by a significant dose of equality and by the satisfaction of basic needs. Vice versa, equality had to be accompanied by liberty, for otherwise it could slide into oppression. It was this belief in liberty that separated him from Plato's ideas on how to create a future society, which were discussed in Chapter 1.

A democratic form of government flowed from his views on human nature and on the values of equality and liberty. Unlike others, however, he insisted that directly participatory democracy was the best form of government for his ideal society. He felt that representative democracy was too distant from the lives of most citizens and was likely to be unstable.

He believed that his vision of the ideal society was possible only in small nation states. Social solidarity, the common good, proximity of the rulers to the ruled, direct citizen participation and efficient government could best be achieved in small countries. Large nation states are too complex, impersonal and inefficient to create a society that puts the common good on a par with the individual interest. It is true that the small state 'was an anachronism from the start' (Sabine, 1963, p 593) but his warnings about the potential of social alienation in large states still holds true. On the other hand, neither Rousseau nor his followers realised the advantages of large organisations – economies of scale, ability to influence demand for their products, the power to have a say in political decisions directly and indirectly, the financial strength to carry out long-term research, and, in the case of large states, the political and military might to dominate small states.

His views on childhood and on education have proved most influential in encouraging a pedagogy that accepts childhood as a stage in development, a much freer form of educational practice, and a broad system of education for all without distinctions of class or political status.

His views on women remain the major reactionary part of his work. He consistently argued that women, though equal to men in many natural ways, are inferior to men, culturally speaking. He was one of the severest critics of inequality but he could not see that gender inequality was anything to worry about. Not unexpectedly, he was severely criticised by Wollstonecraft, as we saw in Chapter 6, and by subsequent writers.

He considered the role of government in society important but he was not an advocate of either the abolition of private property or the confiscation of wealth. Governments have a duty to enable their citizens to look after themselves. Direct government provision is necessary only for those who cannot look after themselves. It was excessive wealth that was unacceptable, for it was the fundamental cause of poverty in society.

Being equal and fraternal, human beings would come to the aid of their fellow citizens. This was not charity but reciprocity – simply good common sense. Society should be so organised that its citizens assist each other willingly in the full knowledge that during their lives they will be both providers and receivers of such help. He was an advocate of a compassionate welfare society rather than of a comprehensive welfare state.

EIGHT

The market, laissez-faire and welfare
Adam Smith (1723–90)

Adam Smith did not write as much about welfare issues, as defined in this volume, as many other thinkers but what he had to say about the division of labour, competition, the invisible hand of the market, economic growth and the limited role of government has had a deep and lasting influence on welfare debates.

His central message was that the unfettered operation of the market was enough to produce the economic growth that was necessary to satisfy the needs of all as well as the demand for luxuries by the few. Any intervention by the state in public affairs should be restricted to those few areas where it was either unprofitable or extremely difficult for the private market to provide. Large-scale government intervention in economic affairs was detrimental to economic growth and hence to human welfare.

Human nature

Although Adam Smith is generally seen as the founder of economics, he saw himself as a philosopher and held an academic chair in moral philosophy. He examined many aspects of economics philosophically and he certainly had a lot to say on the subject of human nature. Smith's theoretical edifice was based on a value system concerning human nature, which he made quite explicit both in his first book – *The Theory of Moral Sentiments* (1759) – and in his major book – *The Wealth of Nations* (1776) – a book that has become a classic not only in the field of economics but in the entire spectrum of the social sciences.

Smith was unequivocally on the side of those, like Hobbes and Rousseau, who believed and argued that differences in innate ability are, on the whole, minimal and that any such differences in life are mostly the result of the environment – family upbringing and education. He rejected the Aristotelian view of marked innate ability differences among human beings. His reason for doing so was that neither parents nor others notice any remarkable differences among children up to the age of eight years; it is only after that age, when children enter very different occupations, that differences in their talents appear and these seem to grow wider with the years 'till at last the vanity of the philosopher is willing to acknowledge scarce any resemblance' (Smith, 1776a, p 120).

It may well be that the professional and upper classes like to satisfy their vanity by believing in significant inherited abilities but this does not reflect reality, argued Smith:

The difference between the most dissimilar characters, between a philosopher and a common street porter, for example, seems to arise not so much from nature as from habit, custom, and education. (Smith, 1776a, p 120)

Like Rousseau, Smith warned that we should not confuse effects with causes. The differences in natural talents among men in different occupations are not only less than people imagine but, on many occasions, they are not 'the cause as the effect of the division of labour' (Smith, 1776a, p 120). On this issue and on most others, Smith was silent on the gender question that concerned so many other philosophers before and after him.

All human beings, irrespective of their abilities, are motivated by a variety of passions – positive, negative and neutral. These passions are part and parcel of their membership of society, their contribution to it and their observance of society's rules (Sugden, 2002). The two passions that are highlighted most in Smith's work and which are directly relevant to welfare debates are self-interest and fellow-feeling. Human beings are by nature self-seeking, anxious to promote their own individual interests. At the same time, however, they all have an inclination to be interested in the fortune of others – to share in the happiness and in the sorrow of others. This compassion is so universal that even 'the greatest ruffian, the most hardened violator of the laws of society, is not altogether without it' (Smith, 1759, p 11).

At a superficial level, this appears similar to Rousseau's human emotions of self-love and compassion, discussed in Chapter 7. The two philosophies of human nature are, however, very different because Smith stresses the power of self-interest very strongly and downplays the significance of compassion equally strongly. It is through the operation of self-interest that an individual will promote both his interests and his relationships with others. It is not love of fellow citizens that activates relationships of exchange between people but rather a quid pro quo premise. In Smith's words: 'Give me that which I want, and you shall have this which you want' (Smith, 1776a, p 118).

Benevolence is a weak motivation in human affairs and it weakens even more the further out we travel from our family circle – into the wider society, let alone the international community. Benevolence is also, according to Smith, a humiliating experience for those on the receiving end for they have nothing to give back in return. Ability to reciprocate reduces dependence while the absence of reciprocity tends to stigmatise the recipient, in the long run. This is why people avoid charity, if they can help it:

Nobody but a beggar chooses to depend chiefly upon the benevolence of his fellow-citizens. (Smith, 1776a, p 119)

Society can, therefore, only function well when people pursue their own interests in a free market and when they normally appeal to other people's self-love rather than to their compassion or benevolence. In Smith's memorable description of social transactions:

> It is not from the benevolence of the butcher, the brewer, or the baker that we expect our dinner, but from their regard to their own interests. We address ourselves, not to their humanity but to their self-love, and never talk to them of our own necessities but of their advantages. (Smith, 1776a, p 119)

Smith was writing at a time when commercial monetary transactions were the rule of the day, when the secular society had just superseded the Church-dominated society, when naked exploitation of the physical and human resources of the colonies was high. His ideas on self-interest and compassion are thoroughly in line with the commercial spirit of his age. Smith saw human nature not in the Hobbesian sense of all against all or in the fraternal sense of Rousseau. Rather, he portrayed men neither as 'devils or angels but only strivers for self-interest' (Sowell, 1979, p 16).

The emphasis on self-interest coupled with the limited role of charity and the minimal role of the state in public affairs that Smith envisages raise serious questions about how those not in employment and those in poverty – and there were plenty in Smith's time – were to cope. Moreover, Smith's individualism could not possibly be used as a base for the creation of a collectivist society of the universal welfare state model, as some of his liberal supporters have claimed.

The division of labour

Economic growth was, for Smith, the major medium for raising living standards for all. He was optimistic that the division of labour that brought about the high rates of economic growth of his time would continue to do so in the future. Increases in productivity resulting from the division of labour were due to three structural reasons that were unlikely to change much in the future. They were as follows:

> 'Firstly, to the increase in dexterity in every particular workman; secondly, to the saving of time which is commonly lost in passing from one aspect of work to another; and lastly, to the invention of a great number of machines which facilitate and abridge labour, and enable one man to do the work of many. (Smith, 1776a, p 112)

Smith's optimism about the enduring good effects of the division of labour stemmed from his belief that it had a firm and enduring base – the division of labour was the result of a gradual process of trial and error by ordinary men pursuing their own interests. It was not the result of some specific government policy or of some abstract theory that might prove wrong or unworkable in the future but the outcome of a long process whereby working men had found out from personal experience that their interests would best be served by specialisation, and this meant division of labour. It was the result of the natural propensity of ordinary people 'to truck, barter, and exchange one thing for another' (Smith, 1776a, p 117).

The division of labour created a more interdependent society than the one that existed before. Few people now produced all they needed to be able to be self-sufficient; most people had to sell either their products or their labour to enable them to buy the things they needed or desired. Money, rather than service or barter, became the common medium of exchange between individuals, groups and nations:

> Every man thus lives by exchanging, or becomes in some measure
> a merchant, and the society itself grows to be what is properly a
> commercial society. (Smith, 1776a, p 126)

As an optimist, Smith viewed economic growth as a surging tide raising all boats in the harbour. Standards of living rose for all with the result that even the poor of his time were better off than the poor of previous centuries as well as the well-to-do of undeveloped countries. Economic growth does not do away with inequalities but it reduces both inequality and poverty, Smith was arguing:

> It may be true, perhaps, that the accommodation of a European prince
> does not always so much exceed that of an industrious and frugal
> peasant as the accommodation of the latter exceeds that of many
> an African king, the absolute master of the lives and liberties of ten
> thousand naked savages. (Smith, 1776a, p 117)

This view of the relationship between economic growth and inequality has become a central issue of debate over the years, particularly in the second half of the 20th century when most colonies gained their independence. All the research evidence seems to suggest that this is not always the case, for a great deal depends on the type of development pursued and the fiscal policies adopted by the government. In many countries that experienced economic growth, inequality did not decline, several groups of people were left behind in poverty; and some of the wealth produced left the country to be paid to shareholders abroad. Moreover, poverty is a relative concept and historical comparisons need to take this into account – something that Smith himself recognised, as we shall see later.

Smith, however, acknowledged the dark side of the division of labour – its dehumanising effects. He argued that the worker who specialises in the performance of one task loses a good deal of his mental, emotional, social and physical aptitudes. His dexterity in his specific job is gained at the expense of the other aspects of his personality:

The man whose whole life is spent in performing a few simple operations of which the effects are perhaps always the same, or very nearly the same, has no occasion to exert his understanding or to exercise his invention in finding out expedients for removing difficulties which never occur. He naturally loses, therefore, the habit of such exertion, and generally becomes as stupid and ignorant as it is possible for a human creature to become. (Smith 1776b, p 368)

Smith stressed that this alienation applied to all the workers involved in industrialisation that was based on the division of labour – it was not an isolated individual pathology but a structural phenomenon affecting all such workers. He was troubled by this, evidenced by the fact that the issue appears in many of his writings over a long period of time (Lamb, 1973).

Both Rousseau before Smith and Marx after him were also concerned with the problem of alienation though they differed in their explanation and their remedy. Rousseau saw it as part of the ongoing commercialisation of society and his remedy involved a rejection of the values and practices of such a society. Marx considered alienation as the result of the exploitation of workers in a capitalist industrial society and his solution lay in the creation of a communist society where the division of labour was replaced by multi-professionalism, as we shall see in Chapter 10. Smith was not prepared to throw away, so to speak, the baby with the bath water. For him the division of labour was beneficial to all in society, and ways had to be found to deal with its undesirable effects on the workers. For the time being, however, workers had to accept that their brutalisation 'was compensated for by their relative opulence' (Bronowski and Mazlish, 1960, p 395).

Smith's long-term solution was to improve the educational standards of the people; he argued for state subsidies to the theatre to provide shows that would entertain the workers and thus relieve the most blatant effects of alienation. Such a proposal says something of Smith's deep concern with the problem, bearing in mind his views on government and the Calvinist environment of Scotland, where Smith lived, that frowned upon theatrical shows. It is, however, a proposal that was unlikely to deal with such a deep-rooted problem, then or now. In the long term, he believed education would prove helpful, though it is difficult to see how.

Laissez-faire and the invisible hand of the market

A society of self-seeking, commercially-minded individuals runs the risk of serious malfunctioning and conflict unless there is a countervailing force to hold in check their rapacious propensities. For Smith, this force is neither the Church nor the state – it is the market itself in the form of unimpeded competition. The 'invisible hand' of the market in the form of open competition ensures that goods are produced in the quantities that society wants and at the prices that society is prepared to pay; and wages are paid at levels that the market makes possible.

A producer who tries to advance his self-interest too far by demanding prices that involve high profit margins will find that other producers will take his custom away from him by asking for similar or even lower prices. If he attempts to pay wages that are too low in a state of high labour demand, he will find that his workers are likely to move elsewhere. The 'invisible hand' of the market can perform this regulatory function better than any government can, provided neither the government nor the employers impede its free operation. For this reason, Smith was against both employers' monopolies and government regulations that restrict competition.

His plea for free trade, both internal and external, can best be understood within the then prevailing conditions. Smith coined the term 'mercantilism' to describe the prevailing system whereby myriad government regulations attempted to control the behaviour of both capital and labour, of trade and employment. He felt that these regulations were the successful result of large companies extracting favourable terms from the government at the expense of the consumers. Mercantilism, according to Smith, served the interests of the merchants rather than the national welfare. Abolition of these regulations, therefore, would have the opposite effect. He was realistic enough to acknowledge that truly free trade is a utopia because of entrenched interests but he hoped that it would go as far as possible.

Smith's hostility to large-scale government intervention in economic and public affairs was based on both specific and general considerations. On the specific side, Rosenberg identifies four weaknesses of the then government in England, which may have influenced Smith's thinking: first, parliament was unrepresentative since 'no more than three or four per cent of the adult population possessed the right to vote'; second, parliament was secretive – it was 'a breach of privilege for newspapers even to divulge the contents of parliamentary debates' (Rosenberg, 1979, p 25); third, parliamentary seats 'were routinely bought and sold, even advertised in newspapers'; and, fourth, 'parliament was both corrupt and inefficient' (Rosenberg, 1979, p 26). Political conditions in other countries were no better – in fact, they were worse in many of them.

It is unlikely, however, that Smith's view of the role of government would have been different if the political environment in England had been healthier. He had deep-seated objections to large-scale government intervention in public affairs.

First, he believed that the men of industry at the local level knew better of what worked or what did not than the men in government miles away. Therefore, decisions taken at the government level ran a higher risk of being wrong than decisions taken by the men of industry at the local level.

Second, he argued that many government regulations interfered with the freedom of the individual and, as such, they were wrong both in ethical and economic terms. He cited the apprenticeship rules that governed the number of apprentices, the years of apprenticeship and the number of workers in certain occupations: these rules created artificial barriers to the free operation of the market, and benefited the masters at the expense of the apprentices. Similarly, the settlement laws that prevented the free movement of people on poor relief were against the sacred freedom of the individual as well as impeding the free movement of labour:

> To remove a man who has committed no misdemeanour from the parish where he chooses to reside is an evident violation of natural liberty and justice. (Smith, 1776a, p 245)

Third, historical evidence convinced him that all governments, monarchical, tyrannical or democratic, had a tendency to spend lavishly on grand projects of luxury. He viewed politicians as 'the greatest spendthrifts in society' because they were spending other people's money and they wanted to live up to the standards set by the affluent sections of the community:

> The taste for some sort of pageantry, for splendid buildings, at least, and other public ornaments, frequently prevails as much in the apparently sober senate-house of a little republic as in the dissipated court of the greatest king. (Smith, 1776b, p 508)

Fourth, all governments were heavily indebted and none managed to pay its debts to the full. They all tried to find ways and means of postponing or even avoiding full debt repayment, often resorting to policies involving the devaluation of their coinage. Despite this, high debts meant high repayment burdens with detrimental effects on the provision of services, taxation policies and economic growth.

Fifth, heavy government involvement in public affairs meant a rise in the proportion of the population employed in what Smith called unproductive labour. He divided the working population into two categories – productive and unproductive. The first increased the value of the commodities it produced while the latter did not. A factory worker increased the value of the goods he helped to produce – he was productive – while a teacher, a doctor, a servant, a soldier, an administrator and many other categories of workers in both the government and the private sector did not – they were unproductive:

> Thus, the labour of a manufacturer adds, generally, to the value of the materials which he works upon, that of his own maintenance, and of his master's profit. The labour of a menial servant, on the contrary, adds to the value of nothing. (Smith, 1776a, p 430)

Smith's general conclusion was that at any one time there was a limit to the number of unproductive workers that the productive sector of the labour force could support without raising taxation levels and without adverse effects on the economy. He thus started a major controversy on what constitutes 'productive' and 'unproductive' labour, which is still going on today. Interestingly enough, he considered education and training as a form of investment that improved productivity at work to the benefit of the national economy, but he classified teachers among the unproductive sector of the labour force:

> The improved dexterity of a workman may be considered in the same light as a machine or instrument of trade which facilitates and abridges labour, and which, though it costs a certain expense, repays the expense with a profit. (Smith, 1776a, p 377)

Experience and research evidence today show that the picture is far more complicated than Smith suggested and that many of what he called 'unproductive' services do, in fact, have positive effects on the economy (George and Wilding, 1984, ch 4). The best example of this, of course, is education, which improves the human capital of society and contributes very substantially to economic growth. Health care services for the working population to the extent that they improve health and reduce illness and work absenteeism also improve productivity; health care services for the retired population obviously do not improve productivity. Actors, whom Smith considered unproductive, do increase the national income, for their product is bought and sold in the market in similar ways to the products of steel workers. Indeed, the economy of most industrial societies is based more on the service than the manufacturing sector – contrary to the position that prevailed in Smith's time.

Smith's belief in market processes as mechanisms for coordinating the various parts of the economy did not imply that he viewed them as perfect – rather that they were 'merely considered superior to political processes' (Sowell, 1979, p 8). Similarly, his support of market men was guarded, though he had a higher opinion of their efficiency and honesty than that of politicians because businessmen were subjected to the pressures of competition, unlike politicians who were a law unto themselves. He reserved his most caustic criticism for politicians:

> His description of the statesman as 'that insidious and crafty animal' is perhaps the most famous swipe at politicians. (Fleischacker, 2004, p 229)

Nevertheless, Smith's portrayal of the economic system as a smooth, well-functioning machine benefiting all in society was contrary to the then prevailing human conditions up and down the country. Heilbroner expresses this contradiction between reality and theory well when he says that beyond 'the elegant lives of the leisure classes, society presented itself as a brute struggle for existence in its meanest from' (Heilbroner, 1969, p 39). Work on the land, in the factories and in the mines was harsh and brutish, with children and women often bearing the brunt of it:

> Children of seven or ten who never saw the daylight during the winter months were used and abused and paid a pittance by the miners to help

drag away their tubs of coal; pregnant women drew coal cars like horses and even gave birth in the dark black caverns. (Heilbroner, 1969, p 39)

Wealth and wages

Smith's work marks the final break with two strongly held beliefs on the nature of wealth: first, that the individual pursuit of wealth was somehow unethical, and, second, that the wealth of a nation rested primarily on its own produce. Smith saw wealth as the natural and welcome result of investment, of good management and particularly of the division of labour; it was beneficial to all in society, for it created jobs, paid wages and raised standards of living for all. One finds no trace in Smith's work of the medieval belief that the individual pursuit of wealth was unethical or unchristian, that profit was a form of exploitation, or that moneylending was usury. He also parted company with Rousseau's thesis that increased economic growth worsens the quality of life – for Smith, economic growth is the yeast that generates improvements in society. Without economic growth, human progress suffers.

Smith also parted company with the mercantilist view that national self-sufficiency should be the goal of government policy with the result that a protective wall of regulations and tariffs was necessary to keep foreign imports out. For him, the wealth of a country depends ultimately on the labour of its people and that foreign trade is to the benefit of all trading countries.

Although Smith never used the notion of class, he saw society in class terms: it was made up of three 'great, original, and constituent orders': 'those who live by rent, those who live by wages, and those who live by profit' (Smith, 1776a, p 356). He had nothing but praise for the working class but he had some harsh words for the other two classes. Those who lived by rent, the landed aristocracy, are often, according to Smith, indolent, ignorant, and incapable of understanding what is in their best economic interests (Smith, 1776a, p 357).

Those who lived by profit, the employers in industry and in commerce, are more interested in their own welfare than that of society, and they have an interest 'to deceive and even to oppress the public'. He, therefore, warned governments to be sceptical and cautious when faced with requests for legislation from this group even if, or rather when, such requests were presented as serving the public interest. Any such proposal 'ought always to be listened to with great precaution, and ought never to be adopted till after having been long and carefully examined, not only with the most scrupulous, but with the most suspicious attention' (Smith, 1776a, p 359). Marx welcomed and highlighted more both of these two criticisms.

The drive for greater wealth was, for Smith, not the result of human desire for an ever-rising standard of living because the rising wages of 'the meanest labourer' were sufficient to achieve this. Rather it was the outcome of the strong human passion to be noticed, to be seen as important in society, to be someone that others want to look up to and imitate. Status and vanity rather than opulence and luxury were the driving forces behind wealth accumulation:

> The rich man glories in his riches, because he feels that they naturally draw upon him the attention of the world, and that mankind are disposed to go along with him in all those agreeable conditions with which the advantages of his situation so readily inspire him. (Smith, 1759, p 61).

Vice versa, poverty is detestable not only because of the physical hardships it entails but also because a poor person is ignored and made to feel ashamed of his condition by the rest of society. While a rich man is 'observed by all the world', the poor man 'goes out and comes in unheeded, and when in the midst of a crowd is in the same obscurity as if shut up in his own hovel' (Smith, 1759, p 62). It is a social psychological model of wealth creation that tends to underemphasise the importance of the search for economic and, hence, for political power as the driving force for wealth creation.

Having proposed a psychological explanation of wealth and poverty, Smith returns to his class conflict model of society when it comes to wages. Bearing in mind the self-interested nature of human beings, it is not surprising that the two sides see things very differently on the issue of wages. Their interests are in structural conflict, according to Smith:

> The workmen desire to get as much, the masters to give as little as possible. The former are disposed to combine in order to raise, the latter in order to lower wages of labour. (Smith, 1776a, p 169)

It is true that both sides needed each other but, in such conflicts, employers clearly had the upper hand in his day for three clear reasons: first, 'being fewer in number, can combine much more easily'; second, 'the law, besides, authorises, or at least, does not prohibit such combinations, while it prohibits those of the workmen'; third, 'in such disputes, the masters can hold out much longer' than the workmen can (Smith, 1776a, p 169).

Smith rejected the then prevailing philosophy among the upper classes, referred to in Chapter 6, that low wages were necessary to act as a spur for higher work effort. He was a supporter of the view that generous wages were necessary to encourage both population growth and productivity at work. Some workers may, indeed, shirk hard or full-time work because they earned enough through part-time work but these were a very small minority. The vast majority of workers behaved very differently, he argued:

> The liberal reward of labour, as it encourages the propagation, so it increases the industry of the common people. A plentiful subsistence increases the bodily strength of the labourer, and the comfortable hope of bettering his position, and of ending his days perhaps in ease and plenty, animates him to exert that strength to the utmost. Where wages

are high, accordingly, we shall always find the workmen more active, diligent, and expeditious than where they are low. (Smith, 1776a, p 184)

His main worry was that workers might work so hard, either of their own volition or through pressure from their employers, that they ran the risk of ruining their health. He thus advised employers to try to hold back excessive work from their employees. In the long run, he argued, both the employee and the employer would benefit from moderate work effort.

True to his principle of laissez-faire, Smith was against any state regulation of wages, including a statutory minimum wage. He theorised that the lowest wages would always be sufficient to meet the basic needs of the worker and his family because it was the only way to ensure the reproduction of the labour force in the future. It was in the interests of employers to do this. Indeed, he felt that the wages of workers in England during his time 'to be evidently more than what is precisely necessary to enable the labourer to bring up a family' (Smith, 1776a, p 176).

The level of wages should be determined through the normal bargaining process between the two sides, unequal though they were in bargaining power, as he himself admitted. Despite this, he felt that the level of wages in any industry would reflect market forces and he pointed to the following five employment characteristics:

> First, the agreeableness or disagreeableness of the employments themselves; secondly, the easiness and cheapness, or the difficulty and expense of learning them; thirdly, the constancy or inconstancy of employment in them; fourthly, the small or great trust which may be reposed in those who exercise them; and fifthly, the probability or improbability of success in them. (Smith, 1776a, p 202)

Neither then nor now is it possible to come up with a list of criteria that will enable one to explain adequately wage differentials in society. The position is that much more complex today with the multiplication of occupations, semi-professions and professions; the growth of companies of varying size and vision; the emergence of trade unions as a force; and the varying complex legislation.

Poverty

Smith condemned the existence of widespread poverty on economic, social and humanitarian grounds. Poverty had adverse effects on the economy, social stability, population growth and it was contrary to any ethical standards of conduct:

> No society can surely be flourishing and happy, of which the far greater part of the members are poor and miserable. It is but equity, besides, that they who food, clothe, and lodge the whole body of people,

should have such a share of the produce of their own labour as to be themselves tolerably well fed, clothed, and lodged. (Smith, 1776a, p 181)

On the economic side, we saw that he considered low wages as detrimental to health and hence as disincentives to work and productivity. Poverty, therefore, undermines economic growth and makes it difficult for the country to flourish. He rejected, as we saw, the view that low wages and poverty act as a spur to greater effort at work.

On the social side, poverty constituted a major reason for the high child mortality rates of the time. Mothers in the Highlands of Scotland who had borne 20 children, he was told, were often left with just two alive; in other areas, half the children died before the age of five; mortality rates were even higher in foundling hospitals and among the children on parish relief. In all these diverse situations, the common factor was poverty. The result was that though birth rates among working-class people were higher than among the rich section of the community, 'a smaller proportion of their children arrive at maturity' (Smith, 1776a, p 182). As regards social stability, Smith argued that 'the avarice of the rich' coupled with the corresponding hatred among the poor and their 'love of present ease and enjoyment' inevitably resulted in conflict between the classes (Smith, 1776b, p 298). Consequently, a major reason for the institution of the state with its judicial powers was the protection of private property – an argument similar to Locke's.

Bearing in mind Smith's view on the near equality of innate ability among human beings, it follows that he would see poverty as, in the main, the result of structural rather than personal factors. He postulated that wherever there is great wealth, there is also great inequality; and where there is great inequality there is poverty – the three are interconnected:

> Wherever there is great property there is great inequality. For one very rich man there must be at least five hundred poor, and the affluence of the few supposes the indigence of the many. (Smith 1776b, p 298)

Smith was one of the first, if not the first, major writer to consider poverty in relative terms. Until then, poverty was viewed in subsistence terms – simply lack of the basic necessities of life. Smith argued that poverty is a relative concept – the list of necessities and the level at which they must be met varies over time and between countries at any one time. Having divided commodities into luxuries and necessities for purposes of taxation, he defined necessities as follows:

> By necessities I understand not only the commodities which are indispensably necessary for the support of life, but whatever the custom of the country renders it indecent for creditable people, even of the lowest order, to be without. (Smith, 1776b, p 465)

All other commodities were luxuries though Smith was at pains to point out that he had no moral objection to their use, provided it was done in temperate terms. He illustrated his relative definition with a series of examples that are worth quoting because they illustrate both the historical transformation of commodities from non-necessities to necessities and the subjective nature of Smith's own relative definition.

His first example was that of a linen shirt. He acknowledged that a linen shirt was not always considered a necessity. Both the Greeks and the Romans, for example, lived quite comfortably without them, he pointed out. Nevertheless in his times, a linen shirt came to be considered a social necessity for even the labourers:

> But in the present times, through the greater part of Europe, a creditable day-labourer would be ashamed to appear in public without a linen shirt, the want of which would be supposed to denote that disgraceful degree of poverty which, it is presumed, nobody can fall into without extreme bad conduct. (Smith, 1776b, p 465)

His second example was the use of leather shoes. Although shoes were not a necessity in previous centuries, they became so in England for both sexes; a necessity only for men in Scotland but not for women because they could 'without any discredit, walk about barefooted'. As for France, leather shoes were not a necessity for either sex because 'the lowest rank of both sexes appearing there publicly, without any discredit, sometimes in wooden shoes, and sometimes barefooted' (Smith, 1776b, p 465).

Thirdly, he considered beer and wine as luxuries even in wine-producing countries because a man of any rank 'may, without any reproach, abstain totally from tasting such liquors' (Smith, 1776b, pp 465–6). Neither physical necessity nor social custom made it indecent for any man to be without such drinks. He held a similar view with regard to tea and sugar: they were luxuries for 'the lowest ranks of people' but necessities for the other sections of the community. On the other hand, salt, leather, soap and candles were necessities.

Fourthly, fuel was a necessity in Britain, he argued, for both reasons of physical health and custom. The severity of winters, the social customs surrounding cooking and because working indoors during the winter necessitated heating meant that fuel was a necessity.

Finally, food is a necessity for all for purely physical health reasons and, therefore, the important question is which food items are necessities and which are luxuries. Smith concentrates on butcher's meat to make his distinction between necessities and luxuries. He does not believe that butcher's meat is in the same category as linen shirts or leather shoes because no one will think ill of a person who does not eat meat since there are adequate, and perhaps better, substitutes:

> Grain and other vegetables, with the help of milk, cheese, and butter, or oil where butter is not to be had, it is known from experience,

can, without any butcher's meat, afford the most plentiful, the most wholesome, the most nourishing, and the most invigorating diet. (Smith, 1776b, p 471)

Personal judgements are inevitable in debates on poverty and this is abundantly clear in Smith's case. Although he always appeals to social custom as the arbitrator between a luxury and a necessity, he in fact decides what social custom dictates. It is his interpretation of the situation rather than the view of the community as to what social custom demands for respectable living. Thus, he feels that a linen shirt is a necessity but leather shoes not necessarily so; that beer and even tea are luxuries even in countries where the consumption of such beverages is general among all sections of the public. In order to get over the problem of subjectivity, recent poverty studies have used public opinion research evidence to ascertain what is considered socially necessary in a society (Mack and Lansley, 1985). This approach does not eliminate the problem of subjectivity altogether but it certainly curtails it.

Smith does not discuss in any direct or coherent way the question of the alleviation of poverty. At times, he seems to imply that poverty will always exist in society, as it is part of inequality; while on other occasions, he appears to suggest that rising economic growth will solve the problem. In some parts of his work, he argues that wages of even the unskilled labourers are high enough to provide for the basic necessities of life for themselves and their families; on other occasions, he discusses the ill-effects of poverty on health and on infant mortality rates in working-class families in Britain and elsewhere.

Although poverty is not a central issue in Smith's work, it has been pointed out by his supporters that several of his proposals on other issues had a positive effect on poverty reduction: his support of public schooling, his advocacy for progressive forms of taxation, his rejection of the apprentices statutes and the laws of settlement for the poor, and his view on the innate equality of talents were all measures of potential benefit to the poor (Fleischacker, 2004, pp 205–8). While all this is true, one can mention just as many other proposals that were potentially detrimental to poverty reduction: his rejection of a minimum wage, his mistaken conclusion that the wages of even the lowest paid workers were sufficient to avoid family poverty, his absolute faith in the power of individualism, his claim that economic growth always reduces inequalities, and so on. The fact is that Smith was not concerned with distributive justice; his main, if not sole, concern was with economic growth, which he saw as the panacea for many of the economic ills of his society (Buchanan, 1979, p 121).

The major positive contribution of Smith's thought on poverty was his strong belief that the poor were no different from the rest of the population in terms of innate ability or willingness to work. Their poverty was the result of structural factors in the economy rather than of individual character failings – a view that was very similar to that of both Wollstonecraft and Rousseau discussed in previous chapters.

Slavery

Slavery had always existed in society, according to Smith, because it was a crude manifestation of man's domineering nature. His view of human nature led him to the conclusion that men like to dominate others and, as a result, they enjoy the unquestioning attitude that slaves have to adopt. Unlike free labourers who can show their dislike of their masters' attitudes and, if necessary, leave for other work, slaves have no option but to obey and appear docile:

> The pride of man makes him love to domineer, and nothing mortifies him so much as to be obliged to condescend to persuade his inferiors. Wherever the law allows it, and the nature of work can afford it, therefore, he will generally prefer the services of slaves to that of freemen. (Smith, 1776a, p 489)

Smith is at pains to explain that slavery and democracy can coexist quite happily. Indeed, he argues that slaves may be better treated in a despotic than in a democratic society because citizens in a democratic society are unlikely to take decisions, such as the abolition of slavery, that go against their perceived interests:

> In a despotic government slaves may be better treated than in a free government, where every law is made by their masters, who will never pass anything prejudicial to themselves. A monarch is more ready to be influenced to do something humanely for them. (Smith, 1776a, pp 96–7)

Smith held steadfastly to the view that 'slavery is a bad institution even for free men' (Smith, 1776a, p 99). It, first, made it impossible for human beings to pursue their own self-interest, to the detriment of themselves and of society as a whole. Secondly, masters were misguided in their belief that slaves were a cheaper form of labour than free labourers. Productivity among slaves was far inferior to that of freemen because they had nothing to aspire to that would act as an incentive for hard work. Since they could not buy any property, all that they were interested in was to work as little as possible and to eat as much as possible. Even under pressure from their employers, their productivity was low and hence the cost to their employers was higher than that of freemen receiving wages:

> It appears from the experience of all ages and nations, I believe, that the work done by freemen comes cheaper in the end than that performed by slaves. It is found to do so even at Boston, New York, and Philadelphia, where the wages of common labour are so very high. (Smith, 1776a, p 184)

The abolition of slavery had always been the result of mainly economic factors rather than of ideology, he argued. He cited the bull of Pope Alexander III in the 12th century, which demanded the emancipation of slaves and which was universally ignored. As he put it, the bull proved nothing more but 'a pious exhortation' to the faithful. He also cited evidence from the various types of plantation in the Americas to support his case. Slaves were used more in the profitable plantations of sugar and tobacco than in the not so profitable corn farms where most of the workers were freemen. This, to him, was evidence that the not so profitable farms could not afford slaves rather than they were unprofitable partly because they did not employ a high ratio of slaves:

> The planting of sugar and tobacco can afford the expense of slave-plantation. The raising of corn, it seems, in the present times, cannot. (Smith, 1776a, p 489)

Finally, he questioned the sincerity of the Quakers in Pennsylvania to free all their slaves. This was not done for ideological or ethical reasons, he argued, but on economic considerations. The number of slaves involved was so small that they could afford to do it. Had the number of slaves been larger and their contribution to the economy of the plantation correspondingly high, 'such a resolution could never have been agreed to' (Smith, 1776a, p 489).

In brief, Smith's general outlook on slavery is similar to his view of poverty. Both conditions are not acceptable on either ethical or economic grounds but their abolition rests on economic rather than on ethical or political considerations. Indeed, in the case of slavery, a monarchical, despotic regime is preferable to a democratic form of government – a point of dubious validity but which flows naturally from his general view of man as predominantly motivated by economic calculus with little humanity evident in his actions.

The family

Smith's views on the family and gender relationships were pretty conventional reflecting the dominant views and practices of his time. It was not an area of central concern to his work and most of the discussion appears in his lectures that were given before he wrote his two main books and which were published after his death.

He saw the role of women in society as being that of the wife, the mother and the housekeeper. This becomes evident from his discussion on education, where he argued that, beyond the elementary stage of education, young women were educated at home by their parents or by their private tutors in the arts that were necessary for their role in society. This form of education spared them the trouble that men suffered of being educated in subjects that would be useless in their adult life:

Every part of their education tends evidently to some useful purpose; either to the natural attractions of their person, or to form their mind to reserve, to modesty, to chastity, and to economy; to render them both likely to become the mistress of a family, and to behave properly when they have become such. (Smith, 1776b, pp 367–8)

He saw marriage as one of the bedrocks of society and, as such, it ought to be a permanent institution. It was the institution responsible for the education and upbringing of children, the inheritance of property and the creation of loving and trusting relationships. Dissolution of marriage ought to be very exceptional, granted mainly in cases of the infidelity of the wife:

The first duty is fidelity of the wife to the husband; breach of chastity is the greatest of offences. (Smith, 1795, p 74)

Because infidelity was such a grave offence, 'an injury to the husband', it was important that unmarried women 'should be laid under restraints' so that they became accustomed to being faithful to their husbands (Smith, 1795, p 76). It also followed that illegitimate children could not inherit the property of their legal father or that of their putative father, for it was often not known who the putative father was. The problems of an illegitimate son are also transmitted to his children:

As a bastard can succeed to nobody, so nobody can succeed to him, as he is not related to any human being. (Smith, 1795, p 89)

These 'disabilities' of illegitimate children followed naturally from the emphasis that society placed on monogamous marriage. If illegitimate children were allowed to succeed their fathers, 'men would hardly subject themselves to the inconveniences of lawful marriage. To have a wife entirely in their power, and to take others when they please, would be more convenient' (Smith, 1795, p 91).

The father was responsible for the upbringing, education and the morals of his children. In return, they were responsible for him during his old age. The mother is invisible in all this:

The father is obliged to bring up his children, and the children, in case of old age or infirmity, to maintain the father. (Smith, 1795, p 94)

The interpretation of Smith's views of women faces the same difficulties as that of Rousseau's. On one hand, his discussion of the equality of innate ability among men of all social classes and between freemen and slaves would imply that he would see a similar equality between the sexes. On the other hand, his view of women in society as individuals, as wives and as mothers strongly suggests that he considered them socially inferior to men.

The role of government

Although Smith was, as a general rule, against government intervention in public affairs, he accepted that certain policies can be pursued by governments better than by private individuals or agencies. He put forward two rules that could justify such government intervention: the state should provide, first, those services that are necessary for the survival of society; and, second, those services that are not profitable to private business. Although both guidelines appear rigorous enough, they can, on reflection, be interpreted both in an expansive and in a restrictive way, depending on the person's own perceptions of the role of the state. It is for this reason that Smith has been seen both as an advocate of minimal government, and as a supporter of the modern welfare state. The view taken here veers towards the first of these two positions because of Smith's views on the importance of self-interest in human affairs, his neglect of distributive justice and his emphasis on low taxation rates.

He listed three areas in public life where government intervention was justified: defence, justice, public works and public institutions.

Defence

Smith makes the security of the realm from foreign aggressors as the first function of government. It is the duty of 'protecting the society from the violence and invasion from other independent societies' (Smith, 1776b, p 279).

In earlier days, the government could rely on private militias that were made up partly of volunteers but this had, by his time, become obsolete as a result of the growing sophistication and expense of weaponry. As he put it:

> A musket is a more expensive machine than a javelin or a bow and arrows; a cannon or a mortar than a ballista or a catapulta. (Smith 1776b, p 296)

All this necessitated the use of regular, well-trained armies that were expensive and could not be paid for by any one individual or group of individuals. The whole nation had to pay for defence in the same way that the whole nation benefited from life in a secure state.

Justice

The second duty of any government is the same as Hobbes' first – that of 'protecting, as far as possible, every member of the society from the injustice or oppression of every other member of it, or the duty of establishing an exact administration of justice' (Smith, 1776b, p 297). Smith follows Locke in arguing that the establishment of a system of national justice became necessary as a result of the rise of private property. It became imperative to protect the property of the owners against the jealous intentions of others. Without such protection, there would be disorder and conflict in society.

Like Locke and Rousseau, Smith was anxious that the executive and the judicial arms of the state should be separate and independent of one another. He feared that when these two branches of government were in the same hands, there would be a real danger that justice would be sacrificed 'to what is vulgarly called politics' (Smith, 1776b, p 310). It was also important to go a step beyond the mere separation of the two branches of government in order to ensure that a judge 'should not be liable to be removed from his office according to the caprice' of the executive power. Only when these two conditions were fully met could the liberty and rights of individuals in society be guaranteed.

Public works and public institutions

It is this category of state services that divides Smith's followers between the minimalist and the almost universalist state supporters. Smith's actual wording, as it appears in the following quotation, can be interpreted both broadly and narrowly:

> The third and last duty of the sovereign or commonwealth is that of erecting and maintaining those public institutions and those public works, which, though they may be in the highest degree advantageous to a great society, are, however, of such nature that the profit could never repay the expense of any individual or small number of individuals, and which it therefore cannot be expected that any individual or small number of individuals should erect them. (Smith, 1776b, p 310)

He further explains that the works and institutions he has in mind are chiefly those that facilitate commerce in society and those that promote the education of both the young and adults. In the first category, he includes 'good roads, bridges, navigable canals, harbours, etc' (Smith, 1776b, p 311). Commerce would suffer if the means of communication of a country were grossly neglected and, as a result, economic growth and human welfare would suffer too. Those who have interpreted Smith liberally would interpret the 'etc' to include such other public utilities as parks, the post office, water supply and other public utilities.

Education should be a state responsibility for a variety of reasons, all but one of which were mentioned by other writers before him: first, education was a form of social capital that benefited both the individual and the state; second, education would strengthen social stability; third, it would enable people to become better judges of politicians' promises; fourth, unless education was compulsory, many poor people would not send their children to school; and, fifth, which is unique to Smith, education would counteract the deadening effects of the division of labour on the workers.

What Smith was essentially proposing was an extension of the existing system of parish and charity schools in England and Scotland. He emphasised his commitment to education by suggesting a scheme of prizes for the children of working-class people who excelled at school; and, more controversially, that no one should be able to obtain the freedom of any corporation or 'be allowed to set up any trade in a village or town corporate' unless he could prove that he was able to read, write, and be numerate (Smith, 1776b, p 372).

In the field of poverty, Smith did not go beyond what was already being provided by the parishes and charitable organisations. As we shall see in Chapter 9, Paine and others during this period began to discuss social security provisions that were similar to those provided today.

Principles of public administration

Smith believed that the few services provided by the state should be administered in ways that encouraged efficiency and quality. The two major ways to achieve this were through user charges for all the services but defence, and through competition. Service charges and competition would raise much-needed revenue, improve the quality and efficiency of the services and encourage consumer sovereignty.

In the case of the justice service, he argued that a judge who receives all his salary from the state has no incentive to be efficient. His salary should therefore be supplemented partly by the fees paid by the offenders, where possible, or by those who benefited as a result of a court case:

> A diligent judge gains a comfortable, though moderate, revenue by his office; an idle gets little more than his salary. (Smith, 1776b, p 310)

It was neither necessary nor conducive to efficiency for the cost of roads, bridges, canals or harbours to be defrayed totally by the government. These services were ideally suited to the use of service charges in the form of tolls. The amount of the toll charge should vary according to the tonnage and the luxury of the vehicle. This meant that heavy luxury coaches for the rich would bear the brunt while non-luxury vehicles carrying goods would be charged very little. Smith welcomed such an outcome for it meant that 'the indolence and vanity of the rich is made to contribute in a very easy manner to the relief of the poor, by rendering cheaper the transportation of heavy goods to all the different parts of the country' (Smith, 1776b, p 312).

Smith's experience as a student at Oxford led him to the conclusion that most professors were more interested in their comfort than in teaching because they received all their salary from endowments irrespective of the quantity or quality of their work:

> In the university of Oxford, the greater part of the public professors have, for those many years, given up altogether even the pretence of teaching. (Smith, 1776b, p 350)

The situation could only be improved if professors' emoluments came mainly from the fees paid directly to them by students, with salaries forming only a small part. In this way professors who could attract students through their good teaching would command a good income while those who neglected their jobs would have to rely on their small salaries.

The emphasis that Smith places on consumer charges stems from his fundamental belief that human beings are by nature inclined to choose the easy life rather than hard work. If they are rewarded by the state without any strings attached, one should not be surprised if they choose to perform their duty 'in as slovenly manner as that authority will permit' (Smith, 1776b, p 350). This applied to all civil servants even though Smith illustrates the principle in relation to teachers and judges.

Since the principles of the private market were, for Smith, largely applicable to the state sector, it was right to expect competition and consumer choice in the state sector too. Monopolies were to be avoided for the same reasons as in the private sector – they are a form of conspiracy against the interests of consumers.

Wherever possible, decisions about the system of funding and the method of administering a service should be left to the local authority because it is in a better position than the central government to know what is needed, how best to supervise and run a service.

Taxation

Smith acknowledged that personal taxation was inevitable if the state was to pay for its services, for he was very much against the prevailing government practice of relying on borrowing to finance public services. Government expenditure in England in 1770 amounted to a mere 10% of national income, made up as follows: 40% was taken by debt service, 33% on the military, 10% on poor relief, and the remaining 17% on miscellaneous, mostly expenditure on the civil service (Musgrave, 1976, p 298, Table 1).

Smith set out four principles that should govern the taxation system of the country – most of which are as valid today as they were then. First, the amount of taxes that people pay should be proportionate to their incomes – 'as nearly as possible in proportion to the revenue which they respectively enjoy under the protection of the state' (Smith, 1776b, p 416). In line with this, he insists that indirect taxes should be laid on luxuries and not on necessities. He does not go into any detail about the level of taxation, or whether the rate of taxation should be the same for all incomes or increase with the rise in income. Payment of taxes according to ability is today a common feature of taxation systems even though it varies in many details.

Second, he was very insistent that people should know in advance the amount of tax that they would have to pay. Arbitrary taxes lead to resentment, corruption and profiteering, he argued.

Third, every tax 'ought to be levied at the time, or in the manner, in which it is most likely to be convenient for the contributor to pay' (Smith, 1776b, pp 416–7). This would make it easier for people to pay their taxes as well as make it more difficult for them to complain about taxes. It has the potential, however, of creating administrative chaos.

Fourth, taxes should be low and should deliver to the treasury the highest possible net proportion of the amount collected. This was a composite principle and Smith broke it down into four subcategories. The administrative costs of the taxation system should be as low as possible; the level of taxes should not be so high as to discourage people from working harder, or from changing jobs to improve themselves; tax evasion should be discouraged; and people should not be subjected too much 'to the frequent visits and the odious examination of the tax-gatherers' in order to avoid tax oppression and tax rebellion (Smith, 1776b, p 418).

Smith also pointed out that taxes are linked to both wages and prices. Direct taxes on wages may, if demand for labour is high, lead to demands for higher wages to compensate for the tax burden, and this could in turn create pressures for higher prices. He also pointed out that high indirect taxes may result in reduced consumption of the taxed commodities, and this in turn to lower government revenues.

He had this timely reminder to those who believed that taxation levels could be raised almost at will:

> Every new tax is immediately felt more or less by the people. It occasions always some murmur, and meets some opposition. The more loudly the people complain of every new tax, the more difficult it becomes, too, either to find out new subjects of taxation, or to raise much higher the taxes already imposed upon them. (Smith, 1776b, p 521)

Despite the progressive nature of Smith's proposals on taxation, they were envisaged to consume only a small proportion of people's incomes, bearing in mind the limited range of public services and the wide use of service charges in his proposals. Smith's taxation proposals could raise the funds necessary for a very minimal welfare state but not of the welfare state as we know it today.

The chequered career of laissez-faire

Smith's doctrine of laissez-faire was a mixture of ideology and empiricism – it was based on Smith's value system and his interpretation of events around him. It contained elements that were critical of the behaviour and interests of the upper classes but it gave theoretical support to the emerging practices in trade and manufacturing that were being pursued by the upper classes. His ideas on competition, the 'invisible hand' of the market and its laissez-faire political viewpoint were welcomed while his views on education or taxation were ignored.

Political elites always try to pick and choose those strands of current social theories that suit their interests.

Parliament in Smith's time was dominated by the landed and commercial classes, and not unexpectedly succeeded in rejecting attempts for legislation to improve wages as well as legislation to allow workers to form trade unions in order to protect their interests, citing in both instances Smith's thesis that such measures would hinder the free operation of the market to the detriment of the whole society (Perkin, 1969, p 188).

As the number of both men and women working in factories or mines increased, the clamour for some legislation to ameliorate the harsh working conditions of children and women intensified, resulting in the various Factory Acts of the early 19th century. During the second half of the century, legislation restricting employers' absolute right in the workplace spread to include men, other aspects of the employment situation, and various public health aspects of the community 'largely undoing the work of Adam Smith in the realm of policy' (Whittaker, 1960, p 124).

By the beginning of the 20th century, Smith's doctrines were widely rejected and few shared his optimism of the virtues of either 'the invisible hand' of the market or of laissez-faire (Gide and Rist, 1913, ch 2). The economic recession of the early 1930s saw the eclipse of Smith's views on laissez-faire and the rise in the belief of the value of government interventionist policies to rectify the weaknesses of the free market:

> By the mid-twentieth century, Smith's star had been eclipsed by Keynes, whose economics of public investment underpinned a broad political consensus in Britain. (Robertson, 1984, p 146)

As in the case of other serious ideologies, laissez-faire survived to make a comeback when the conditions in society were more favourable. The substantial expansion of state activity in all aspects of the public sector during the post-war period in all advanced industrial societies coupled with the decline of economic growth rates in the early 1980s led to the re-emergence of laissez-faire doctrines. Universal state welfare provision, it was argued, undermines the spirit of competitiveness and the individual's will to look after themself – to pursue their own self-interest to the full, as Smith had postulated. Governments embarked on a series of denationalisation measures as well as incremental reductions in state welfare but at the end of the 20th century public expenditure still accounted for about 40% of the gross national product in these countries – about four times higher than in Smith's time (George and Taylor-Gooby, 1996). While the rhetoric had all the right laissez-faire phrases, governments remained very interventionist, though in different ways and degrees.

Conclusion

The world of today is so very different from Adam Smith's world that only fragments of his theory can be relevant. The small workshops that Smith described so perceptively are no longer a dominant feature of the national economy. Rather, the national and international economy is dominated today by large multinationals whose economic and political power can set the economic agenda of a country. They are near monopolies that influence demand, prices, employment and governments. The open competition between the small enterprises that Smith identified as the driving force behind economic growth is of only historical interest today.

The world has also changed politically. Parliament is not in the hands of a small clique of the upper classes but has a much wider political base reflecting in varying ways and degrees the competing interests in society. Governments are not always subservient to the interests of the upper classes today as they were in Smith's time.

The balance between population and resources has also changed considerably, making Smith's vision of the individual pursuing his economic self-interests unimpeded into a nightmare. In a world of low population with vast unexplored lands and seemingly infinite physical resources the freedom of the individual to roam at will to the benefit of all, may have made some sense. In today's overpopulated globe with finite physical resources, such a policy can only speed up the process of resource exhaustion to the detriment of all.

Smith's insistence that the unregulated operation of the market serves the public interest and that any government intervention has adverse effects on both the market and the public interest have been shown to be mistaken by events in many countries during the past two centuries. Without government intervention in the various facets of the market, it is more than likely that the market itself would suffer; and the public would suffer even more. His belief in the positive contribution of economic growth to human prosperity was correct; his implied conclusion that economic growth by itself can deal with the problem of poverty has been shown to be incorrect historically and comparatively.

Smith's advice that most government services should be administered by the private sector and that user charges should be the rule rather than the exception had not had much success until the last quarter of the 20th century. Today, however, there is a greater willingness in advanced industrial societies to contract out government services to the private sector and to charge fees in some instances, though not to the extent that Smith envisaged.

After two centuries, we have come to accept that there is a place for both private and government initiatives in society. Human welfare is derived from both the workplace and government services. The real question is not a choice between public and private but rather what mixture of the two can best be used to serve human welfare. Both Smith's unregulated capitalism and Marx's blanket nationalisation of all the means of production and distribution, discussed in Chapter 10, have been shown by history to be contrary to human welfare.

NINE

Democracy and welfare
Thomas Paine (1737–1809)

Paine was the first major figure to argue for a fairly comprehensive system of social security benefits to prevent and alleviate poverty and has, as a result, been described by some as the 'prophet of the modern welfare state' (Canavan, 1963, p 658). To most people, however, Paine is known for his political ideas: as the staunchest supporter of democratic government against monarchical rule – he was 'the prophet of democracy' (Hearnshaw, 1931, p 140). His social security programme was tied to his political system, for he strongly believed that it could only be fulfilled in a democratic society. Vice versa, democracy, he argued, would be enhanced and strengthened by the implementation of a social security system. In brief, he supported the idea that became widely accepted from the second half of the 19th century onwards that a degree of economic equality is an essential ingredient of political liberty. Political and welfare rights go together, he argued.

He took part in both the American and the French Revolution, and did his utmost to enlighten the public in England so as to bring about a republican government. Unlike most thinkers, Paine was a radical political activist; and unlike most revolutionaries, he was a thinker. He excited both devotion and hatred. He was idolised by millions and his books sold hundreds of thousands of copies; but he was also hated by millions, and his major book, *The Rights of Man* (1791/2) was proscribed by the government in England – it was burnt in public, those who sold it were imprisoned or exiled; and those who propagated its ideas were punished. He was a major figure in the revolution in France, but was later imprisoned for pleading to save the king from execution; he contributed immensely to the success of the American Revolution, but was later disowned because he was considered an atheist for his deist views; his popularity among the radicals and the working class in England was second to none, but he was also tried for sedition and sentenced to become an outlaw.

Human nature

As with all other writers, Paine's views on welfare and politics were influenced by his personal beliefs on human nature. His philosophy of human nature is based on at least four basic assumptions. First, all human beings are God's creatures and as such they 'are born equal, and with equal natural right' (Paine, 1791, p 117). There are no inherent reasons for treating some persons as superior or inferior to others because of their race, sex, class or religion. It is a view of equality of human nature that is very similar to Rousseau's and very different from Aristotle's.

Equality of worth and equality of consideration for all human beings took centre stage in Paine's political and social philosophy.

Second, all human beings possess certain fundamental natural rights given to them by God – the right to life, to free thought, to free worship and basic sustenance. These natural rights should not be suppressed or taken away or even surrendered – they are part of a person's identity as a human being. As we shall see later, some of these natural rights are turned into civil rights with the people's agreement but they still remain theirs, fundamentally speaking. Paine was not, of course, the first to use the notion of rights. The debate on rights can be traced back to Classical Greek philosophy, right through the late Middle Ages, and finally to the work of Hobbes and Locke (Freeden, 1991). In the 18th century, debates on rights were commonplace. What made Paine's work on rights so appealing to the general public was its connection with the American and French Revolutions, its use to attack monarchy, its relationship to social security rights, and the bold but plain language used by Paine that made his work intelligible to a much wider circle than that of most other writers.

From this equality of human nature and natural rights, Paine developed his third and fourth assumptions: the individualism and the sociability of human beings. All human beings have a duty to maintain themselves but they do this in conjunction with others to their mutual benefit. This chain of interdependence holds society together so long as all citizens play their part properly. In words first written in 1776 that were later echoed by Adam Smith, Paine illustrates this mutually beneficent interdependence as follows:

> The landholder, the farmer, the manufacturer, the merchant, the tradesman, and every occupation prospers by the aid which it receives from the other, and from the whole. (Paine, 1792, p 214)

Paine's fourth dimension of human nature is its sociability. Human beings are not just individuals who are equal to one another, possessing equal natural rights and pursuing their self-interest in conjunction with others; nature has also implanted in man 'a system of social affections, which, though not necessary to his existence, are essential to happiness. There is no period in life when this love for society ceases to act. It begins and ends with our being' (Paine, 1792, p 214).

Human beings, in brief, are equal to one another; they are endowed with the same basic natural rights; they are neither totally individualistic nor altruistic; and they can live peacefully together in societies to their mutual advantage most – though not all – of the time.

Society and government

Paine was the first major writer to delineate clearly the difference between society and government or society and the state. The tendency till then was to confuse, to ignore, any differences between them or to treat them as one and the same concept. For Paine, society is the fundamental unit of human life; government is an addition made necessary because some human beings do not always behave according to their natural sociability.

Society is created because human beings cannot by themselves satisfy all their wants, let alone their desires. They need to live in stable communities where they can cooperate with one another, exchange their products and communicate socially with one another for their mutual happiness. Although they are equal in rights, 'they are not equal in power; the weak cannot protect themselves against the strong' (Paine, 1796, p 403). There are, therefore, situations either of misbehaviour or where society is not able to act conveniently or impartially, and it is these undesirable situations that make government necessary:

> Society is produced by our wants, and governments by our wickedness;
> the former promotes our happiness *positively* by uniting our affections,
> the latter *negatively* by restraining our vices. (Paine, 1776, p 5)

The implication of Paine's views on society and government is that in a well-organised society where people behave according to their nature, only a modicum of government is needed. Government is simply a necessary evil: it was rendered necessary 'by the inability of moral virtue to govern the world' (Paine, 1776, p 7). Civil society, rather than government, is the main provider of the means of sustenance, of social life and of security. Government is only needed when society fails to provide these. It is a limited view of government, and Paine had to enlarge it in his later writings when he acknowledged that society was not dealing adequately with the problem of income inequality and poverty. He then attributed to government the major duty of raising the necessary revenues through taxation in order to provide social security benefits that would reduce both poverty and income inequalities.

Paine's distinction between civil society and government has served as a reminder that, on one hand, government non-intervention in societal affairs is tantamount to abrogation of governmental duties. On the other hand, however, intervention beyond a certain point or beyond certain areas becomes oppressive and counter to natural rights. The difficulty has always been that there are no agreed criteria to measure the type and the degree of acceptable government intervention.

The first form of government, according to Paine, was participatory, of the Athenian model. People got together under 'some convenient tree', exchanged views and decided to set up a government to implement their decisions. In order to do this, they entrusted some of their natural rights to the government for enforcement – they turned them into civil rights. Natural rights, according to Paine, are those which 'appertain to man in right of his existence'; while civil rights are those which 'appertain to man in right of his being a member of society' (Paine, 1791, p 119). Examples of the first are 'the rights of thinking, speaking, forming and giving opinions', while examples of the second are those of 'personal protection, or acquiring and possessing property' (Paine, 1789, p 81).

Paine never accepts that either natural or civil rights are gains made by people in their everyday political struggles. For him, they are God-given even though the government is entrusted with the enforcement of some of them. Paine's notion of natural rights was criticised by his conservative opponents as being mystical, metaphysical, abstract, theoretical, impractical and destructive (Burke, 1790). His reply was that rights were very practical and constructive concepts, evidenced by the fact that they were incorporated in the declarations of both the American and the French Revolutions.

Since then the notion of rights has become generally accepted even though there are differences of opinion as to their nature and origin. From an absolute perspective, rights are essentially demands by disadvantaged groups for a better life; from a relative perspective, they amount to 'the demand that everybody in a society should enjoy as a right what some only enjoy as a privilege' (McClelland, 1996, p 391). It is the disadvantaged and not the dominant groups in society who have always appealed to the concept of rights to improve their condition either absolutely or relatively or both.

Rights always imply duties. Paine stresses this repeatedly by pointing out that if a person wishes others to acknowledge his rights, he or she has a corresponding duty to do likewise for theirs. He reminded Americans, for example, that if they wanted England to grant them their freedom, they had a duty to do the same for their slaves:

> A Declaration of Rights is, by reciprocity, a Declaration of Duties also. Whatever is my right as a man, is also the right of another; and it becomes my duty to guarantee, as well as to possess. (Paine, 1791, p 165)

Acceptance of the premise that rights imply duties leads to the conclusion that rights are never absolute. My freedom to free speech must be tempered by the consideration that it should not cause undue offence to others; my freedom to own as much property as I can master must be tempered by my concern for my less affluent fellow citizens; and so on. Although Paine did not face squarely this restriction to absolute rights, he often referred to it when discussing other topics. The crucial issue with many of the rights is how far to curtail their absolute nature in order to take account of the interests of other people. Libertarians might take the view that 'only in very exceptional circumstances' should rights be narrowed; others, might prefer to err on the side of security rather than liberty (Ayer, 1989, p 79).

Hereditary monarchy versus elective democracy

Although the first form of government was democratic, strong men gradually usurped power to install themselves as chiefs, tyrants and kings and to establish hereditary forms of monarchical government. Aristocracy grew around monarchy to create a hereditary class of parasitic power, wealth and prestige. The contempt with which Paine held both monarchy and aristocracy is clear throughout his writings. The following quotations are just illustrations of this attitude:

> Of more worth is one honest man to society, and in the sight of God, than all the crowned ruffians that ever lived. (Paine, 1776, p 19)

> The first aristocrats in all countries were brigands. Those of later times, sycophants. (Paine, 1796, p 401)

If Paine considered monarchs and aristocrats as tyrants living on the toil of ordinary people, several conservative opponents of his time considered the general working-class section of the community as incapable of rational thinking, let alone able to participate in the political affairs of the nation. In their view, 'the common man did constitute the swinish multitude' (Aldridge, 1960, p 138).

Paine gives a long list of reasons why he thinks that hereditary monarchy and aristocracy lack legitimacy and are against the common interest:

- hereditary governments are tyrannical by nature since they are imposed on rather than elected by the people;
- the idea that the ability to rule is hereditary is as absurd as the claim that the ability to be a good mathematician or poet is necessarily hereditary;
- many kings proved themselves totally incapable of carrying out their duties;
- monarchies do not have the trust of the people 'because a body of men holding themselves accountable to nobody, ought not to be trusted by any body' (Paine, 1791, p 134);
- monarchies are inefficient – since monarchs surround themselves with a class of aristocratic sycophants, they never get to know the real problems or the feelings of ordinary people;
- a hereditary form of government breeds both insolence on the part of the rulers and apathy or subservience on the part of the public;
- Paine rejected out of hand the notion that hereditary government brought order and stability to society (indeed, the opposite was the case, he argued – monarchies and aristocracies constantly waged wars that had to be funded out of the taxes exacted from ordinary people; they wage wars 'to prevent people looking into the defects and abuses of government' [Paine, 1792, p 321]);
- the authoritarianism of monarchical rule spreads into the other institutions of society – the family, the Church, business and so on (in his words, 'Every place has its Bastille, and every Bastille its despot' [Paine, 1791, p 98]);
- monarchies are grossly extravagant in lifestyles, in the midst of abject poverty;
- no generation has the right to impose its decision on subsequent generations on what form of government they should have; every age must decide for itself. In Paine's memorable sentences:

> The vanity and presumption of governing beyond the grave is the
> most ridiculous and insolent of all tyrannies.... It is the living, and not
> the dead, that are to be accommodated. (Paine, 1791, p 92)

The only legitimate form of government for Paine was democracy. He rejected
not only monarchy but the Aristotelian view that mixed forms of government
were superior to others for they cancelled out each other's flaws – democracy
led to anarchy, and monarchy led to oppression. Paine believed, with a great
deal of justification, that the mixed forms of government of his generation were
dominated by the monarchy and the aristocracy. In England, only 5% of the
adult population could vote and these were mostly the landed and the educated
elites – working-class males, the emerging commercial groups and all women
were excluded.

Although he envied the Athenian model of participatory democracy, he realised
that it was no longer practical in view of the large geographical size of modern
nations. He thus put all his faith in elected, representative democracy. The right
to vote should be granted to all irrespective of property qualifications – a very
radical view at that time:

> To take away this right is to reduce a man to a state of slavery, for slavery
> consists in being subject to the will of another, and he that has no vote
> in the election of representatives, is in this case. (Paine, 1796, p 398)

Paradoxically, however, he does not plead the case of women being granted the
right to vote. There is enough 'contextual evidence' in his writings to show that
he acknowledged sexual equality (Keane, 1988, p 46), but not to the point of
extending the right to vote to women. His view on the fundamental significance
of the right to vote makes his lack of interest in women's suffrage 'strikingly
myopic' (Philp, 1995, p xxi).

Although Paine acknowledged that republican governments have their own
problems, he played down the seriousness of many of them. Experience has
shown that several of the problems he attributed to monarchies have plagued
democratic governments just as badly. Wars, for example, have been just as frequent
since the advent of democratic rule as before. Paine failed to realise that in the
geographically expanding world of his time commercial interests were frequent
causes of war – instead, he attributed them solely to the greed or machinations
of monarchs. As Ayer puts it:

> It is strange that it did not occur to Paine that it might be in the interest
> of manufacturers to promote wars, in order to obtain raw materials
> more cheaply, or acquire, to the point of monopolizing, new markets
> for their goods. (Ayer, 1989, p 93)

Paine's over-optimism on the benevolence of republican government stemmed from his simplistic understanding of the social structure of society – it was made up of the nobility and the people. He could not see that there could be divisions of interest among the various sections of 'the people' or among the various groups of the upper class. For this reason he came to believe that 'republican government, once properly established, would automatically work with efficiency and justice' (Fennessey, 1963, p 30).

He was also over-optimistic about the speed with which monarchies would collapse to be replaced by republics, for he underestimated the tenacity with which people cling to traditional forms of conduct – 'a failure which he shared with the natural rights theorists in general' (Adkins, 1953, p xlii). He cautioned against the use of violence in bringing about change: 'it would be an act of wisdom to ... produce revolutions by reason and accommodation, rather than commit them to the issue of convulsions' (Paine, 1791, p 197). To be doubly sure, he insisted that even a republic must have a written constitution that lays out in detail people's rights so that people can know and demand the fulfilment of their rights.

Finally, Paine envisaged that, with the collapse of monarchies and the creation of democracies, international cooperation would be far easier. Conflicts of interest between nations would be lessened and they could be resolved through international arbitration rather than wars – hence, a more peaceful world would emerge. Looking to the future, he foresaw that 'all Europe may form but one republic' (Paine, 1792, p 262) and that an international body for arbitration would come about. He may have been proved correct with regard to the emergence of the European Union and the United Nations organisations but he has also been proved wrong with regard to the incidence of wars, and the rational efficiency, let alone economic justice, of republican rule. Many of Paine's misjudgements stemmed from the fact that he did not understand how a capitalist system works – perhaps justifiably, because industrial capitalism was just emerging.

Despite the many criticisms that can be levied against Paine's onslaught on monarchical rule and his over-optimism of republican rule, there is no doubt that the broad picture of his doctrine has been generally accepted. Absolute monarchies have no support today, and the monarchies that still exist are bereft of any significant overt political power. Elective democracy is the ideal that countries aspire to all over the world today.

Slavery

The 18th century witnessed the highest levels of the slave trade. An estimated six million slaves were forcibly transported from Africa to the Americas, almost treble the number so transported during the previous two centuries. Slavery became part and parcel of the American way of life – in the family, the community and the economy. Paine was one of the most eloquent advocates in America for the abolition of slavery. Soon after his arrival in America, he wrote strongly against the cruelties of the slave trade and the abomination of slavery as an institution.

His arguments against slavery were detailed and they can be summarised under five headings.

First, the natural rights argument: all human beings are endowed with natural rights, and personal freedom is one of them. No one has the right to deprive others of their freedom. Second, the Christian argument: it is hypocritical of Christians to pray to their God and at the same to openly disobey one of His basic tenets – the equality of human beings. Third, the political argument: how could Americans justify keeping other human beings as slaves at a time when they were themselves fighting for their political independence from England? Fourth, the family argument: slavery split families asunder by 'an unnatural separation and sale of husband and wife from each other and from their children, an injury, the greatness of which can only be conceived by supposing that we were in the same unhappy case' (Paine, 1780 p 30). Fifth, the colour-blind argument: although people in various parts of the world are distinguished 'by a difference in feature or complexion', there is no justification in concluding that one colour or feature is superior to another because 'the most fertile as well as the most barren parts of the earth are inhabited by men of complexions different from ours, and from each other' (Paine, 1780, p 29).

As clerk to the government of the state of Pennsylvania, Paine took a very active part in formulating the legislation that led to the abolition of slavery in that state in 1780. The legislation was the first of its kind and, inevitably, it was a compromise measure, involving many weaknesses – it was certainly more timid than the abolitionists wanted: Paine's plan was to free all slaves who reached the age of 21 – not 28 as the law stipulated; freed slaves should be given some land to become independent farmers – the law gave them nothing; elderly and disabled slaves who could not benefit from their freedom should continue to be provided for by their masters – the law ignored this.

Pennsylvania had few slaves in comparison to many other states, particularly in the South – 6,000 compared to 200,000 in Virginia. Inevitably, it took many more years before states with large number of slaves followed Pennsylvania's example. Despite its many weaknesses, the American legislation 'signalled that in a republic, black slavery was a historical anomaly and should ultimately be abolished' (Keane, 1995, p 196).

Trade, private property and the common good

Paine, initially, shared with Adam Smith the belief that trade was the best medium for raising individual and national standards of living. Free trade, untrammelled by the labyrinth of government regulations, was to the best advantage of all concerned – individuals and nations. Foreign trade benefited all nations: indeed, 'the prosperity of any commercial nation is regulated by the prosperity of the rest' (Paine, 1792, p 266). The most that governments can and should do to encourage trade is to avoid wars and maintain the peace – something that monarchies find difficult to do.

Unlike Rousseau, who deplored the growth of luxury that accompanied trade, Paine welcomed economic prosperity though he became increasingly worried about its inegalitarian effects. By the time he came to write his last major book, *Agrarian Justice* (1797), he was convinced that economic growth was exacerbating material inequalities. It was this realisation that led him to reappraise the role of government in public affairs, as we shall see later. He came to adopt a much more interventionist role for government than Smith would have approved of; on the other hand, he continued to value economic growth and affluence, which Rousseau had rejected. This is how he described what he saw as the contradictory situation of mass poverty amid growing wealth in 'civilised' countries.

> On one side, the spectator is dazzled by splendid appearances; on the other, he is shocked by extremes of wretchedness; both of which he has erected. The most affluent and the most miserable of the human race are to be found in the countries that are called civilized. (Paine, 1797, p 416)

Although Paine was the strongest advocate of political levelling, he did not support economic levelling. He accepted that private property and wealth had a place in society provided they were acquired honestly and they were put to such use that the common good also benefited. He railed against the profligacy of the monarchy and the aristocracy but he never went as far as to advocate the confiscation of their properties. He simply argued that they should share their good fortune with those less fortunate than themselves – and if they were not prepared to do so on their own accord, the republican state should force them to do so through a series of taxation and welfare measures.

During the first two stages of civilisation when human beings earned their living as hunters and shepherds, land ownership was not relevant, argued Paine. It was during the third stage when human beings began to earn their livelihood through land cultivation that land began to be important and private ownership was established. Paine uses this historical development to argue for two types of property: natural and artificial property.

Natural property – land, air, water – was given to all human beings by God to be owned and used in common. Artificial or acquired property was the invention of human beings – it was the pattern of private land ownership that emerged during and after the stage of land cultivation. Two separate land rights thus emerged: the right to natural land that all possessed and the right to improved cultivated land that only the cultivators possessed. While natural property was owned equally, artificial property could not be owned equally because 'to attribute it equally it would be necessary that all should have contributed in the same proportion, which can never be the case' (Paine, 1797, p 411).

Paine accepted that land cultivation increased the value of land – by tenfold, he estimated – because of the rise in productivity. At the same time, it set up the concentration of cultivated land in a few hands, thus creating 'the greatest evil':

> It has dispossessed more than half the inhabitants of every nation of
> their natural inheritance, without providing for them, as ought to have
> been done, as an indemnification of that loss, and has thereby created
> a species of poverty and wretchedness that did not exist before. (Paine,
> 1797, p 419)

How could this social dilemma be resolved? Despite his radicalism, Paine refrained
from advocating communal land ownership, as several socialist writers of the
period had done. Instead, he advocated the taxation of all land and the revenues
to be used in order to establish a special fund that would be incorporated into
his general social security scheme, to be discussed later. He envisaged two types
of taxes: death duties and an annual 'ground rent' for the land that a person held
– these taxes would reduce both land concentration and income inequalities and
poverty in society. In this way, he managed to reconcile his belief that people had
a natural right to own property and a right to the basic necessities of life.

The structure and culture of poverty

It is generally agreed that Paine's family and community background had a
profound influence on his attitude towards poverty and what should be done to
deal with it (Collins, 1969, pp 10–12). Born of Quaker parents of very modest
means, Paine left school at the age of 13 to work with his father as a stay-maker.
He saw at first hand the destructive effects of the enclosure movement on the
dispossessed families of his native East Anglia. He thus experienced and witnessed
poverty at first hand from his early life to his middle age. Although he rejected
several aspects of Quaker faith – its pacifism and its mystical approach to religious
life – he supported its views on education and poverty, its hostility to the aristocracy
and its general egalitarianism.

In one of his first jobs, Paine found himself being the spokesman of his fellow
workers – excise men – making the case for higher wages in a pamphlet that
contained his first ideas on poverty (Paine, 1772); he was dismissed as a result and
soon afterwards he emigrated to America. His family background and his early
working life ingrained a deep hatred of poverty and of those societal institutions
that he considered as being responsible for it.

Paine's account of the causes of poverty is complex and it is scattered throughout
his writings. It contains elements of both the structure and the culture of poverty,
but it is primarily a structural explanation. To begin with, he rejected the argument
made by clerics and others that poverty and wealth were God's creation, and that,
consequently, they were both just and unalterable:

> It is wrong to say that God made Rich and Poor; he made only Male
> and Female; and he gave them the earth for their inheritance. (Paine,
> 1797, p 414)

Wealth and poverty are conditions created by human action. Their coexistence creates the right conditions for unrest and disorder in society; it offends human dignity and decency; and it holds back individual and national economic and political progress. In his colourful language:

> The contrast of affluence and wretchedness continually meeting and offending the eye, is like dead and living bodies chained together. (Paine, 1797, p 425)

The major cause of poverty, for Paine, is 'the march of civilisation', by which he means the political economy of economic growth that had taken place over the years. In the state of nature, there was no poverty even though standards of living were low for all. As most people lost their right to live off the land and became slaves, serfs or workers, they also lost their basic means of sustenance. He supported this argument with the evidence from America where, he claimed, there was no poverty among the Indian tribes even though their level of comfort and luxury was low. They simply worked the land and lived off its produce in a collective way. The 'march of civilisation' made life easier for the rich but it also made the life of another part of society more wretched – worse than the condition of the Indian in America:

> Poverty, therefore, is a thing created by that which is called civilized life. It exists not in the natural state. On the other hand, the natural state is without those advantages which flow from Agriculture, Arts, Science, and Manufactures. (Paine, 1797, p 416)

Second, Paine relates both the nature of economic growth and the extent of poverty to the type of government that had prevailed for centuries in Europe, that is monarchical and aristocratic rule that helped to create and perpetuate poverty:

> When in countries that are called civilized, we see age going to the workhouse and youth to the gallows, something must be wrong in the system of government. (Paine, 1792, p 271

Monarchies, he always argued, are wasteful of national resources: they spend too much on the luxuries and frivolities of the court circle and on wars but they neglect the needs of the majority of the population. Instead of the nation's resources being used to instruct the young and to support the elderly, they were 'lavished upon kings, upon courts, upon hirelings, imposters, and prostitutes' (Paine, 1792, p 271). If only resources were redirected from the luxurious living of the ruling group to the needs of the people, they would be 'more than sufficient to ... benefit the condition of every man in a nation, not included within the purlieus of a court' (Paine, 1792, p 271). This cannot happen, however, until the people establish their own democratically elected government, he maintained.

Third, the social divisions of society are re-inforced by the residential segregation of the nobility from the rest of the population. In this way the upper classes do not have to face every day the wretchedness of impoverished neighbourhoods; and they also avoid having to pay for the expense of relieving poverty. He has this to say, in relation to the aristocracy:

> Their residences, whether in town or country, are not mixed with the habitations of the poor. They live apart from the distress, and the expense of relieving it. It is in manufacturing towns and labouring villages that those burthens press their heaviest; in many of which it is one class of poor supporting another. (Paine, 1792, p 278)

Fourth, Paine pointed to the low wages of working-class people. Wages had been so low that the families of most working-class people ended up in poverty; this became a particularly acute problem during periods when inflation was higher than wage rises. He thus advocated the control of inflation because he believed that it would benefit the poor more than the rich. The system inaugurated by the Speenhamland magistrates in 1795 of linking poor relief rates to bread prices was an attempt to protect those on poor relief from rising prices. Not unexpectedly, the system soon spread to the rest of England until it was abolished later.

Fifth, Paine related the low wage rates to the high indirect taxation that fell upon the ordinary working-class people. He pointed out that the tax on beer fetched about as much revenue to the government as the land tax but it did not affect the aristocracy because they brewed their own beer (or rather their servants did!) thus evading the payment of duty. Only beer sold in either the public houses or elsewhere was liable to tax – and this is how ordinary people obtained their beer. Poor rates weighed more heavily on the middle classes than the aristocracy, and, as we shall see later, he wanted to abolish them.

Sixth, Paine, in various parts of his work, refers to the contribution that culture makes to the perpetuation of poverty. He begins with the claim that poverty in all European countries became 'hereditary' with more people falling into it than getting out of it:

> The great mass of the poor, in all countries, are become an hereditary race, and it is next to impossible for them to get out of that state themselves. It ought also to be observed, that this mass increases in all countries that are called civilized. More persons fall annually into it, than get out of it. (Paine, 1797, pp 426-7)

This increasing mass of impoverished people is subjected to all sorts of penal measures including death. 'Why is it', he asks, 'that scarcely any are executed but the poor?' (Paine, 1792, p 271). Having no prospects in life and being 'bred up without morals', poor people commit offences the penalty of which could be death. Structure and culture combine to perpetuate poverty from one generation to the next. The culture of poverty is but a way of coping with the harsh realities of life. People who are so badly paid that they cannot make ends meet are unlikely to do their jobs properly and may well find themselves involved in dishonest dealings or even thieving to maintain themselves and their families. This may sound incredulous to the well-paid and the affluent but 'could they descend to the cold regions of want, the circle of polar poverty, they would find their opinions changing with the climate' (Paine, 1772, quoted in Clayes, 1989, p 22). People's behaviour is affected by their ideas, which, in turn, are influenced by their circumstances. Harsh economic realities can evoke unpleasant responses, even when these are contrary to established societal norms:

> Poverty, in defiance of principle, begets a degree of meanness that will stoop to almost nothing. A thousand refinements of argument may be brought to prove that the practice of honesty will be still the same, in the most trying and necessitous circumstances. He who never was ahungered may argue finely on the subjection of his appetite; and he who never was distressed, may harangue as beautifully on the power of principle. But poverty, like grief, has an incurable deafness, which never hears; the oration loses its edge; and '*To be, or not to be*' becomes the only question. (Paine, 1772, quoted in Aldridge, 1960, p 22, Paine's emphasis)

All this is not to suggest that Paine considered the poor dishonest by nature; this would be contrary to his broad philosophy. What he meant was that severe and chronic poverty can lead people to dishonesty. In the abstract, he considered the morals of the poor and the rich to be not too dissimilar, even though they present themselves differently:

> Wealth is no proof of moral character; nor poverty the want of it. On the contrary, wealth is often the presumptive evidence of dishonesty; and poverty the negative evidence of innocence. (Paine, 1796, p 398)

Although Paine was the harshest critic of poverty, he accepted that a certain degree of income and wealth inequality was both natural and inevitable. This is the result not only of exploitation but also of natural differences in 'talents, dexterity of management, extreme frugality, fortunate opportunities or the opposite', and of differences in attitudes towards material wealth: some people are keener to save and to accumulate wealth than others – some make it 'the sole business of their life' – others are satisfied to accumulate just enough for their 'wants and independence' (Paine, 1796, p 399). Although he accepted the inevitability of income and wealth inequality, he was against excessive inequalities and particularly when they were used without any concern for the common good:

> Though I care as little about riches as any man, I am a friend to riches because they are capable of good. I care not how affluent some may be, provided that none be miserable in consequence of it. (Paine, 1797, p 425)

A universal welfare state

Paine was the first to sketch out a plan for a universal welfare state, that is, a system of state welfare provision that was based on citizenship rights and not on proof of need through harsh individual means tests. His fundamental principle was that, as far as possible, benefits should be paid to all who belonged to a certain population or occupation or age group, irrespective of income, gender or race, as a recognition of their right as citizens and not out of charity, pity or social control that usually involves a personal test of means and needs:

> It is not charity but a right – not bounty but justice, that I am pleading for. (Paine, 1797, p 425)

He gave a number of reasons for his choice of universalism versus means testing. First, people paid their taxes either as land taxes, poor rates or indirect taxes when they purchased things in the market. Government revenues, therefore, had a very broad social base: they did not derive from the rich only but from the hard work of all, including the poor.

Second, people had a right to compensation as a result of the land that their ancestors once owned by right but were dispossessed of; third, the rich made their wealth partly by exploiting their workers – the least they can do is to use their wealth to pay for a system of universal benefits; fourth, it is best to pay benefits as of right, rich or poor, 'to prevent invidious distinctions' or in the more recent phrase 'to avoid stigmatisation' (Paine, 1797, p 420); and, fifth, in a novel way, Paine reminds the rich that their wealth is the 'effect of society; and it is impossible for an individual to acquire personal property without the aid of Society.... Separate an individual from society, and give him an island or a continent to possess, and he cannot acquire personal property' (Paine, 1797, p 428). This implied a clear duty on the part of the rich to contribute to a generous welfare programme.

Paine tried to reassure the competing interest groups that his plan 'would benefit all, without injuring any' (Paine, 1797, p 427). The poor would receive benefits as an acknowledgement of their contribution to society and as a compensation for the losses they suffered over the years; the middle groups would receive more in benefits than they paid in taxes; and the upper groups would gain 'a degree of security, that none of the old governments of Europe, now tottering on their foundations, can give' (Paine, 1797, p 427).

How would such a universalist system of welfare provision be funded? Paine spent considerable time attempting to reassure his audience that his proposals were not extravagant and could be easily funded. Bearing in mind his attitude to poverty and excessive inequality, it is not surprising that he ended up with a vertically redistributive system of taxation. His scheme entailed the abolition of the prevailing system of poor rates, which were paid by householders of middle and higher incomes – 'by about a quarter to a third of the population' (Philp,1995, p 480).The amount of rates varied according to the number of poor in the parish that had to be relieved, with the result that parishioners often tried to evict any person who was either poor or likely to become poor but did not belong to the parish – a practice that Paine condemned. His scheme also envisaged the abolition of taxes on houses and windows because they weighed heavily on households with middling incomes.

These taxes would be replaced by a progressive system of taxation and by death duties. His system of progressive taxation meant that 'all estates of the clear yearly value of fifty pounds, after deducting the land tax, and up' would pay a gradually rising rate of tax (Paine, 1792, p 304). Any income above £22,000 would be subject to a 100% income tax. He hoped that such a progressive tax would not only reduce income inequalities, but would also encourage or even force the large landowners to hive off part of their land to their younger siblings. This would improve the productivity of the land, and would reduce political corruption, for it would 'extirpate the overgrown influence arising from the unnatural law of primogeniture, and which is one of the principal sources of corruption at elections' (Paine, 1792, p 307).

In addition to progressive taxation of incomes from all sources – not just land – Paine suggested a system of death duties on wealth. When the wealth passed on to the heirs of a deceased person, it would be subject to a 10% tax, payable 'within the space of one year, in four equal payments, or sooner, at the choice of the payers' (Paine, 1797, p 431). Although he was criticised by radicals then and since that such a low rate of death duty would do little to break up the large estates, it has to be remembered that he was anxious to ensure the support of all sections of society for his plan.

Paine was also certain that under a republic the amount of expenditure on what he considered unnecessary government functions would reduce: the pomp and ceremony of democratic governments would be far lower than the expenditure lavished on kings and courts; with the more peaceful conditions that would exist between democratic governments, there would be a substantial peace dividend that could be used for social policy measures. He calculated that under the monarchy in England, 'not a thirtieth, scarcely a fortieth, part of the taxes which are raised are either occasioned by, or applied to, the purposes of civil government' (Paine, 1792, p 265).The rest was used by the monarch and his court or was eaten up by military expenditure.

In these ways, Paine believed that he created a fairer and a more egalitarian system of taxation that would provide the revenues that were necessary to finance his social security system. His list of benefits – together with his plan for tax reform – are contained in the second part of his *Rights of Man* and in his *Agrarian Justice*. It is clear that both his tax proposals and his social security measures became more radical by the time he came to write *Agrarian Justice*. They are, however, presented here jointly, pointing out only the major differences between the two sets of proposals.

Whatever Paine may have written about the relative roles of civil society and government, he acknowledged from the start of his plan for social security that the state had to take the major responsibility for the relief of poverty. Such non-governmental organisations as 'benefit clubs, which, though of humble invention, merit to be ranked among the best of modern institutions' could only deal with the incidental, minor groups in poverty (Paine, 1792, p 293). Similarly, private charity was equally incapable of coping with the major groups in poverty. A charitable individual 'may give all that he has, and that all will relieve but little' (Paine, 1797, p 425). Only society through the government is up to the task of dealing with the problem of poverty – and this is best done by making 'society the treasurer' to guard and to manage the fund accumulated from the monetary contributions made by all sections of the community (Paine, 1797, p 428).

The most innovative and most universalist of his proposals was the payment of £15 to every person when they reached the age of 21 'as a compensation in part, for the loss of his or her natural inheritance, by the introduction of the system of landed property' (Paine, 1797, p 419). He hoped that such a grant would be useful in helping young people set up employment for themselves and thus prevent them from falling into poverty:

> With this aid they could buy a cow, and implements to cultivate a few acres of land; and instead of becoming burthens upon society, which is always the case, where children are produced faster than they can be fed, would be put in the way of becoming useful and profitable citizens. (Paine, 1797, p 426)

In his *Rights of Man*, Paine estimated that one fifth of the population of England, that is, 1,400,000 persons, were so poor as to be in need of government benefits for their survival. Estimates of poverty have always depended on the definition, which in turn has always been largely a matter of personal judgement. Paine does not explain how he arrived at his estimates, though it appears he was influenced by the financial constraints involved in relieving poverty. The two major groups in such poverty were, he claimed, large families and the elderly: of the estimated 1,400,000 persons in such poverty, 10% were elderly and the remaining 90% were members of large families. He made no mention of the single unemployed or the single mother with one child only, for example, because he considered these as minor groups to be taken care of by the various voluntary benefit clubs or charitable institutions. His estimate, therefore, of one fifth of the population being in official poverty is an underestimate since it excluded these 'minority' groups in poverty.

On a very impressionistic basis, he estimated that the elderly, that is, those aged 50 or over, comprised one sixteenth of the population. Of these, he further estimated that 30%, that is, 140,000 persons, were poor enough to be in need of government support. For benefit purposes, he further divided the elderly into two groups – those aged 50 to 60 years and those above 60. The first group retained their mental faculties intact but found it difficult to cope with the hard physical work and less able to compete with younger workers – he likened a person in this group to 'an old horse, beginning to be turned adrift' (Paine, 1792, p 294). The second group, those aged 60 and over, should certainly cease work, unless they themselves wanted not to do so, because they were not physically capable:

> It is painful to see old age working itself to death, in what are called civilized countries, for daily bread. (Paine, 1792, p 295)

Pensions should be paid as of right to all the 140,000 elderly in need but the amount of the pension should vary between the two age groups: the sum of £6 per annum to those aged 50 to 60, and the sum of £10 per annum to the second group aged 60 and over. Paine based this distinction of pension amount on the belief that the first group might still be earning small amounts from occasional work while the second group would not.

Having gone into all this detail on the elderly in need, their age groups and their pension rates, Paine does away with it all five years later in his *Agrarian Justice* by advocating a far more generous provision. He now proposes that all those above the age of 50, rich or poor, should get the higher pension of £10 per annum:

> The sum of Ten Pounds per annum, during life, to every person now living, of the age of fifty years, and to all others as they arrive at that age. (Paine, 1797, p 420)

Paine's proposals on old-age pensions are pretty radical even though the amounts offered may not be. It has been calculated that 'a lowly manual labourer and his wife were likely to be earning about £22 p.a.' in 1777 (Philp, 1995, p 481). In other words, the pension amounts proposed by Paine were in line with the living standards of the lowest paid worker. This may sound miserly – and it is – but experience has shown that state benefits that are not based on insurance contributions tend to reflect the living standards of the low-paid in society. There has always been the fear that more generous benefits will undermine work and savings incentives.

The radicalism of Paine's pension plan is shown when compared with the provisions of the first Old Age Pensions Act, introduced in Britain in 1908. The Act provided a non-contributory pension to all those who were 70 years or more, who had incomes that did not exceed an annual limit, and who satisfied certain moral standards of behaviour – they had worked regularly, had not been convicted of drunkenness, and so on. As a result of all these restrictions many did not qualify, and bearing also in mind that few people lived beyond the age of 70 at that time, only a small proportion of the population benefited from it. Despite this, the amount of pension it provided was not much higher than Paine's in absolute terms: five shillings a week, that is, £13 per annum, compared to £10 in Paine's plan. In relative terms, taking account of inflation or the rise in wages, it may even have been less generous.

Paine acknowledged that many of the elderly would be disabled and would receive the old-age pension. Those of the disabled below the retirement age of 50 years who were incapable of earning a livelihood would also qualify for the same amount of pension – £10 per annum. In this way, he pointed out, 'three classes of wretchedness', that is, 'the blind, the lame, and the aged poor', would be lifted out of poverty (Paine, 1797, p 425).

The largest group in poverty, totalling 90% of the poor, comprised families with children. Paine estimated that 630,000 children under the age of 14 lived in families that needed state support to make ends meet. To these families, he offered a system of child allowances amounting to £4 per year per child under the age of 14. Those above that age could either work or they could be apprenticed. Such child allowances were not introduced in Britain until 1945 but they were payable in respect of all children in the family, bar the first, irrespective of parental income.

The payment of child allowances was conditional on the child attending school and a requirement was placed on 'the ministers of every parish to certify jointly to an office, for that purpose, that this duty is performed' (Paine, 1792, p 294). Paine also recognised that parents with incomes just above the poverty line may also find it difficult to send their children to school. A provision in the plan was, therefore, made for 'ten shillings a year for the expense of schooling, for six years each' and 'half a crown a year for paper and spelling books' (Paine, 1792, p 297).

Like almost all other reformers, he stressed the importance of education to both the individual and the state in a republic. Education enhanced a young person's ability to obtain a job, to complete an apprenticeship and to improve his or her career. In this way, education acts also in a preventive way against poverty:

> Many a youth, with good natural genius, who is apprenticed to a mechanical trade, such as a carpenter, joiner, millwright, shipwright, blacksmith, &c. is prevented getting forward the whole of his life, from the want of a little common education when a boy. (Paine, 1792, p 294)

Paine insisted throughout his works that a democracy needs educated citizens who can take an active part in civic life. This could only be achieved if people were at least literate. Education enhanced people's rationality, which he considered essential in the decision-making process of a democracy. Only a monarchical and aristocratic government 'requires ignorance for its support', he believed (Paine, 1792, p 297).

A number of other innovative proposals were included in Paine's welfare plan. A maternity grant of 20 shillings was included but Paine hoped that only those who needed it would apply. Similarly, a marriage grant of the same amount was included but, again, it was urged that only those in need should apply for it. His instinct was to make such benefits universal but he was realistic enough to acknowledge that funds were limited. This is why for the first time he introduces a benefit with an annual budget: a national sum of £20,000 for the funeral expenses of persons travelling for work and dying at a distance from their parish of origin. This was motivated both by humane considerations and also by a desire to reduce the parish practice of ejecting all those 'outsiders' who might prove a burden on the rates.

Paine made no financial provisions for the single unemployed or low-paid because he felt they were the responsibility of civil society. But he did make suggestions for the employment of young unemployed people in London, where the problem was at its worst. He suggested the building of two or more workhouses in London where young unemployed people could go on their own accord. There, they would be put to work, fed and paid a wage. They would be free to leave whenever they wished and any wages left after paying for their lodging would be given to them. He hoped that such a scheme would enable those in difficulties 'to recruit themselves, and be enabled to look out for better employment' (Paine, 1792, p 300).

Throughout his plan, Paine was at pains to make clear that the costs would not be considerably higher than current government expenditure and they would thus be affordable. Expenditure on the royal court and on wars had to be curtailed to make room for his proposals, however.

Paine often condemned the current practice of the low wages and high profits that existed in his time. It was, therefore, not unexpected that he came out strongly against the legal regulations in force 'for regulating and limiting workmen's wages'. All he asked for was the removal of such regulations in order to allow workers and employers to bargain freely for wages. Like Adam Smith, he called for this on grounds of workers' personal freedom, but, unlike Smith, he hoped this would lead to higher wages, instead of simply arguing for government-free industrial practices:

> Personal labour is all the property they have. Why is that little, and the little freedom they enjoy to be infringed? But the injustice will appear stronger, if we consider the operation and effect of such laws. When wages are fixed by what is called a law, the legal wages remain stationary, while every thing else is in progression. (Paine, 1792, p 310)

There are, of course, many gaps in Paine's welfare state plan – no provision for many of the unemployed, no reference to health care or housing and so on. Such omissions may be understandable bearing in mind the prevailing socio-economic circumstances and the fact that Paine was anxious that his plan should be considered affordable. It is difficult, however, to explain the absence of any proposal to limit 'the evils of laissez-faire in the field of industrial development' (Hearnshaw, 1931, p 138), in view of the deteriorating working conditions in the mushrooming factory workshops. Indeed, despite the laissez-faire doctrine of governments, the first half of the 19th century witnessed the introduction of government regulations to protect workers at work in Britain, even though the legislation was not always enforced.

Despite these weaknesses, it is impossible not to admire Paine's spirit of reform. It went beyond all other proposals that could be taken seriously as politically feasible one day. His own wish was that his scheme would make a real contribution in dealing with poverty, as the following moving quotation shows:

> By the operation of this plan, the poor laws, those instruments of civil torture, will be superseded, and the wasteful expense of litigation prevented. The hearts of the humane will not be shocked by ragged and hungry children, and persons of seventy and eighty years of age begging for bread. The dying poor will not be dragged from place to place to breathe their last, as a reprisal of parish upon parish. Widows will have a maintenance for their children, and not be carted away, on death of their husbands, like culprits and criminals; and children will no longer be considered as increasing the distress of their parents. (Paine, 1792, p 301)

Paine's plan is a good example of the problems involved in labelling an idea or a proposal as 'utopian'. His plan appeared utopian to many of his contemporaries but it has proved a very practical proposition in the 20th century.

Religion and welfare

In his penultimate major book, *The Age of Reason* (1794), Paine takes a critical look at organised religion and human welfare. What he has to say applies to all organised religions even though the examples he uses to illustrate his arguments come from Christianity – the Old and the New Testament.

He makes it abundantly clear that he believes in a God who is humane and almighty, for He created the human species and the cosmos. There is, he argued, no other logical explanation for the creation of the world. His belief in God and hence his religious beliefs reflected broadly his moral values on how human beings should live and how they should behave towards one another:

> I believe in one God, and no more; and I hope for happiness beyond this life. I believe in the equality of man; and I believe that religious duties consist in doing justice, and endeavouring to make our fellow creatures happy. (Paine, 1794, p 7)

Although he believed in one God, he also believed that any relationship between the individual and God can only be direct. There was no need for any organised religion, be that Christianity, Judaism, Confucianism, Islam or any other religion. Indeed, he went further to argue that organised religion with its quest for money, fame and power made it impossible to achieve true faith. It is best for the individual to communicate directly with his or her maker. Hence his much-quoted statement: 'My own mind is my own church' (Paine, 1794, p 8). Organised religious institutions 'appear to me to be no other than human inventions, set up to terrify and enslave mankind' (Paine, 1794, p 8). The Bible, the Koran and other such books are nothing more but the works of ordinary humans. He described the Bible and Old Testament as 'impositions and forgeries' (Paine, 1794, p 190).

Paine's views on religion did him no favours. They were widely interpreted as atheistic and, as such, they strengthened the hand of his critics who presented him as a radical atheist whose political views should also be rejected. It made it difficult for his supporters to promulgate his political and welfare views. Nevertheless, his religious views contributed to the growing body of opinion arguing for religious freedom and the separation of state and religion – both of which are widely supported today in the West.

Conclusion

Paine's radical ideas in politics and welfare became very influential in working-class politics in England till the latter part of the 19th century when socialist and Marxist radicalism began to take over:

> Until the 1880's, it was, by and large, within the Painite framework that working class radicalism remained transfixed. (Thompson, 1991, p 105)

Paine's legacy consists of three fundamental ideals: first, the notion of universal rights: the belief that all human beings have certain basic rights irrespective of class, race, religion or sex or any other criterion. It is true that not everybody today claims that these are God-given rights; many would argue that these are rights won in the political arena in some countries, which ought to be expanded to all other countries. Few, however, would question the legitimacy of the universality of rights today.

The second was the notion of democracy and political representation as the best form of government: the belief that every citizen has a right to join in the election of the government of the country for a specific period. Paine's insistence that representative government and monarchy cannot be combined may, perhaps, have been proved wrong but only by stripping the monarchy of most of its formal power. The yearning for democratic government was a major factor in the collapse of Soviet-style government and the same yearning is apparent in all undemocratic countries today.

Third, Paine can rightly be called 'the father of the welfare state'. His views were radical for his day and remained so for at least a century and a half before the welfare state came to be the main way of reducing poverty and humanising the excesses of capitalism. The welfare state, despite its many failings, is one of the major social advances of the 20th century.

Paine's major weakness was his underestimation of the tendency of unregulated capitalism to create both wealth and poverty. He came close to recognising this in his last major work but he still tended to apportion most blame for the endemic poverty of his time to political factors – monarchy and aristocracy. He failed to recognise that poverty can remain a major problem even in democratic societies. It is ironic, for example, that the republic that he helped to create – the USA – occupies a top position today among advanced industrial countries in both the wealth and the poverty leagues.

Paine is the last of the four figures of the 18th-century Enlightenment discussed in this volume. Although they differed in their ideals, they were similar in one way: independence of mind (Porter, 2001). Indeed, at least two of them – Wollstonecraft and Paine – were prepared to suffer as a result of their independent stand on the issues they championed. In the next chapter, we move on to the 19th century, which witnessed the full growth of industrialisation in many European countries, the establishment of working-class movements and the emergence of Marxist and modern theories on welfare.

TEN

Classical Marxism and welfare
Karl Marx (1818–83)
Frederick Engels (1820–95)

The arrival of Marxism reflected the industrial transformation of northern Europe and the rise in the size and power of the working class. By the 1840s when the publications of Marx and Engels began to appear, the industrialisation of England had been well and truly established – a historical fact so important that, in Engels' view, it had 'no counterpart in the annals of humanity' (Engels, 1845, p 50). Advancing capitalist industrialisation had 'a centralising effect' on many other aspects of life: capital began to be concentrated in fewer hands; the workforce started being amassed in factories rather than in the myriad of workshops that dotted the villages; the rural exodus to the towns gained momentum so that by the 1851 census half the population in England lived in towns; the heart of the nation's economy shifted from agriculture to industrial production; and the industrial working class was beginning to flex its political muscle (Engels, 1845, pp 54–5).

Marx and Engels consistently considered capitalist industrialisation as having both positive and negative effects on human welfare. On one hand, it facilitated technical innovation, it encouraged productivity, it opened new markets, it created new products and, with these, the general standard of living rose. On the other hand, working conditions deteriorated in the factories, workers became alienated from their workplace, inequality widened, housing standards in the urban working-class ghettos became utterly inhuman, community spirit declined and the class antagonism between workers and employers sharpened, with the fear of revolution always in the air.

Marxism sought, first, to interpret these changes within a materialist theoretical framework; and, second, to use the same conceptual framework to explain the emergence of the good society – communism – that would put an end to the evils of capitalism, while retaining the technology that fuelled productivity and economic growth. Marx and Engels tried to distinguish themselves from other socialists by claiming that their theories on capitalism, socialism and communism were 'scientific', objective and practical rather than 'ideological', subjective and, hence, utopian. It is an assertion that does not stand up to any serious examination not only because their proposals have not been implemented anywhere but also because we have come to realise that the writers' views on human nature, on what is desirable in life and what is not, always influence their 'theoretical' edifices. 'No political philosopher', wrote Wright Mills, 'can be detached; he can only pretend to be' (Wright Mills, 1963, pp 11–12).

Marx and Engels' writings on welfare issues were often part of their broader political debates. Issues of poverty were treated as part of the effects of capitalist accumulation; education was discussed in relation to industrialisation; crime as part of the capitalist ethos or the alienation debate; and so on. Their theories, however, of how the capitalist society functions and how their ideal society would be organised were rich in their welfare implications.

Human nature and human needs

Marx and Engels rejected the approach that ran from Aristotle to the contract theorists that before the dawn of civilisation, in the state of nature, human beings possessed certain characteristics that were universal, timeless, sometimes God-given and, hence, formed the basis for claims for certain rights or duties and for certain political regimes. For Hobbes, for example, human beings were aggressive by nature and needed strong monarchical governments to ensure that peace and security prevailed in society. For Rousseau, human beings were born free and though governments trod over their freedom over the years, they still retained their right to freedom because it was natural and timeless, and human beings could best thrive in a democratic society. Marx ridiculed Jeremy Bentham's claim that his theory of utilitarianism, which justified conservative policies, was based on a timeless and unchanging type of human nature:

> With the driest naivete he takes the modern shopkeeper, especially the English shopkeeper, as the normal man. Whatever is useful to this queer normal man, and to his world, is absolutely useful. This yard-measure, then, he applies to past, present, and future. (Marx, 1867, p 488)

Marx and Engels did not speculate about human nature in the state of nature and how it changed over time. Instead, they argued that human nature reflects the cultural, social and economic conditions that human beings find themselves in. But they were not simple social determinists, for they argued that individuals, in turn, influence their society so that a dialectical relationship exists between individual and society.

Although they adopted a historicist approach to human nature, they did not preclude the existence of certain characteristics that they considered special to human beings. They did not make a list of such features of human nature, as other writers had done, and one must glean these either from their views of human beings in a communist society, or from Marx's critique of alienation and loss of humanity under capitalism, or from passing comments. As Duncan observes, 'any account of dehumanisation presupposes a notion of what is human or truly human' (Duncan, 1973, p 56).

First and foremost, they see human beings primarily as creative workers – labour is essential to men and women, to their self-development and self-satisfaction, provided it is free rather than enforced labour. The history of humankind is the history of work. Human nature fulfils itself and changes itself through free labour. Second, human freedom is essential to human beings but this must be freedom not only in the sense of political rights but also economic rights and social rights – the freedom of individuals to fulfil their abilities and talents. Marx was forthright in his rejection of the argument that in a democracy both workers and employers possessed equal rights: 'Between equal rights', he snapped, 'force decides' (Marx, 1867, p 151). Third, the creativeness of human beings can only be fulfilled in a society where they can decide for themselves the kind of jobs that they enjoy doing. As we shall see later, Marx was very critical of the alienating working conditions that human beings endured under capitalism. Under communism, he argued, human beings will have the freedom to do the kind of jobs that they are interested in – though they will have no freedom to be idle. Fourth, both Marx and Engels often stressed the ideal of the 'total man' who combined in his personality both mental and physical attributes. They hoped that in their communist society the distinction between mental and physical labour would disappear. Fifth, human autonomy and freedom was not something individualistic, 'but with people, by people and for people. Man can only achieve real happiness and perfection when he associates his own happiness and perfection with those of others' (Fritzhand, 1967, p 158). Finally, there is a strong emphasis not only on individualism but on equality at the same time. Marx and Engels stressed the 'original goodness and equal intellectual endowment of men' (Marx and Engels, 1845, p 9).

The development of history is, in essence, the ongoing human struggle to satisfy human needs. Marx spends some time elaborating this theme. In the early days of civilisation, human beings struggled to produce enough simply to satisfy their biological needs in order to survive – 'eating and drinking, a habitation, clothing and many other things' (Marx, 1845a, p 48). During this period, human needs were not very different from those of animals – they were basic in character and few in number. But in the process of production for the satisfaction of biological needs, human beings created new products and, hence, new needs; and the process continued throughout history. Satisfaction of needs at one level leads to the creation of new needs that may not be necessary for biological survival but are seen as essential for social survival. In this way, the time comes when 'man's needs have no limits and are completely elastic' (Marx, 1867, p 397). Marx was one of the first theorists to analyse this interrelationship between production and social needs – to advocate a materialistic expansion of human needs. He set it out as follows:

> Hence production produces consumption: 1. by providing the material of consumption; 2. by determining the mode of consumption; 3. by creating in the consumer a need for the objects which it first presents as products. (Marx, 1845a, p 133)

Marx also illustrates how relative deprivation feelings emerge when a need that was satisfied in a traditional way is seen in comparison to the same need being satisfied in a new and more luxurious way as follows:

> A house may be large or small; so long as the surrounding houses are equally small it satisfies all demands for a dwelling. But let a palace arise beside the little house, and it shrinks from a little house to a hut. The little house shows now that its owner has only very slight or no demands to make; and however high it may shoot up in the course of civilization, if the neighbouring palace grows at an equal or even greater extent, the occupant of the relatively small house will feel more and more uncomfortable, dissatisfied and cramped within its four walls. (Marx, 1849, pp 93–4)

It is not, however, home production only that expands the range of social needs; foreign trade, too, has the same effect. This became particularly evident as a result of the discovery, colonisation and exploitation of the New World. The process of globalisation gained momentum, and both production and consumption gained a more cosmopolitan outlook in the rich countries:

> In place of the old wants, satisfied by the productions of the country, we find new wants, requiring for their satisfaction the products of distant lands and climes. In place of the old local and national seclusion and self-sufficiency, we have intercourse in every direction, universal inter-dependence of nations. (Marx and Engels, 1848, p 6)

In brief, a vibrant relationship is created between human production and human consumption at both the national and the international level so that human needs become essentially social in character and, over time, the distinction between need and desire becomes blurred:

> Our desires and pleasures spring from society; we measure them, therefore, by society and not by the objects which serve for their satisfaction. Because they are of a social nature, they are of a relative nature. (Marx, 1849, p 94)

It is not simply that new social needs are added to the catalogue of existing social consumption. Even the satisfaction of biological needs changes its social character over time to create new needs:

> Hunger is hunger; but the hunger that is satisfied by cooked meat eaten with knife and fork differs from hunger that devours raw meat with the help of hands, nails and teeth. (Marx, 1859, quoted in Duncan, 1973, pp 61–2)

Despite their theorising on the relative nature of needs, both Marx and Engels never lost sight of the fact that most workers of their day did not earn enough to satisfy even their basic, biological needs. Thus the debate within Marxism as to whether Marx was a historical 'relativist' or whether he maintained an 'essentialist' view of human needs is unbalanced, for he clearly took a stand that made room for both (Sayers, 1998). Relative needs supplement and expand basic needs but they never totally supplant them.

Finally, Marx became increasingly aware that his proposals for the free satisfaction of all needs for all in a communist society would come to grief if there were no control over the range and quantity of social needs to be satisfied. He came close to arguing for a distinction between false and real social needs – an attempt that was bound to end in failure, for who is to make and enforce that distinction? We shall return to this issue later in the chapter.

The materialist conception of history

Perhaps the most important contribution to social science that Marx and Engels made was around our understanding of the historical process. Until then, the general view was that abstract ideas, theories, great historical figures and divine intervention were the propelling forces behind the development of human civilisation. For Marx and Engels, historical development is nothing more but the result of the human struggle, against nature to begin with and against entrenched interests later, to eke out, sustain and improve living standards. Work rather than thought was the driving force of human civilisation. They referred to this as the materialist conception of history though others have labelled it as 'historical materialism' or 'dialectical historical materialism':

> The central idea of the materialistic conception of history was that
> the key to change in society was to be found in the way men produce
> their life in common. (McLellan, 1971, p 135)

The theoretical model of the materialist conception of history was based on the twin notions of 'economic structure' and 'superstructure'. The economic structure of society is nothing more but the materials and the tools used by the workers for production, while the superstructure is the legal system, the nature of politics, dominant ideology, literature, art, educational system, and so on. In general, it is the economic structure that determines the character of the superstructure. There is, thus, a broad congruence between the general features of the structure and the superstructure of society. In the field of welfare, it can be argued that the welfare state, with its universal retirement pension schemes, compulsory education, free health care and so on, can only come about in industrial, affluent societies for both economic and political reasons. The details of such schemes, however, will vary depending on the particular situation in an industrial country.

In his widely debated Preface to *A Contribution to the Critique of Political Economy* (1859), Marx expresses this relation between structure and superstructure as follows:

> In the social production which men carry on they enter into definite relations that are indispensable and independent of their will; these relations of production correspond to a particular stage of development of their material forces of production. The sum total of these relations of production constitutes the economic structure of society – the real foundation, on which rise a legal and political superstructure and to which correspond particular forms of consciousness. The mode of production in material life determines the social, political, and intellectual life processes in general. It is not the consciousness of men that determines their being, but, on the contrary, their social being that determines their consciousness. (Marx, 1859, pp 328–9)

Marx and Engels intended this conceptual framework as an explanation primarily of how society developed from slavery, to feudalism, to capitalism and how it would eventually grow into a socialist and communist society. They did not expect that this could be used to explain every event and detail in history – for both Marx and Engels, the details of any future programme are to be settled by the people themselves involved in the particular economic and political situation.

If the basic driving force of historical development was the nature of the material base of society, the mechanism involved for this transformation was the ongoing conflict between the two main social classes in society: slaves against slave owners, serfs against nobles, workers against employers. In the memorable words of Marx and Engels:

> The history of all hitherto existing society is the history of the class struggle. (Marx and Engels, 1848, p 3)

In the field of welfare, both Engels and Marx referred to the constant conflict between the workers and the employers over the introduction of factory legislation and the curtailment of the excessively long hours of work in factories in England during the 19th century. The clearest comment on this comes from Marx:

> The creation of a normal working day is, therefore, the product of a protracted civil war, more or less dissembled, between the capitalist class and the working class. (Marx, 1867, p 180)

The materialist conception of history has been criticised as grossly overestimating the significance of economic factors, downplaying the importance of politics and treating the individual as an automaton of economic interests. There is a degree of truth in this claim, particularly in view of some careless remarks by both

Marx and Engels on this issue. The following comment by Marx, for example, is tantamount to technological determinism:

> The hand-mill gives you society with the feudal lord; the steam-mill, society with the industrial capitalist. (Marx, 1867, p 763, cited by Fischer, 1973, p 83)

Yet, overall, neither Marx nor Engels claimed that economic factors were the only factors in historical development. They both acknowledged the importance of political factors not only because they were both political activists but also because their theoretical framework clearly stated that the socialist society of the future would only come about through protracted and concerted political action by the organised working class in advanced industrial societies. They were, however, ambivalent about the relative weight of economic versus political factors and Engels' attempt to clarify this by claiming that the economic factor is 'in the last analysis' the determining factor in history only helped to muddy the waters further (Engels, 1884, p 71). It simply shifted the point of dissension as to what constitutes 'final analysis'.

Similar debates have ranged over the importance of the individual actor in history. Both Marx and Engels rejected the 'great historical figure' thesis of history but they accepted the significance of individual actors provided they were placed within the existing socio-economic conditions of the period. Individuals are important in history but they are also shaped by history, as was argued earlier. Their actions are not to be seen as the outcome of their own independent thoughts but as the result of their ideas that are shaped by the history and culture of their society:

> Men make their own history, but they do not make it just as they please; they do not make it under circumstances chosen by themselves, but under circumstances directly found, given and transmitted from the past. (Marx, 1852, p 225)

Finally, the very division of society into structure and superstructure raises also the question of which institutions or groups belong to one rather than the other sector. Does labour as factory hands belong to the structure while labour as trade union members belong to the superstructure? Marx and Engels were very vague about such details.

In brief, Marx and Engels rejected both idealism and economic determinism; they proposed a synthesis of economic and political factors where the economic usually dominates the political; they were unable to be more specific about this relationship and occasionally contradicted themselves; in the end, they were left with a formula that was too vague: the economic structure usually dominates the superstructure of society though there are occasions when the latter can act independently. Despite this weakness, the merit of Marxism has been to bring to the fore the importance of economic factors that were previously neglected when discussing historical developments, including the growth of welfare state provisions.

The claim that class conflict was the major mechanism for social and political change in history is clearly an exaggeration. Numerous examples of changes can be cited where the conflict between the oppressed and the oppressing class played a major and determining role but, equally, as many examples can be given where class conflict was a peripheral force. The collapse of the feudal system, for example, had more to do with the emergence of the new class of entrepreneurs bolstered by the discoveries of the New World than with the conflict between serfs and nobles. In the field of welfare, factory legislation had a good deal to do with class conflict between workers and employers, as pointed out earlier, but health legislation to combat epidemics emanating from insanitary housing and living conditions in the towns of 19th-century England had more to do with the self-interest of the upper classes, as Engels himself acknowledged. As soon as it was scientifically shown, he argued, that epidemic diseases could not be confined to the working classes and that they would spread to bourgeois neighbourhoods, 'the philanthropic bourgeois became inflamed with a noble spirit of competition in their solicitude for the health of the workers. Societies were founded, books written, proposals drawn up, laws debated and passed, in order to stop the sources of the ever-recurring epidemics. The housing conditions of the workers were investigated and attempts made to remedy the most crying evils' (Engels, 1887, p 578).

Above all, however, the class conflict thesis ignores the importance of other major structural conflicts in society – of gender and race – which were not generally recognised in Marx's time but which are central to today's social science and social policy debates. The Marxist claim that gender and ethnicity are always mere subdivisions of class is a misrepresentation of reality. The relationship between gender and class and the Marxist attitude towards gender issues will be further discussed later in the chapter.

The critique of capitalism

Both Marx and Engels made it abundantly clear that their criticisms of capitalism were directed primarily at the system itself and not at the individual capitalists. Indeed, on occasion, they considered capitalists themselves as victims of the system over which they deemed themselves as masters. Moreover, throughout their writings they viewed the capitalist system as possessing advantages and disadvantages even though they devoted more time and energy in analysing its disadvantages and planning for its downfall. All the advantages and disadvantages stemmed from the central, basic feature of the capitalist system – the hunger for increased profitability:

> The directing motive, the end and aim of capitalist production, is to extract the greatest possible amount of surplus-value, and consequently

to exploit labour-power to the greatest possible extent. (Marx, 1867, p 202)

The pursuit of profit in an increasingly competitive world inevitably meant that the two major constituents of productivity – labour and technology – had to be exploited to the full. While previous economic systems managed to survive with technological stagnation, capitalism relied for its survival on continuous technological innovation. It was this that accelerated the division of labour within the factories – a process that was considered necessary for increased profitability. Technological innovation and the division of labour boosted profitability for the employers, but they had significant adverse effects on the living conditions of workers, as well as for the rest of society. The two major consequences were alienation and increased impoverishment for the working class:

> It is true that labour produces for the rich wonderful things – but for the workers it produces privation. It produces palaces – but for the worker, hovels. It produces beauty – but the worker deformity. (Marx, 1844, p 73)

Alienation

Alienation was, for Marx, the centrepiece of his attack on capitalism; vice versa, the abolition of alienation was the central feature of a communist society. Like Adam Smith before him, Marx was bitterly critical of the alienating effects of the division of labour on the workers, though the two differed completely on its meaning and its abolition. From his early to his late writings, Marx maintained the same critical stance, rating alienation as a worse evil than impoverishment. His views on alienation make sense only if they are seen in conjunction with his views on human nature, discussed earlier. Human beings are by nature creative, freedom-loving and considerate of others: all these qualities are smothered and distorted by the employment conditions imposed on them in factories.

Alienation as a human affliction consisted of three closely interwined strands. First, 'labour is *external* to the worker, that is, it does not belong to his essential being' (Marx, 1844, p 74; author's emphasis). What he produces belongs not to him but to the employer; his products bring profit to others but not to him; he often is unable to buy them; they come to dominate his life even if he does not profit from their production. Second, alienation means that in his employment, the worker 'does not affirm himself but denies himself, and does not feel content but unhappy, does not develop freely his physical and mental energy but mortifies his body and ruins his mind' (Marx, 1844, p 74). This is the meaning that Adam Smith had in mind – a reference to the loss of physical and mental function suffered by the workers in factories based on the division of labour. A clear by-product is that workers seek their fulfilment not at work but outside during their leisure time, which was precious little at Marx's time. Third, the competitive nature of the division of labour means that the worker loses his sociability, his concern for others – he is alienated from his fellow human beings, from his species.

This is how Marx summarises the combined effects of these three strands of alienation on the worker:

> As a result, the man (the worker) no longer feels himself to be freely active in any but his animal functions – eating, drinking, procreating or at most in his dwelling and in dressing up etc; and in his human functions he no longer feels himself to be anything but an animal. What is animal becomes human and what is human becomes animal. (Marx, 1844, p 74)

The detestation that Engels and Marx had of the regimented factory system went beyond the issue of alienation to cover the whole authority structure of employment. This was not because of their yearning for the old cottage system of industry but because of the vision of the more fulfilling system of work that they had for the communist society of the future:

> Masses of labourers, crowded into the factory, are organized like soldiers. As privates of the industrial army they are placed under the command of a perfect hierarchy of officers and sergeants. Not only are they slaves of the bourgeois class, and of the bourgeois state; they are daily and hourly enslaved by the machine, by the overlooker, and, above all, by the individual manufacturer himself. (Marx and Engels, 1848, p 10)

Although alienation afflicts the workers directly, its depressing ethos spreads to society in general to affect social relationships among the general public. Moreover, alienation affects employers themselves, who have little or no option but to behave the way they do towards their workers and towards each other if their enterprises are to survive and increase their profitability in a competitive economic environment. Marx makes the point that industrial practices of his day did not depend 'on the good or ill will of the capitalist. Free competition brings out the inherent laws of capitalist production' (Marx, 1867, p 166). In a capitalist society, alienated human beings behave towards each other not in a spirit of fellowship but as competitive individuals belonging to different social strata.

Both Marx and Engels attributed alienation to the private ownership of the means of production and to the division of labour. They, therefore, felt that its abolition would follow naturally from the abolition of both those two practices. What they did not consider was whether it was at all possible for the division of labour to be abolished in complex industries or whether alienation was part and parcel of complex industrial production even if it were possible to ameliorate the strict application of the division of labour.

Poverty and the immiseration of the working class

One of Marx's first publications was an article in a German newspaper in 1842 on the issue of poverty. It concerned the new law in Prussia that made it an offence for the poor to collect fallen wood for fuel – a practice that they, as well as the poor in England, had used for years.

Lubasz's analysis of the article points out that Marx based his defence of the poor on the concept of 'conflicting property rights', that is, while the rich had a right to their property, the poor also had a right to survival – an argument similar to the Christian principle that we discussed in Chapter 3. Lubasz points out that Marx based his article on three theses: first, 'so far from the poor being a problem to state and civil society, it is the state and civil society themselves which constitute the problem'. Second, he rejected the traditional view of the poor as amoral; instead he saw the poor as exceedingly human: 'what they have, they share in common'. Third, those who made property rights so sacrosanct as to force others into a danger of death situation 'are dehumanised by their property-fetishism' (Lubasz, 1976).

Engels' classic study of the living conditions of the working class in England both drew some of its evidence from and also lent support to the numerous official government reports that poverty was rife and dehumanising. It inevitably drew a grim picture of working-class living conditions. Only some of the main findings can be summarised here.

First, Engels accepted that not all the sections of the working class lived under the same conditions: some did better than others but in the worst sections what one found was 'bitter want, reaching even homelessness and death by starvation. The average is much nearer the worst than the best' (Engels, 1845, p 106).

Second, the poor were on the whole geographically segregated from the affluent in the large cities of England:

> True, poverty often dwells in hidden alleys close to the palaces of the rich; but, in general, a separate territory has been assigned to it, where, removed from the sight of the happier classes, it may struggle along as it can. (Engels, 1845, p 59)

Third, the clothing, the diet and the housing conditions of many of the poor were so sub-standard that life was far shorter than that of the affluent sections of the community. It was not the lack of goods in the market that was the problem but the lack of money to pay for them:

> In the great towns of England everything may be had of the best, but it costs money and the workman, who must keep house on a couple of pence, cannot afford much expense. (Engels, 1845, p 102)

Fourth, children were most vulnerable to this form of severe privation and many of those who survived early death became 'weak, scrofulous, and rachitic in a high degree' (Engels, 1845, p 132). Three of Marx's six children died very young. Life expectancy was low. According to the Report of the Medical Officer of Health for Manchester, 'the average age at death of the Manchester upper middle class was 38 years, while the average age at death for the labouring class was 17 years; while at Liverpool those figures were represented as 35 against 15' (Marx, 1867, p 359).

Fifth, poor communities developed a way of life, a culture of their own, as a way of coping with their poverty. The culture was not the cause but the result of poverty. In words that are reminiscent of Disraeli's description of the two nations, Engels has this memorable description of the chasm between the upper- and the working-class culture:

> In view of all this, it is not surprising, that the working class has gradually become a race wholly apart from the English bourgeoisie. The bourgeoisie has more in common with every other nation of the earth than with the workers in whose midst it lives. The workers speak other dialects, have other thoughts and ideals, other customs and moral principles, a different religion and other politics than those of the bourgeoisie. Thus they are two radically dissimilar nations, as unlike as difference of race could make them. (Engels, 1845, p 157)

Sixth, Engels was certain that the state and voluntary society provision that existed for the poor was far too inadequate for the size of the problem. Indeed, for him and for Marx, poverty could not be abolished in a capitalist system:

> The poor rates are insufficient, vastly insufficient; the philanthropy of the rich is a rain-drop in the ocean, lost in the moment of falling, beggary can support but few among the crowds. (Engels, 1845, p 121)

The Marxist interpretation of the existence of poverty amid rising economic growth was that they were both the result of the same economic system and that poverty was necessary for the growth of wealth. 'Accumulation of wealth at one pole is at the same time accumulation of misery ... at the opposite side' (Marx, 1867, p 362). It was this contrast that was so obvious to so many that gave support to the Marxist interpretation then and later:

> The work of Marx taken as a whole is a savage sustained indictment of one alleged injustice; that the profit, the comfort, the luxury of one man is paid for by the loss, the misery, the denial of another. (Wright Mills, 1963, p 35)

Marx and Engels maintained that this impoverishment would get deeper with the passage of time as capitalism lurched from one crisis to another, as unemployment increased, and as the employers tried to increase profitability by squeezing wage rises. The bourgeoisie might increase its wealth but the worker would sink deeper into misery:

> The modern labourer, on the contrary, instead of rising with the progress of industry, sinks deeper and deeper below the conditions of existence of his own class. He becomes a pauper, and pauperism develops more rapidly than population and wealth. (Marx and Engels, 1848, p 15)

It is not really clear whether the thesis of immiseration meant that the working class would become poorer in absolute terms; or in relative terms to the general rise in living standards; or whether it referred to a rise in inequality between the incomes of the workers and of the bourgeoisie. In all these meanings, it has been proved wrong at the national level of the advanced industrial societies. Absolute poverty has declined to the point of extinction, relative poverty remains high but lower than at Marx's time, and wealth and income inequalities have narrowed since the 19th century.

Some have argued, however, that there may be some truth in it if one speaks of the working class at the global level. Fischer makes this point as follows:

> In the global sense his (Marx's) historical vision proved correct when he pointed out that in assessing the situation of workers it was necessary to consider the world market as a whole, and that the wages of some would rise only because others were starving. (Fischer, 1973, p 124)

Such an interpretation, however, flies against the fact that Marx usually referred to the situation in the industrial countries. Moreover, it would be impossible to prove or disprove at the international level for at least purely methodological reasons: the lack of statistical evidence, how to treat the mass of rural workers, which countries to include in the calculations, and so on. What evidence there is, insufficient and unreliable though it may be, suggests that subsistence poverty declined in some parts of the developing world but increased in others during the second half of the 20th century (George, 2004).

Globalisation

The theoretical framework of the capitalist system adopted by Marx and Engels inevitably led them to the conclusion that national boundaries would not deter private capital from seeking to increase its profitability wherever possible including in foreign countries. They already drew attention to the fact that the discovery of the New World had provided a great stimulus to commercial, industrial and cultural expansion, usually at the expense of the New World countries. It was only a step further from this to argue that the bourgeoisie would chase foreign markets with or without the support of the national state. Bearing in mind their definition of the state – nothing more 'but a committee for managing the common affairs of the whole bourgeoisie'– state involvement in the commercial activities of large companies was normal:

> The need for a constantly expanding market for its products chases the bourgeoisie over the whole surface of the globe. It must nestle everywhere, settle everywhere, establish connections everywhere. (Marx and Engels, 1848, p 6)

Although Marx and Engels concentrated on the economic aspects of globalisation, they had a few words to say about the intellectual and cultural effects. In the same way that economic expansion abroad created a 'universal inter-dependence of nations', they felt that the same process was taking place in the intellectual domain so that a world literature was in the making:

> The intellectual creations of individual nations become common property. National one-sidedness and narrow-mindedness become more and more impossible, and from the numerous national and local literatures, there arises a world literature. (Marx and Engels, 1848, p 7)

On the cultural side, Marx described in very graphic terms how British trade in India had destroyed local cultures in the pursuit of profit. He was, however, not totally sorry for that because he believed that, by doing so, English trade had also undermined the very authoritarian, traditional social structures of India and thus helped to prepare India for industrialisation. In his words:

> England has to fulfil a double mission in India: one destructive, the other regenerating – the annihilation of old Asiatic society, and the laying of the material foundations of Western society in Asia. (Marx, 1845a, p 494)

Marx saw the introduction of the railways in India as both a great venue of exploitation – a facilitator of trade for the benefit of the British companies seeking to export Indian agricultural goods such as cotton to England in order to return them as manufactured goods eventually – and as a basis of future industrialisation – 'truly the forerunner of modern industry' – in India and, with this, the dissolution of 'the hereditary divisions of labour, upon which rest the Indian castes, those decisive impediments to Indian progress and Indian power' (Marx, 1845a, p 497). From the short-term point of view, however, it was the first function that became obvious because the export of cotton from India resulted in the collapse of the Indian home manufactures, the expansion of British manufacture, the rise in unemployment in India and the growth of employment in England. As Marx put it:

> British steam and science uprooted, over the whole surface of
> Hindustan, the union between agriculture and manufacturing industry.
> (Marx, 1845a, p 491)

Economic globalisation, emanating mainly from the most industrial country of
Europe, England, was irresistible. It battered down 'all Chinese walls'; it drew into
the European orbit 'even the most barbarian' nations; it forced such countries
'to adopt the bourgeois mode of production'; it created 'a world after its own
image'; and thus made 'barbarian and semi-barbarian countries dependent on the
civilized ones, nations of peasants on nations of bourgeois, the East on the West'
(Marx and Engels, 1848, p 7).

One of the major international effects of capital was thus to force the colonies
into becoming providers of raw material for the industries of the European
countries, as in the case of cotton from India and wool from Australia. This type
of trade encouraged industrialisation in Europe, ruined any chances of the same
process taking place early in many of the colonies and thus created the basis for
the economic gap that widened between the two sets of countries:

> A new and international division of labour, a division suited to the
> requirements of the chief centres of modern industry springs up,
> and converts one part of the globe into a chiefly agricultural field
> of production, for supplying the other part which remains a chiefly
> industrial field. (Marx, 1867, p 274)

Marx could not have been more prophetic on this issue. He provided the
theoretical framework for several Marxian views on development issues of the
second half of the 20th century, particularly the dependency thesis, which viewed
the dependence of developing countries on the industrial affluent West as an
unequal, exploitative relationship that sank developing countries further into
debt and poverty (Frank, 1967).

Marx's predictions on the globalisation of capital have come true. His
prediction, however, that the internationalisation of capital would also lead to the
internationalisation of the labour movement that would eventually overthrow
international capitalism has not come true and looks unlikely to do so in the
foreseeable future. Labour movements in different countries have spent more
time protecting their own individual national interests than coordinating their
activities to rein in, let alone overthrow, international capital.

Reform or revolution

Marxist theory had as one of its central tenets that every social system contains
within it the seeds of its own destruction. It was argued, for example, that the
advance of capitalism meant the creation of a working class that would get larger
over the years, that it would become more concentrated in factories, more alienated

and impoverished, and, as a result, more politicised, viewing the bourgeoisie as a hindrance to further socio-economic development. In the words of Marx and Engels:

> What the bourgeoisie, therefore, produces, above all, is its own grave-diggers. Its fall and the victory of the proletariat are equally inevitable. (Marx and Engels, 1848, p 16)

What was at issue, therefore, was not whether, but when and how, the collapse of capitalism would come about, to be followed by socialism. Clearly, it could only come about in advanced industrial societies where the conditions mentioned above were fulfilled and where there was also economic affluence. Without the latter, socialism could only mean the redistribution of poverty, Marx and Engels warned several times. It is in this respect that they considered the full development of capitalism as essential to the birth of socialism.

It is incorrect to interpret Marxism as being totally opposed to gradualism and to social reform. Both Marx and Engels stated that reforms were useful in two senses: they brought improvements to the working class and they politicised the proletariat, for they saw reforms not as willingly given by parliaments but as concessions wrung by the working class from an unwilling bourgeoisie. Parliaments were good on debates about abstract rights, which were nothing more but vacuous rhetoric. As the following quotation shows, Marx would rather have action, even if it consisted of small reform measures:

> In the place of the pompous catalogue of the 'inalienable rights of man' comes the modest Magna Charta of a legally limited working-day. (Marx, 1867, p 182)

The general principle for both Marx and Engels was 'reform where possible, revolution where necessary'. They felt that conditions were ripe in four countries for the reformist road to socialism: England, the United States, France and the Netherlands. Engels, who outlived Marx by several years, became more convinced that the revolutionary path to socialism was strewn with very severe difficulties; hence the gradual road was the better alternative, provided care was taken not to lose sight of one's original objectives. Duncan puts this well when he says that Engels became convinced that the revolutionary road had become 'to a large extent obsolete, as development in weapons, the professionalisation of the armies, and the change in the lay-out of the cities, made it extremely costly to the workers, and, more importantly, because proletarian ends were now being secured by other means' (Duncan, 1973, p 160).

Marx and Engels were both certain that the ruling class would resist such radical measures as the nationalisation of the means of production and distribution and would use both its ideological and repressive powers to resist them. It was not just the police and the army but the judiciary, and other state agencies too, that would oppose radical change. Marx referred to the ways in which judges sitting in tribunals negated the intentions of the Factory Acts in England – in these tribunals, 'the masters sat in judgement on themselves' (Marx, 1867, p 175). This was a natural outcome of the Marxist view that the state includes not only the government but other apparatuses in society, too, and they all act in unison when the interests of the ruling class are threatened. On the ideological front, Marx and Engels believed that on matters of significance to the status quo, there is a dominant ideology that reflects and protects the interests of the ruling class. It is this ideology that is contained in the workings of state agencies:

> The ruling ideas of each age have ever been the ideas of the ruling class. (Marx and Engels, 1848, p 24)

In retrospect, Marx and Engels underestimated the public support that reformed capitalism came to enjoy; they overestimated the degree of working-class idealism; they were too reticent about the possibilities for change through the parliamentary method; and, Marx in particular, placed too much faith in the 'scientific' interpretation of the historical process that made the arrival of socialism almost an inevitability. Their approval of the use of violence to achieve political ends may have been acceptable in their time – the age of revolutions in Europe – but the idea gradually lost public support when people were granted the right to choose their governments and thus exert some influence on government policies.

The position of women in society

Contemporary literature on the relevance of Marxism to feminism falls into three broad types. First, there are those writers who consider Marxism as irrelevant and even hostile to feminism. MacKinnon, for instance, insists that the two theoretical approaches are based on two different theoretical frameworks and they lead to two different, and sometimes conflicting, policy solutions. While feminism's theoretical base is sexuality, Marxism's core lies in class; the result is that they must follow different paths towards the achievement of their ideal society:

> Feminists charge that Marxism is male dominated in theory and in practice, meaning that it moves within the world view and in the interest of men. Feminists argue that analysing society exclusively in class terms ignores the distinctive social experiences of the sexes, obscuring women's unity. Marxist demands .... could be (and in part have been) satisfied without altering women's inequality to men. (MacKinnon, 1982, p 4)

Second, there is the marxist–feminist position that stands in opposition to this essentialist feminist line of attack on Marxism. Although it does not claim that Marxism contains a coherent theory of feminism, it argues that the core concepts of Marxism are helpful to feminism and that the two movements cannot achieve their goals on their own – they need each other. Thus Guettel maintains that both women and men have a common enemy – capitalism and its ruling class – and that a non-sexist socialist society is the goal of both:

> Women are oppressed by men because of the forms their lives have had to take in class society, in which both men and women have been oppressed by the ruling class. (Guettel, 1974, p 2)

The third position attempts to steer a middle course between the first two. It claims that, despite all the valid criticisms that can be levied at Marxism, 'Marx's thought does have something valuable to say to modern feminism and can be used to develop feminist theory' (Kain, 1993, p 376). It is this position that is supported by the few and scattered comments made by Marx and Engels on women's position in society.

To begin with, Marxism rejects the traditional claims that male superiority stems from either divine pronouncements or from natural biological differences and, as such, they are timeless and unalterable. In line with the general Marxist thesis of historical materialism, gender social relations are socially structured, they have changed over the years and they will continue to change in the future. More precisely, private property and the capitalist form of production are the major determinants of gender relations and, hence, sexism can only be abolished in a communist society where both those institutions will be put to rest.

Both Marx and Engels occasionally stated that 'the propagation of the species' is part of the structure of society and thus is one of the factors influencing the superstructure. On closer examination, however, this turns out to be nothing more but a throwaway comment, soon forgotten in their general historical analysis. Had they been serious about it, they would have made the development of the family as one of the major factors determining other aspects of society. Instead, as will be shown later, the development of family patterns is treated as simply the result of material and other factors.

Apart from this general line of thinking, Marx's statements on gender issues are few and far between and they are usually found as part of his discussion of other themes. Engels wrote more extensively on gender issues in one of his major publications (Engels, 1884), although, as always, he was less coherent and theoretical than Marx. His basic claim was that existing anthropological evidence showed that the way people earned their living influenced sexual practices and the prevailing system of family patterns. In the early days of civilisation, men and women lived in groups that looked for their food together and practised full sexual freedom, with equality between men and women and with no structured family lives:

> Among all the savages and all barbarians of the lower and middle stages, and to a certain extent of the upper stage too, the position of women is not only free, but honourable. (Engels, 1884, p 113)

The introduction of monogamy was gradual and was the result of economic changes that brought more wealth to society through the work of men. These economic changes were, first, 'the domestication of animals and the breeding of herds' to be followed by 'metalworking, weaving, and, lastly, agriculture' (Engels, 1884, p 118). The result of such changes was that 'it was the man's part to obtain food and the instruments of production for the purpose' while women looked after the house and the children (Engels, 1884, p 119). Until that time, family descent was by the mother; now, with their superior economic power, men changed the rule so that family descent began to be by the father. Engels described this as a major historic change that left its imprint on subsequent gender and family relationships:

> 'The overthrow of mother right was the *world historical defeat of the female sex'* (Engels, 1884, p 120, author's emphasis)

After this historic change, the man became the ruler of the household, and the wife 'became the slave of his lust and a mere instrument for the production of children'. In historical terms, this type of gender and family pattern was well and truly established by the Classical Greek period, as we saw in Chapter 1. Monogamy, family descent through the male line, division of labour in the household, male superiority, female degradation and family conflict became the pattern of gender relations, according to Engels.

> The first class opposition that appears in history coincides with the development of the antagonism between man and woman in monogamous marriage, and the first class oppression coincides with that of the female sex by the male. (Engels, 1884, p 129)

Neither Marx nor Engels develops the implications of this statement. Instead, they move on to argue that with the arrival of capitalism women's position began to deteriorate in some ways and to improve in others. The deskilling of factory work and the division of labour meant that women were suited as much as men for employment because physical strength was no longer an advantage. Indeed, argued Engels, physical strength was a disadvantage in those industries such as clothing 'where "flexibility of finger" is needed, something that women and children are better at than men' (Engels, 1845, p 169). Thus one of the early results of industrialisation was an increase in the number of women employed in factories, so much so that in some clothing factories they outnumbered men.

The increase in the number of women employed outside the home brought with it increased economic and social independence. Both Marx and Engels maintained that this was a prerequisite for the emancipation of women – 'for a higher form of the family and of the relations between the sexes' (Marx, 1867, p 294). They did not claim that economic independence leads automatically to equality between the sexes, for they were not economic determinists; rather that economic independence made possible other forms of independence. In other words, though they accepted the significance of other factors, they argued that without economic independence women's liberation from men would not get far. Engels makes this fairly clear when he says that though the economic reason for male supremacy may disappear, the force of culture and tradition may still persist:

> And now that large-scale industry has taken the wife out of the home onto the labour market and into the factory, and made her often the breadwinner of the family, no basis for any kind of male supremacy is left in the proletarian household, except, perhaps, for something of the brutality toward women that has spread since the introduction of monogamy. (Engels, 1884, p 135)

Paid employment for women, however, had its drawbacks: for the women themselves, for their husbands and for their children, at a time when child care and school facilities were pretty well non-existent, when the male breadwinner was the cultural norm, and when sexual norms were very different from the situation today. Factory employment accentuated the problems faced by mothers trying to combine paid employment and housework; it had a deleterious effect on the children when both parents were at work; and it led to the wage exploitation of women by unscrupulous employers. These are pretty uncontroversial criticisms, though correct. It is when Marx and Engels moved into gender issues per se that their criticism is open to question. Engels comments that young girls in paid employment have no time to prepare themselves for the housework and child care duties that await them when they get married (Engels, 1845, p 175); concentration of male and female employees in the same room 'is not calculated for the favourable development of the female character' (Engels, 1845, p 176); and an employer will take advantage of young girls sexually – 'his mill is also his harem' (Engels, 1845, p 177).

The emphasis on paid employment as a liberating force implied that working-class women were freer than middle- and upper-class women who were not usually in paid employment. Although there is an element of truth in this, there is also an element of untruth, bearing in mind the differences in the economic situation between working-class and upper-class women. Be that as it may, Marx and Engels believed, in brief, that paid employment was a major force in female independence from men but it was not the only factor involved. The following quotation from Engels refers to possibilities not inevitabilities – other forces have to play their part:

> The emancipation of woman will only be possible when woman can take part in production on a large, social scale, and domestic work no longer claims anything but an insignificant amount of her time. (Engels, 1884, p 221)

Marx and Engels in their different ways believed that only in a communist society with the abolition of private property, with the provision of free schooling for all children, paid employment for all according to need, substantial welfare service provision, as well as rising and changing public consciousness on many issues, would gender equality become a reality. A communist society 'will make the relation between the sexes a purely private relation which concerns only the persons involved, and in which society has no call to interfere' (Engels, 1847, p 20).

In one of his earliest writings, Marx considered progress towards gender equality as the best sign of human progress, a view expressed by others, too, at that time. But he went further to claim that, 'The direct, natural, and necessary relation of person to person is the *relation of man to woman*' (Marx, 1844, p 101, author's emphasis). In other words, gender equality is the best example of humanistic social relationships. When men and women treat one another as equal, in the same way that men consider other men as equal and women do likewise with other women, the human species will live free and fulfilling lives. Such an ideal state of affairs could only exist in a communist society, he argued.

In conclusion, one can raise several objections to the views of Marx and Engels concerning the position of women in society: Engels' anthropological evidence was suspect (Carver, 1985); Marx's emphasis on class dwarfed any interest he showed in gender issues; both Marx and Engels occasionally expressed views that from today's standards appear sexist; and so on (Held, 1976; Bryson, 1992, pp 73–5). But, on the whole, one has to conclude that their writings are both supportive of gender equality and helpful in understanding the historical evolution of gender relationships. Indeed, the real issue is not whether Marxism is supportive of feminism but whether its ideal society of communism where gender equality could only thrive is achievable; for, if it is not, one either has to question the Marxist view that gender equality is impossible in a capitalist society, or to conceive of some other political system where it is possible, or try to unpack the notion of equality in order to see which strands of equality are desirable.

A communist welfare state

Both Marx and Engels insisted that communism would not burst onto the world scene instantaneously but would emerge slowly from within the structures of advanced capitalism. Between advanced capitalism and communism, however, lay socialism, with features of both the other two systems. In Marx's words, socialism is:

> in every respect, economically, morally, intellectually, still stamped with the birth marks of the old society from whose womb it emerges. (Marx, 1875, p 32)

Communist society

Communism would take a long time emerging from socialism. The vision of communism was of a society 'in which the free development of each is the condition for the free development of all' (Marx and Engels, 1848, p 26). This vision is a far cry from the 'barrack communism' of the now defunct soviet states. At the heart of communism, argued Marx and Engels, was the individual as a free, social human being, a product and a producer of society, a member of a society of like-minded individuals, working for himself or herself as well as for others.

Although both Marx and Engels often stated that the details of communist society could not be listed in advance, they sketched out its broad outline sufficiently for an assessment. They produced a similar sketch of socialism (Marx and Engels, 1844, pp 25–6) but, here, we will concentrate on their plan for a communist welfare state. It is important to make clear from the outset that Marx did not see communism in simple egalitarian terms but in 'the creation of new wealth, of new needs and of the conditions for their satisfaction' (Avineri, 1968, p 64).

On the economic front, a communist society is, first, technological, for without technology economic affluence is impossible; indeed the more technology is used, the more it will be possible to reduce the working week and provide more leisure time to workers. Second, the private ownership of the means of production and distribution would be abolished and, 'in its stead, there will be common use of all the instruments of production, and the distribution of all products by common agreement' (Engels, 1847, p 17). The abolition of private property would reduce class conflict in society as well as encourage a spirit of fellowship that would be helpful for both social and economic reasons.

Third, Marx believed that, apart from the problem of alienation, the division of labour with its narrow specialisation had become a hindrance to increased productivity and should, therefore, be scrapped; people should be trained to be competent to do several jobs according to their interests; this would also enable the distinction between mental and manual labour to disappear. The development of industry and society in a communist society called for:

> the fully developed individual, for a variety of labours, ready to face any change of production, and to whom the different social functions he performs, are but so many models of giving free scope to his own natural and acquired powers. (Marx, 1867, p 292)

Fourth, all adults would be employed unless there were reasons exempting them – reasons that were previously agreed by the state. Unemployment would be a thing of the past, partly as a result of better economic planning and partly because of the requirement that all should work.

For all four reasons, industry in a communist society would be more productive than in a capitalist society: it would be more technological, it would make better use of its labour resources, it would use workers with all-round training and it would encourage workers to exert more effort at work since they would be aware that their labour benefited them and their fellow workers, not the owners of industry as in a capitalist system. Marx and Engels did not deal with the issue that the owners of industry may have gone but the managers of industry would have arrived and they could be as rapacious as their predecessors.

On the political front, many of the various state apparatuses of the capitalist state would wither away and their place would be taken by a new kind of people's institutions that were concerned with the administration of public life only and not with government or repression. This was a far easier proposition at the time when Marx and Engels were writing than today, for the state provided very few services in those days, beyond the justice system, the police, the army, rudimentary education and poor relief. Since wars against other countries would not be necessary in a communist society, a regular army would not be necessary either and would be replaced by a people's militia. A communist state would be slimmer, cheaper and run with more participation from the citizens and less by paid professionals. Like Rousseau before them, Marx and Engels fail to convince on this issue, for the distinction between administration and government is never clear; and the need for some repressive measures will always exist in large societies.

In the social field, the major feature would be that people's wages would be based not on the amount or centrality of their work, as under socialism, but on their needs. This could only take place in the higher phase of communist society when the division of labour disappeared, when affluence was at its highest and when people discarded their acquisitive inclinations so that they did not hanker after each and every social need. As Marx put it:

> only then can the narrow horizon of bourgeois right be crossed in its entirety and society inscribe on its banners: From each according to his ability to each according to his needs! (Marx, 1875, p 34)

Again, there are obvious elements of uncertainty: first, about the definition of need and, second, about the compatibility of the goals that people are encouraged to achieve. Most probably, Marx had in mind that only those needs stipulated by the people's state would be taken into account when deciding a worker's level of wages – perhaps the number of children, perhaps disability, and so on. The formula also sends conflicting messages to the workers: on one hand, workers are encouraged to be productive, while, on the other, they are encouraged not to be too consumer-oriented. Obviously, the intention was that people should be satisfied with basic, 'real' needs only. The distinction, however, between 'real' and 'false' needs is a matter of personal judgement, however much the leading institutions of society try to influence people in one direction rather than in another. Neither Marx nor Engels attempted to provide any specific guidelines on 'real' as against 'false' needs – an impossible task at any time.

Government expenditure

The amount of wages according to need, however, would depend on how much was left in the government funds after payment for a variety of government services. These are divided into two groups, each comprising three groups of services. The first group includes:

- 'Cover for replacement of the means of production used up';
- 'Additional portion for expansion of production'; and,
- 'Reserve or insurance funds to provide against accidents, dislocations caused by natural calamities, etc'.

The second group consisted of:

- 'General costs of administration not belonging to production';
- An amount 'which is intended for the common satisfaction of needs, such as schools, health services, etc'; and,
- 'Funds for those unable to work, etc. in short, for what is included under so-called official poor relief today' (Marx, 1875, p 31).

There is no discussion on such important details as the level of cash benefits or the standards of education, the coverage of health services, and so on. As always, these details were left to the general public in the particular communist society. There is no provision, either, for the expenses of the police, army, prisons or judiciary, because such services would not be needed – a serious shortcoming in large, complex societies, as we pointed out earlier. We now proceed to look at Marxist views on education, housing and crime in order to gain a better insight of their views on social policy issues.

Education

Marx and Engels did not develop a theory of education in the way that Locke or Rousseau before them did. Nevertheless, their general theory of the individual, of society and of work has clear implications for a Marxist theory of education.

We saw earlier that Marx saw work as essential to human development; that he considered specialisation and the division of labour as incompatible with either human development or work productivity; that he wished the distinction between mental and manual labour to disappear; and that he believed that human beings learn as much by doing as by abstract thinking. It is, therefore, reasonable to assume that he would not have supported a specialised, abstract system of education.

Marx was well aware of the socialising and indoctrinating effects of education. Since he believed that the dominant ideology of a capitalist society is the ideology of the ruling class, he would have wanted to change the ideology that was propagated through the school system. He would have strived for a school system that would act as an agent of socialist change. It was the duty of the educators to do this. In his words:

> The philosophers have only *interpreted* the world, in various ways; the point is to *change* it. (Marx, 1845b, p 123, author's emphasis)

In brief, Marx's central idea of a theory of education was that of revolutionary 'praxis': a theory that stressed the interaction between theory and practice, between ideas and actions, in order to promote socialist change. He supported an educational system in which 'theory enriched by practice, and practice guided by theory', was the dominant principle (Hawkins, 1974, p 10). He referred to the schools that Robert Owen established in his communes as the model of his type of schooling:

> Robert Owen has shown us in detail, the germ of the education of the future, an education that will, in the case of every child over a given age, combine productive labour with instruction and gymnastics, not only as the methods of adding to the efficiency of production, but as the only method of producing fully developed human beings. (Marx, 1867, p 290)

Marx also believed that the results of recent government school provision for children at work supported his choice of a school system that tried to fuse theory with practice. The schools set up under the provisions of the Factory Act in England for working-class children also showed the same way forward, he claimed:

> Though the Factory Act, that first meagre concession wrung from capital, is limited to combining elementary education with work in the factory, there can be no doubt that when the working-class comes into power, as inevitably it must, technical instruction, both theoretical and practical, will take its proper place in the working-class schools. (Marx, 1867, p 293)

Both Marx and Engels were, as expected, critical of the inadequacies of the then existing educational provision. The findings on schools that emerge from Engels' survey of working-class conditions in England are indicative of their criticism, and they can be summarised as follows:

> The means of education in England are restricted out of all proportion to the population.

> The few day schools at the command of the working-class are available only for the smallest minority, and are bad besides.

Compulsory school attendance does not exist.

The evening schools are almost abandoned or attended without benefit.

Sunday schools … are most scantily supplied with teachers, and can be of use to those only who have learnt something in the day schools. (Engels, 1845, p 140)

Marx's emphasis on polytechnical education was a corrective to the previous emphases by other thinkers: Aristotle on abstract education; Rousseau on 'natural' education; Locke on education for the sons of the nobility. Nevertheless, it raises an array of difficult questions. First, how exactly would that system of education change the dominant class ideology that permeated, as he feared, the school system? His reply might be that the radical changes in society – the abolition of private property, the institution of multi-occupations, payment according to need, and so on – would have created a new dominant ideology in tune with the new socio-economic system. All that the school system had to do was simply to propagate this new ideology. This is logical as far as it goes, but history shows that enforced changes in the structure of society do not necessarily lead to changes in its culture – the structure does not always determine all aspects of the superstructure, certainly not in the short term.

Second, would teachers be full-time professionals or would they, too, submit to the Marxist notion of doing more than one occupation in order to do away with the distinction between mental and manual labour? The Maoist experiment of sending academics to the fields for the harvest was not one of the successes of that regime; and it is equally doubtful whether sending workers to teach for part of their working life only would improve the educational system.

Third, it is not clear how combining theory with practice would work in some subjects. Using philosophy or politics where Marx specialised, what kind of meaningful practice would pupils or students be involved in that would enrich their theoretical development? In the case of politics, Marx might argue that involvement in everyday politics is the answer; after all, he was involved in several of the revolutions of his time. It is more difficult to suggest practical experience in the case of philosophy, classics, history, literature, and so on, particularly for the younger age groups.

Marx's failure to develop a systematic theory of education inevitably led to different and conflicting interpretations of his views among educational sociologists (Sarup, 1978). Nevertheless his views encouraged some interesting social policy debates: the influence of social class on schooling, the relevance of education to economic development, the problem of alienation in schools, the content of teacher training curricula, the question of who trains the trainers, and so on.

Housing

Almost all the writing on housing comes from Engels' work in England and in Germany. He was one of the first to speculate on the nature of social problems, using housing as an example. His thesis was that an undesirable condition may exist for centuries but it is not treated as a social problem by governments unless it satisfies two related criteria: public visibility and upper-class vulnerability.

Inadequate housing had been a feature of all 'oppressed classes' for centuries, he argued (Engels, 1887, p 557), but no government took notice. The industrialisation process of the 18th and 19th centuries, however, witnessed such a massive exodus from the villages to the towns that the inadequate housing conditions of the rural areas were not simply transferred to the cities but concentrated in certain parts of the cities, making the housing problem far more visible than before. What changed the situation politically, however, was, first, the fact that the shortage of housing 'is not confined to the working class but has affected the petty bourgeoisie as well' (Engels, 1887, p 557); and second, as was pointed out earlier, the epidemics of the slums began to threaten the affluent neighbourhoods. Only then, the authorities began to take some palliative action.

In true Marxist style, Engels argues that the housing problem 'is one of the innumerable *smaller*, secondary evils which result from the present-day capitalist mode of production' (Engels, 1887, p 558, author's emphasis). It is just one aspect of the ugly face of capitalism, though capitalism also has a more acceptable face – the fact that it increased 'the productivity of labour a thousandfold' (Engels, 1887, p 564).

Engels' account of the shocking housing conditions in the working-class areas of the cities of England is supported by many government reports. The following is just one of many such accounts:

> In a word, we must confess that in the working-men's dwellings of Manchester, no cleanliness, no convenience, and consequently no comfortable life is possible; that in such dwellings only a physically degenerate race, robbed of all humanity, degraded, reduced morally and physically to bestiality, could feel comfortable and at home. (Engels, 1845, p 96)

Despite this, those with a permanent roof over their heads were to some extent lucky. It was the homeless who bore the worst brunt of the housing problem, particularly the roofless. Homeless people had to look for a bed each night in one of the many lodging-houses in the cities where conditions were even worse:

> These houses are filled with beds from cellar to garret, four, five, six beds in a room; as many as can be crowded in. Into every bed four, five, or six human beings are piled, as many as can be packed in, sick

and well, young and old, drunk and sober, men and women, just as
they come, indiscriminately. (Engels, 1845, pp 64–5)

Engels rejected two explanations of the housing problem that were making the
round in his day: the culture of the poor, and ignorance on behalf of both labour
and capital. As regards the first, he rejected out of hand the attempt to blame the
shocking housing conditions on the drinking, smoking and gambling habits of
working-class people. He argued the exact opposite:

> Under the existing circumstances, drunkenness among the workers
> is a necessary product of their living conditions, just as necessary as
> typhus, crime, vermin, bailiff, and other social ills. (Engels, 1887, p 584)

The claim that labour and capital did not fully realise the implications of bad
housing was nothing more, he argued, 'but the old phrases about the harmony
of interests of labour and capital' (Engels, 1887, p 584). It was nothing more but
an excuse for the absence of any government effort to deal with the problem.

As far as Engels was concerned, the housing problem was, in all its dimensions,
the inevitable result of the capitalist system, concerned with profit maximisation,
irrespective of the ill-effects this might have on the health and welfare of the
workers. The pattern of his discussion on solutions followed naturally from his
account of the causes.

On both practical and ideological grounds, he rejected the suggestion of non-
Marxist socialists that the state and industry should help workers buy their own
houses: not all workers could benefit from such a scheme; home ownership posed
problems in a mobile society with chronic unemployment; and the scheme was
contrary to socialism because of its emphasis on possessiveness. He also disagreed
with those who claimed that owning a house would increase the wealth of
working-class people because for him a house did not constitute disposable wealth
that a person could use. He saw capital as 'the command over the unpaid labour
of others' (Engels, 1887, p 586).

Another suggestion that he disliked was company housing for workers. Such a
scheme had a number of practical difficulties but above all it would undermine
'the revolutionary movement of the urban proletariat' (Engels, 1887, p 570). He
approved of workers' self-help projects but believed that they could cater for a
small minority of workers only.

His analysis of the state in capitalist society led him to the conclusion that
neither local authorities nor central government could or would do much to solve
the housing problem because of opposition from entrenched interests. A certain
amount of 'superficial palliation' could be implemented but no more than that.

> The state is nothing but the organised collective power of the
> possessing classes, the landowners and the capitalists, as against the
> exploited classes, the peasants and the workers. What the individual

capitalists do not want, their state also does not want. (Engels, 1887, p 604)

The solution to the housing problem lay in the abolition of capitalism and the creation of a socialist society. The new socialist state, to begin with, would have to employ some draconian measures: since there were enough dwellings for all, provided they were rationally utilised, he proposed 'the expropriation of the present owners, that is, by quartering in their houses homeless workers or workers excessively overcrowded' (Engels, 1887, p 571).

In the long run, the influx to the towns should be stopped and, in view of the affluence of a communist society, and its distributional principle based on need, the shortage of adequate housing could be corrected. No set of policies could solve the housing problem in a capitalist society, Engels argued, even though reforms may help to ameliorate it a little.

Crime

The thesis that capitalism is the basic cause of all social ills extends to the case of crime. Chronic poverty, induced by the capitalist system, lay at the roots of such behaviour as alcoholism, gambling and crime. Marx and Engels wrote very little about crime but we can, nevertheless, identify two or perhaps three ways in which the capitalist system bred crime, particularly economic crime that was the major form of crime in their day.

First, crime was seen as the result of want. People did not have enough to pay for the necessities of life and were understandably driven to stealing:

> Want leaves the working-man the choice between starving slowly, killing himself speedily, or taking what he needs where he finds it – in plain English stealing. And there is no cause for surprise that most of them prefer stealing to starvation and suicide. (Engels, 1845, p 145)

Second, crime was sometimes seen as a form of rebellion by working-class people against an oppressive, alienating regime. Engels referred to the constant 'social war' that went on between the proletariat and the authorities – crime was part of this ongoing war, alongside the breaking-up of machinery, unofficial strikes, and, more recently, organising trade unions or joining radical political parties. Workers, however, soon realised that stealing as a form of political protest got them nowhere as it brought onto them the full force of the state. Trade unions came to be seen as the better way forward but even so with limited success against an entrenched economic and political system:

> The history of trade unions is a long series of defeats of the working-men, interrupted by a few isolated victories. (Engels, 1845, p 243)

Third, crime was considered as the effect of the demoralisation of a section of the working class that degenerated into a habitual anti-social group – the lumpenproletariat. Marx, in particular, had some harsh words for this group, not because it included among its ranks 'vagabonds, criminals and prostitutes' but because it often served the interests of the capitalist class – 'it furnishes to capital an inexhaustible reservoir of disposable labour-power' (Marx, 1867, p 359).

The treatment of crime by both Marx and Engels is incoherent largely because they did not feel it was a major problem for political economy. Indeed, they felt that the 'institutional crime' committed by the state against working-class people was a more serious problem, even though it went unrecognised because it was a crime of the bourgeoisie, albeit a crime by omission rather than by commission:

> But when society places hundreds of proletarians in such a position that they inevitably meet a too early and unnatural death, one which is quite as much a death by violence as that by the sword or the bullet; when it deprives thousands of the necessaries of life .... knows that these thousands of victims must perish, and yet permits these conditions to remain, its deed is murder just as surely as the deed of the single individual. (Engels, 1845, p 126)

Marx did not consider that crime was an inevitable part of people living together in a society, as others, such as Durkheim, did. He rejected the idea that crime will always exist in any society (Taylor et al, 1973, p 213). He argued that crime might continue in a reduced form during the transitional stage of socialism but it would disappear in a communist society. There would be no economic necessity for it; and people's consciousness would have changed sufficiently to discard any anti-social form of behaviour:

> Without classes and without poverty, crime and laws against crime would wither away, and law would be replaced by self-imposed restraints. (Duncan, 1973, p 190)

Even Marxist criminologists agree that the views of Marx and Engels on the causes of crime leave much to be desired. They could not be seriously seen today as an adequate explanation of crime in affluent societies. What Marx and Engels contributed to our understanding of crime is their treatment of the judicial criminal process as an ideological and repressive arm of the state. Instead of seeing the legal system as a totally impartial code of laws, enforced by a totally disinterested group of judges, one should at least recognise the possibility of class partiality being involved in the process, even if one does not accept the entire Marxist view that the whole legal process is biased towards preserving the capitalist system, as the following quotation suggests:

Moreover, the legal system is an apparatus that is created to secure the interests of the dominant class. Contrary to conventional belief, law is a tool of the ruling class. The legal system provides the mechanism for the forceful and violent control of the population. (Quinney, 1975, pp 192–3)

Conclusion

Marxism put social class at the very centre of its social theory. In the field of welfare, it has been both a major contribution as well as a major handicap. On one hand, the influence of social class in the formulation, administration and delivery of social services has been widely accepted; similarly the connection between one's status in the labour market and one's welfare position when not at work has been well-documented. On the other hand, the exclusive stress on social class has meant that, until recently, the importance of other social divisions – ethnicity, gender, disability, age, and so on – was either ignored or underestimated. It was Marx's strength to introduce class in such debates and it was also his weakness to ignore non-class factors.

Many of Marx's predictions of the future of capitalism have come true but his major prediction has not. Capitalism has become a global force; capital has been concentrated in large multinational organisations; the world is roughly divided between the affluent and the impoverished world; capitalist industrialisation is a major consumer and waster of natural resources; and economics often override politics; as Marx argued. On the other hand, Marx's predictions that capitalism would collapse to be replaced, first, by a socialist and gradually by a communist society have not come true – and this is the principal failure, for it was the major theme and prediction in all the writings and political activities of both Marx and Engels.

The materialist interpretation of history was a major contribution to our understanding of the development of civilisation. It has many weaknesses but it has, nevertheless, made it impossible to ignore the economic or material factors when examining historical or contemporary events, as was the case before Marx. Similarly, the contribution of political figures to historical events was placed by Marx in a far better conceptual framework than was the case before him. The real issue today is how to disentangle the effects of the various factors, let alone attribute to them different weights. In major societal changes this may well be nigh impossible.

Marx's stress on the historically developing character of human nature was broadly correct but again he erred too strongly on the unselfishness and community spirit of individuals; he paid far too little attention to the other side of human nature – personal greed and insatiable desires. The Marxist vision of the distribution of resources according to need corresponds well with the ideals of many religions but, on the evidence so far, it is likely to remain a dream towards which society may strive but, probably, never reach.

The refusal of both Marx and Engels to get involved in the details of their theories and policy proposals has proved a major weakness, for it has created uncertainty and dissension among both their supporters and their opponents. It also stopped them from scrutinising their own grand ideas and allowed them to commit errors that they might not have committed had they paid more attention to details. Often the detail is just as important as the general principle.

During the past few decades, there has been a rejection of Marxism in both theory and policy. It has come to be believed that capitalism can solve the major problems at the global and national level. Yet, a cautionary note is most certainly needed for this over-optimistic assessment of capitalism. It is, to say the least, uncertain whether global poverty, environmental degradation or world migration movements can be solved by unbridled capitalism. It needs to be accepted that 'the major problems of late capitalism require collective solutions' (Hampsher-Monk, 1992, p 560). Moreover, the capitalist emphasis on unlimited consumption may well pose serious problems for the environment.

Marx's views on the centrality of work in human life, the alienating effects of factory employment and the need for personal satisfaction at work have been generally accepted. Working conditions have been improved over the years but it is still an open question whether many workers get much satisfaction from their employment. Marx's belief that the division of labour at work was a handicap to increased productivity has been proved false over the years.

In the field of social welfare provision, the views of both Marx and Engels were neither original nor detailed. Many of their proposals were made by others before them, notably Paine; they have since been introduced as social reforms by governments both of the left and the right, in a gradual way rather than as part of a coherent grand plan. Welfare reforms made capitalism more acceptable to the public, strengthened it as a result and helped it to survive. It is for this reason that many feel that the universal welfare state may well prove to be the nearest point that societies will ever get to Marx's vision of a communist society.

ELEVEN

Positive freedom and state welfare
T.H. Green (1836–82)

By the last quarter of the 19th century, the ideology of laissez-faire was beginning to loosen its grip on government policy in the industrial countries of Europe. Successive governments in England had already introduced considerable legislation that went against the philosophy of government non-intervention in economic and social affairs: factory legislation that restricted the number of hours of work, or attempted to make working conditions less unsafe; public health legislation designed to prevent or limit the effects of epidemics in cities; several education acts that tried to improve the scope and level of education in the country; and legislation that extended the franchise to more groups of the adult male population.

Government intervention in social affairs had truly begun and could not be stopped or reversed, due to the rising political power of the emerging working class, if for no other reason. There was, thus, an urgent need for a new dominant ideology to encourage and legitimise government intervention in public affairs. The two new ideologies – Marxism and socialism – could not fill the gap because their demands were totally unacceptable to the ruling groups of society as well as to many groups of the populace, for they both demanded the abolition of the capitalist system itself, though in different ways. Green's ideas were a response to this need and filled the gap admirably – they pointed the way towards the reform but not the abolition of capitalism. Green's argument was for a welfare liberal society or, in today's language, for a welfare capitalist society, a welfare state of a sort.

Green was a liberal by political conviction, a university professor of philosophy by profession and a political activist at the local level. He aimed his philosophy as much at academia as at the political establishment of his party – it had the ambitious aim of not merely explaining the world but of changing it, too, to use Marx's notable phrase. It is a mistake, however, to put too much emphasis on the role of ideas as the force behind the reforms that have led up to today's welfare state. The first major welfare reforms in Europe were introduced not by a left-wing but by a right-wing politician, Chancellor Bismarck of Germany, in an effort to undermine the political radicalism of the working class.

Positive freedom

The centrepiece of Green's political theory was the concept of positive freedom. The classical liberal view, beginning with Locke, saw freedom as the absence of government intervention in public affairs, as a buttress against despotism. Human beings, it was argued, possessed a right to be free, to carry on with their affairs without government intervention and oppression. Individuals and institutions, added Smith, should be free to manufacture and to trade freely without government regulations. It was a view of freedom that came to be known as negative freedom, or as freedom from, as opposed to positive freedom.

Green acknowledged the contribution that the negative notion of freedom had made to the welfare of citizens in the past – it enabled the development of democracy in Western Europe. At the same time, however, it also legitimised the exploitation of the weak by the strong in society. A labour contract agreed 'freely' between employer and worker, for example, would in effect give the upper hand to the employer, bearing in mind the unequal economic and social power possessed by the two sides. As evidence of this, Green pointed to the long hours of work, unsafe working conditions and low wages of children, women and men in factories. The freedom of parents to do as they pleased with their children often meant severe child cruelty in the family and many children being sent to work in order to enhance the family wage rather than being sent to school, as the law required. More controversially, the freedom of the individual to drink as much as they liked sometimes resulted in alcoholism, with inevitable grave consequences for the individual, their family and society at large.

By the second half of the 19th century, the major threat to human welfare in Britain was not despotism but naked exploitation and poverty. Green was perceptive enough to realise this and, as a result, he was led to the belief that the notion of freedom did not mean, merely, the absence of coercion in life:

> We do not mean merely freedom from restraint or compulsion. We do not mean merely freedom to do as we like irrespectively of what it is that we like. We do not mean a freedom that can be enjoyed by one man or one set of men at the cost of a loss of freedom to others. (Green, 1890b, pp 370–1)

Total absence of government intervention in public affairs was, of course, never advocated by anyone outside the anarchist movement. Even Smith, the first major advocate of laissez-faire, supported government intervention in several aspects of life, as we saw in Chapter 8. What was at issue, therefore, was the degree of government intervention and the justification for it. Green was neither a socialist nor a laissez-faire advocate – he occupied a position between the two. He, therefore, believed that negative freedom should be supplemented, but not supplanted, by positive freedom. It is the combination of these two types of freedom that is the hallmark of his ideal society.

But what is positive freedom? Green uses the notion of positive freedom in two related senses: the ability of the individual to realise his or her capacities to the full; and the ability of the individual to contribute to the common good as a result of self-realisation. Unlike negative freedom, which is an individualistic concept, positive freedom is a social concept – the achievement of negative freedom is aimed at enhancing primarily the welfare of the individual concerned, while the implementation of positive freedom aims at benefiting both the individual and the other members of society:

> When we speak of freedom as something to be so highly prized, we mean a positive power or capacity of doing or enjoying something worth doing or enjoying, and that, too, something that we do or enjoy in common with others. We mean by it a power which each man exercises through the help or security given him by his fellow-men, and which he in turn helps to secure for them. (Green, 1890b, p 371)

Government intervention in public affairs is absolutely necessary if the individual is to be enabled to fulfil his capacities to the full, according to Green. He accepts that the application of positive freedom can restrict the negative freedom of some individuals but it enhances the negative freedom of many others. The provision of compulsory and free education for all by the state, for example, may curtail the freedom of those individuals who are opposed to it in principle or who have to pay taxes against their wishes to finance education, but it enhances the freedom of all those who benefit from education as well as society in general. Government legal coercion is a necessary evil in the midst of a plethora of private forms of coercion.

> The justification of legal coercion is precisely that it offsets and neutralises other forms of coercion which are less tolerable. (Sabine, 1963, p 734)

The distinguishing mark of a truly free society, according to Green, is not merely the absence of government coercion but the enabling of the majority of individuals to fulfil their capacities to the full to the benefit of all. Green had no objection in principle to the view that this enabling is best done by individuals themselves, though in practice he felt it was unlikely to happen – 'we must take men as we find them', he cautioned. Those few employers, for example, who were willing to introduce good labour standards voluntarily ought to welcome government legislation as 'a powerful friend', for it made life easier for them and protected them against unscrupulous employers who would not follow the voluntary road. Similarly, he did not believe that charities had the resources or the authority to replace the state in enabling individuals to fulfil themselves, bearing in mind the low living and educational standards of the majority of the population. It may well be that the day would come, he argued, when living and educational standards would be high enough so that state intervention could be replaced by voluntary effort but for the time being it was not only an unrealistic proposal but a socially destructive one, too:

> Left to itself, or to the operation of casual benevolence, a degraded population perpetuates and increases itself. (Green, 1890, p 376)

Green also rejected the argument that state legislation weakened self-reliance and increased state dependency. Indeed, he claimed that the social legislation of previous decades had achieved the opposite – strengthened the spirit of independence and self-reliance in society. By removing some of the worst social abuses, social legislation enabled its beneficiaries to gain more self-confidence than they had before:

> The dead weight of ignorance and unhealthy surroundings, with which
> it would otherwise have had to struggle, being partially removed by law,
> it was more free to exert itself for higher objects. (Green, 1890b, p 386)

Green's view of positive freedom became the rallying cry, the rhetorical justification, for social reform in Britain for decades. The two major social reform periods in Britain were the Liberal government's reforms in social security during 1908–14 and the Labour government's establishment of the welfare state during 1945–48. On both occasions, the spirit of positive freedom was used as a justification for the changes, as the following two quotations show.

Asquith, a follower of Green and the Liberal Prime Minister during 1908–16, had this to say in one of his speeches as Home Secretary in 1892:

> I am one of those who believe that the collective action of the
> community may and ought to be employed positively as well as
> negatively, to raise as well as to level; to equalise opportunities no less
> than to curtail privileges; to make freedom of the individual a reality
> and not a pretence. (Quoted in Wempe, 2004, p 195)

Fifty years later when plans for the post-war welfare reforms were hotly debated in Britain, an editorial in *The Times* on 1 July 1940 appealed again to the spirit of positive freedom to galvanise public opinion in support of major reforms:

> If we speak of democracy, we do not mean democracy which maintains
> the right to vote but forgets the right to work and the right to live. If
> we speak of freedom, we do not mean a rugged individualism which
> excludes social organisation and economic planning. If we speak of
> equality, we do not mean a political equality, nullified by social and
> economic privilege. If we speak of economic reconstruction, we think
> less of maximum production (though this too will be required) than
> of equitable distribution. (Quoted in George and Wilding, 1976, p v)

The notion of positive freedom has inevitably had its critics. Berlin's work is the best-known, the most perceptive and worth discussing in some detail. He agrees with many of Green's comments on negative freedom: first that it was used by the strong and the unscrupulous in society against the weak and the humane. In his words: 'Freedom for the wolves has often meant death for the sheep' (p xlv);

second, that without a minimum standard of living in society, negative freedom is 'of little or no value to those who may theoretically possess it. For what are rights without the power to implement them?' (Berlin, 1969, p xlvi). Third, and as a result of the previous two arguments, the case for government intervention to achieve a national minimum standard for all 'is overwhelmingly strong' (Berlin, 1969, p xlvi).

Nevertheless, Berlin insists that negative freedom is the basic value while positive freedom is an important addition to it. This is the lesson of history, he argues, even though in contemporary democratic societies it may be thought otherwise:

> The fundamental sense of freedom is freedom from chains, from imprisonment, from enslavement by others. The rest is extension of this sense, or else a metaphor. (Berlin, 1969, p lvi)

Berlin is critical of Green for being far too vague about the extent of government intervention implied in his notion of positive freedom. As we shall see later, there is some justification in this even though Green's actual proposals for government intervention did not amount to much. Berlin fears that a government that takes to heart the idea of positive freedom can become so omnipotent as to be oppressive, even though in a well-meaning way. Generally, he wrote:

> all paternalistic governments, however benevolent, cautious, disinterested and rational, have tended, in the end, to treat the majority of men as minors, or as being too often incurably foolish or irresponsible. (Berlin, 1969, p lxii)

Interestingly enough, Green, too, had voiced this fear of an omnipotent central government, and he always preferred the provision of services to be in the hands of local authorities.

In brief, Green rightly argued that negative freedom at both the individual and the state level gave priority to self-interest while positive freedom stressed the collective interest, with different implications for the different classes in society (Dimova-Cookson, 2003, p 513). In everyday life, however, the real issue today is not a choice between negative and positive freedom but the degree of each, the manner in which they interconnect, and the way in which they are expressed and administered in government policies.

The common good

Green's notion of positive freedom could only thrive in a society that placed the common good above individual and sectional interests. Positive freedom and the common good are causally interrelated, for each benefits from as well as promotes the other. Like Rousseau's general will, Green's common good is hard to define but, in general, it refers to a societal situation where each individual pursues his self-realisation to the benefit of himself and to the benefit of others, and where he is assisted by others and by the state to realise his abilities. The principle of self-realisation is not simply an individual but a collective goal – this is why it is closely connected with the principle of non-exploitation. These two principles, according to Simhony, form the moral basis of Green's societal structure (Simhony, 1989).

Through the notion of the common good, Green was attempting to construct a moral framework in which self-interest and benevolence could be combined in both the actions of individuals and the policies pursued by the state. Central to this moral goal was the idea of mutual interdependence in society, when human beings treat each other as equals, not as means but as ends. In Green's words:

> it is only in the intercourse of men, each recognised by each as an end, not merely as a means, and thus having reciprocal claims, that the capacity (that is, of conceiving himself and the bettering of his life as an end to himself) is actualised and that we really live as persons. (Green, 1883, sec 183, quoted in Simhony, 1993, p 230)

Green acknowledged the problems and the dilemmas involved in the implementation of the common good. He understood that the social divisions of British society made the acceptance of the common good as a guiding principle difficult; he accepted that human beings can be both selfish and benevolent; but he believed that since human beings are above all rational, they would come to realise and to accept that mutual social interdependence is to the benefit of all. In the final analysis, he wrote, 'where the selfishness of man has proposed, his better reason has disposed' (Green, 1883, sec 216, quoted in Carter, 2003, p 31).

He combined his notion of the common good with a social approach to the notion of rights. He rejected the claim by previous liberal writers that rights are either given to human beings by God or that they are somehow part of their nature as human beings. Instead, he argued that rights are social creations; that men and women have rights only as members of the same society; that the possession of rights is based on the acknowledgement that others possess the same rights, too; and that the individual who demands the satisfaction of his or her rights must agree that others, too, have a right to the fulfilment of their rights. Rights only make sense in a society where human beings recognise one another as equal and behave accordingly:

> Rights do not belong to individuals as they might be in a state of nature, or as they might be if each acted independently of the others. They belong to them as members of a society in which each recognises the other as an originator of action in the same sense in which he is conscious of being so himself, and thus regards the free exercise of his own powers as dependent upon allowing an equally free exercise of his powers to every other member of society. (Green, 1890a, p 449)

Like freedom, rights are of two kinds: negative rights that secure the individual's negative equality before the law, and positive rights that secure the individual's positive freedom in the access to minimum standards of living. Both types of rights are important, though Green stresses more the second than the first in the same way that he stresses positive over negative freedom. In effect, Green's work is associated with the idea of social rights rather than with the idea of legal or political rights, which belong to Locke and others before Green.

Inherent in Green's conception of social rights is the idea of social duties. An individual has the right to expect the assistance of others, through the state, in his efforts for self-realisation but he also has a duty to respond in similar ways to the efforts and needs of others. Green does not go so far as to stress duties over rights but it is difficult to understand his ideas on rights without involving the idea of duties in society.

The strength of Green's conception of social rights is that it highlights human interdependence, mutual help and a government commitment to make the fulfilment of rights possible. They are not merely abstract notions to be invoked from time to time in order to defend a position or to make certain claims on society – they are a major force in conducting the affairs of a society. Working together, people construct their society, from which they all benefit, even though unequally.

Green's conception of rights, however, suffers from a major weakness – what happens when the majority in society do not recognise the rights of a minority group even to exist, as happened, for example, in Nazi Germany? As Thomas puts it: 'Did Jewish rights depend on their explicit legal endorsement by the Third Reich?' (Thomas, 1987, p 351). Although Green recognised the problems posed by social divisions in society, he seemed to have based his ideas about rights on social harmony. As one of his sympathetic critics has put it:

> For Green conflicts of interest, and indeed of duties, are apparent, not real. This flies in the face of the economic fact of scarcity. (Simhony, 1991, p 319)

Green's claim that human beings are equal should not be understood to mean equality of outcome, for he never advocated – indeed, he opposed – any measures to achieve such a state of affairs. What he had in mind was equality of opportunity but of a special kind. Normally, equality of opportunity means the equal chance of everyone to fulfil his or her abilities and to benefit from that. Green may have been happy with the first but not with the second part of this statement. People should have an equal chance to fulfil themselves not for their sole benefit but so that both they and their fellow citizens should benefit. He accepted inequalities in principle but qualified this acceptance by insisting that such inequalities should be shown to benefit society – 'inequalities were justifiable only if they served the common good' (Carter, 2003, p 35). The problem with such a statement is that there are competing ways of assessing the condition that inequalities should serve the common good. Many on the right, for example, have claimed over the years that inequalities generated by the market always serve the common good because they encourage hard work, self-reliance and the spirit of enterprise.

Self-realisation, according to Green, depends on both the person's internal abilities and the external conditions prevailing in society. People with severe mental disabilities will not be able to reach normal societal standards, however good society's structural opportunities may be. Vice versa, slaves and women, despite their high internal abilities, never managed to reach the educational level of men over the centuries prior to Green because of discrimination against them. Self-realisation is, therefore, only possible when normal internal abilities and favourable external conditions combine.

Green, like many others before him, fails to bring out the complex interrelationships between internal abilities and external conditions that affect a person's social achievements. He does not acknowledge that a person's abilities can be partly due to the social conditions and family life he finds himself in; hence, if governments wish to provide equal opportunities for self-development they may well have to apply measures that discriminate positively in favour of the socially weak groups in society – as was acknowledged by governments in Britain during the 1970s with the introduction of positive discrimination in primary schools. What Green does well is to stress that it is the responsibility of governments to provide the conditions that enable all individuals alike to fulfil themselves in a non-exploiting way so that not only they benefit but their fellow citizens benefit, too, or at least they do not lose out.

The interventionist state

Green's argument for more government intervention in social affairs is based on his firm belief that both the feudal and the capitalist economic system had served the interests of a small class at the expense of the mass of the population. Indeed, he wondered whether the 'underfed denizen of a London yard' was that much better off than the slave of Athens had been. All this injustice had been perpetrated on what he thought was the perverse argument that the state should not interfere in the contracts freely entered into between employers and workers, landlords and tenants, ignoring the unequal bargaining power between the two parties:

> No contract is valid in which human persons, willingly or unwillingly, are dealt with as commodities, because such contracts of necessity defeat the end for which alone society enforces contracts at all. (Green, 1890b, p 373)

The state had a duty to rectify this situation so as to enable each individual to enjoy both the material and the spiritual wealth of their country. It is only when people are in a position to benefit from the material and spiritual progress of their country that true citizenship can be said to exist for all. Only then can the state expect all its citizens to behave in ways that are in line with the common good. There is no point in the state trying to make ordinary people behave in morally correct ways through force. This would be both oppressive and counterproductive. Rather, the duty of the state is to remove those obstacles in life that make it difficult for people to behave morally, to treat one another as equal, to be mutually helpful to one another and to fulfil themselves. In his words:

> the effectual action of the state, that is, the community acting through law, for the promotion of habits of true citizenship, seems necessarily to be confined to the removal of obstacles. (Green, 1890a, pp 514–5)

Green's list of areas where the state should intervene by removing obstacles covered work, education, property, family, crime and alcoholism. It was not a long list of obstacles because he believed, like Marx, that future generations would have their own agenda. He was only concerned with the pressing matters of his day.

Policies at work

Green did not accept the then prevailing economic view that labour is a commodity to be bought and sold just like any other commodity without any government interference or regulation. He believed that labour is different from other commodities in the sense that it 'attaches in a particular manner to the person of the man' and it was therefore both necessary and legitimate for the government to regulate its sale and use 'in order to prevent labour from being sold under conditions which make it impossible for the person selling it ever to become a free contributor to social good in any form' (Green, 1890b, p 373). Unregulated labour markets cannot contribute to the common good, and may even undermine it, he maintained.

Society is quite within its rights to intervene in the case of men, women and children working in unsafe and insanitary conditions that are detrimental to health. He warned that the health of the worker is not simply an individual concern but a public issue as well. Private injuries become public issues under these circumstances, in Green's estimation:

> Every injury to the health of the individual is, so far as it goes, a public injury. (Green, 1890b, p 373)

He also believed that the state was justified in prohibiting the employment of women or young persons beyond certain hours because it demonstrably resulted in 'physical deterioration' and 'a lowering of the moral forces of society' (Green, 1890b, p 373). Interestingly enough, he did not include men in this, either because they were considered the breadwinners of the family, or because he subscribed to the view that men were able to look after themselves on this.

He applied the same logic of the justification of government intervention in the case of 'the purchase or hire of unwholesome dwellings'. The health of residents of such dwellings would suffer. The object of any moral society, he argued, was to enable individuals to make the best of themselves, in a collective manner; and this could only be achieved if all contracts of service that went against this principle were prohibited by law – 'the deliberate voice of society' (Green, 1890b, p 373). He was certain that ordinary men and women would welcome such legislation in the same way that they welcomed previous similar legislation.

Education

If the first duty of the state was to improve the health and safety of the working class, its second duty was to get the working class 'out of the pub and into the classroom' (McClelland, 1996, p 512). Like all writers reviewed so far, Green valued the contribution of education on the usual economic, political, social and moral grounds, though he, perhaps, stressed the latter most. He rejected the view that it was the responsibility of the parents to decide whether their children went to school or not. On such an issue, the state was justified in overriding parental authority because the lack of education harmed society as a whole. An uneducated individual, he maintained, 'is as effectually crippled as by a loss of a limb or a broken constitution. He is not free to develop his faculties', to the detriment of himself and of society (Green, 1890b, pp 373–4).

Green had a good knowledge of the workings of the educational system, partly because of the active interest he took in the affairs of several schools and partly because he served as assistant commissioner on the Royal Commission on Education of 1864. He spent some time interviewing and talking to headmasters, teachers, guardians and parents, as well as writing reports on education.

Beginning with elementary education, he accepted that the number of children going to school increased considerably during the century and would increase at a much faster rate as a result of the Education Act of 1870 that made elementary education free and compulsory for all children. It was the quality of elementary education that worried him most. Most elementary schools were grossly under-provided for and in many of them, he remarked, 'the only apparatus of instruction was often the stick' (Green, 1890c, p 415). The net result was that the majority of children leaving school at 13 may have been able to sign their name but they were 'without anything like a complete command of the elementary arts of reading, writing, and calculating' (Green 1890c, p 450).

Secondary and university education were determined more by the parents' ability to pay, by 'the accidents of birth and wealth' (Green, 1890d, p 461) than by the children's intellectual talents or interests. The result was not only an educational disaster but a social one, too. Secondary schooling both reflected and reinforced the class divisions of the country. The best secondary schools attracted pupils from the affluent sections of society and, in turn, provided the students for the two most prestigious universities of the country – Oxford and Cambridge – that became the repository of class privilege. Green accepted that social class distinctions inevitably exist in any society but he lamented the fact that 'in England these separations have been fixed and deepened by the fact that there has been no fusion of class with class in school or at the university' (Green, 1890d, p 458).

He supported the reform proposal by several Government Commissions and by individuals for a 'ladder in education' stretching from the elementary school to the university – a unified system of state education:

> He wished to straighten out the tangle of endowed schools, charity schools, schools run for commercial profit, and to establish a national system of secondary education, national standards, and national inspection. (Brinton, 1962, p 221)

He tried to allay fears that such a ladder of education would lead to a levelling down rather than levelling up – one of the main objections to the reform of education voiced at the time:

> A properly organised system of schools would level up without levelling down. It would not make the gentleman any less of a gentleman in the higher sense of the term, but it would cure him of his unconscious social insolence just as it would cure others of social jealousy. (Green, 1890d, p 460)

At the base of the ladder, the elementary school would be compulsory and free to all up to the age of 13. After that, there would be those secondary schools that took children up to the age of 16, when they would leave and 'be put into some business'; the last rung on the ladder would take children up to the age of 18, when 'they will pass on to the universities' (Green, 1890c, p 460). Since secondary schooling would not be free, it was necessary to have a system of bursaries for those children who excelled at the exams and whose parents could not pay. Bursaries would also be used in the same manner for universities, the number of which should be increased to accommodate the demand from the rising middle classes.

The 'ladder of education' would have not only educational but social and moral benefits as well. Green believed that when children rub shoulders at school, they would be less snobbish as adults, social divisions would become less sharp and the common good would benefit:

> Common education is the true social leveller. Men and women who have been at school together, or who have been at schools of the same sort, will always understand each other, will always be at ease together, will be free from social jealousies and animosities however different their circumstances in life may be. (Green, 1890d, pp 457–8)

Despite this strong emphasis on the all-round value of education, Green did not recommend government finance of secondary education, let alone of universities. He relied on private finance and on charitable bursaries despite the fact that he considered charitable funding inefficient.

From today's standpoint, Green can be easily criticised for setting ambitious educational targets without willing the financial means to achieve them. This would be too harsh a judgement of him, because he was aware of the futility of any such financial proposals. He pointed out that the recommendations for an education ladder, even without government financial support, by previous government reports had come to nothing because 'there was no developed popular knowledge or opinion ... strong enough to countervail the vested interests which the enactment of these recommendations at least seemed to threaten' (Green, 1890e, p 388).

He also knew that many upper-class families would not send their children to the state elementary schools but he looked forward to the day when 'most of our elementary schools will become, as many of them are already, places where children might be sent without scruple from the most refined and carefully managed homes' (Green, 1890d, p 462). He, therefore, would argue that his financial proposals for a system of bursaries was the only politically realistic proposal of his time.

Green's vision of a ladder of education, free and compulsory for all, did not materialise in Britain until the educational reform of 1945, supporting the view that social reform is usually piecemeal but, nevertheless, the 'utopias' of one period can become the realities of another. Change is usually gradual but, cumulatively, over a long period, it can achieve the unthinkable.

Wealth and poverty

Green had no objection, in principle, to property or wealth, because he believed that it was the inevitable result of the different abilities and efforts of private individuals. This was particularly the case with the new class of factory owners and businessmen more than with the aristocratic landowners, many of whom obtained their land by force or royal favour in the first place:

> Considered as representing the conquest of nature by the effort of free
> and variously gifted individuals, property must be unequal. (Green,
> 1890a, p 527)

But though private property, whether in land, factory or business, is acceptable, it must not be used in such a way as to make it impossible for others either to amass wealth or to hold property. When this happens 'it may be truly said that "property is theft"' (Green, 1890a, p 526), and it justifies government intervention to rectify the situation. He believed, however, that the concentration of industrial and commercial wealth was not so heavy as to debar wage-earners from amassing wealth and becoming capitalists themselves:

> There is nothing in the fact that their labour is hired in great masses by great capitalists to prevent them from being on a small scale capitalists themselves. (Green, 1890a, p 531)

Indeed, he pointed out that this had already happened in the case of many skilled workers in the better-paid industries. Many such workers 'do become capitalists, to the extent often of owning their houses, and a good deal of furniture, of having an interest in stores, and of belonging to benefit-societies through which they make provision for the future' (Green, 1890a, p 531). His definition of 'capitalist' is rather idiosyncratic, however, for on that definition the majority of the population in contemporary advanced industrial societies would be classified as capitalists. What, perhaps, he had in mind was that the economic system was not totally closed, that it was not a caste system and that small-scale upward social mobility was possible through hard work and enterprise.

Green viewed wealth in the form of land owned by the aristocracy, however, very differently from industrial wealth for three reasons. To begin with, aristocrats came to own their vast estates not through hard work but either through force or as a reward for services rendered to the Crown – 'the original landlords have been conquerors' (Green, 1890a, p 532). Secondly, while industrial and commercial wealth was potentially unlimited, land was, by its very nature, limited in area. As he put it: while 'the increased wealth of one man does not naturally mean the diminished wealth of another', there is a natural limit to the amount of land (Green, 1890a, p 530). The concentration of land in a few hands, therefore, made it impossible for others to become landowners. Thirdly, the custom of primogeniture whereby the estates of a deceased aristocrat went to the eldest son meant that land remained concentrated over the years. There was, thus, a strong case for government intervention in the management and inheritance of land.

He rejected out of hand any suggestion for land nationalisation. He followed Aristotle, whom he admired, to argue that private ownership serves the common good better than state ownership: In his words:

> the earth as appropriated by individuals under certain conditions becomes more serviceable to society as a whole, including those who are not proprietors of the soil, than if it were held in common. (Green, 1890a, p 533)

If land was to remain in private hands, it had to abide by certain rules that would make it more productive as well as more widely held. First, the system of primogeniture should be abolished not only because it was inefficient but also because it perpetuated economic and political power, fostered arrogance and 'hindered the formation of that mainstay of social order and contentment, a class of proprietors tilling their own land' (Green 1890b, p 378). Second, the state had a duty to intervene and to modify the conditions included in the contracts between landlords and their tenants because, as in the case of wage-earners and employers, these contracts reflected the unequal power between the two parties and operated against the best interests of the tenants. Eviction was the fate of any tenant who did not agree with the contracts drawn up by his landlord. Third, the state could not allow the owners to do as they pleased with their land because of its very special social nature. The state should both have a say in the use made of the land by its owners as well as have the power to compulsorily purchase any land that it needed for public purposes, provided it compensated generously its owners – as it had, indeed, done on a grand scale in the building of roads and railways.

In brief, Green wanted industry, commerce and agriculture to remain in private hands but to be used with the common good in mind. He believed that the laws of the country, however, had allowed both the landlords and the employers far too much freedom of action at the expense of the workers, the labourers and the land tenants. The result was all too clear for all to see:

> Their health, housing, and schooling were unprovided for. They were
> left to be freely victimised by deleterious employments, foul air, and
> consequent craving for deleterious drinks. (Green, 1890a, p 534)

It was, therefore, no surprise that poverty was so widespread in 19th-century Britain. Green does not deal with the issue of poverty directly, but it is clear from his other writings that he considered it a social and moral evil that needed to be abolished. His belief in equality of opportunity, his stress on self-realisation and non-exploitation, the central place of the common good in his philosophy, his tendency to liken the impoverished of London with the slaves of Classical Athens – all these and other aspects of his work clearly show his strong objection to poverty.

He saw the causes of poverty in the practices of competitive capitalist accumulation and in the feudalist practices of the landed aristocracy. He referred several times to the fact that laissez-faire capitalism with its relentless emphasis on competition meant that the poor 'are left to sink or swim in the stream of unrelenting competition, in which we admit that the weaker has not a chance' (Green, 1883, sec 245, quoted in Carter, 2003, p 39). Unlike Marx, he did not believe that poverty was the inevitable result of capitalism – rather of the remnants of the feudal 'legacy from the middle ages' (Richter, 1964, p 274), and of the practices of laissez-faire capitalism. His whole philosophy was based on the strong belief that government intervention could rectify the excesses of capitalism.

He viewed the poverty of the tenant farmer as the result of feudalism rather than capitalism, despite the fact that feudalism had disappeared by his time. The state had allowed landlords a free hand in the running of their estates with the result that they exploited their tenant farmers in the same way that employers exploited their workers. Poverty among the rural population 'is really due to the arbitrary and violent manner in which rights over land have been acquired and exercised, and to the failure of the state to fulfil those functions which under a system of unlimited private ownership are necessary to maintain the conditions of free life' (Green, 1890a, p 534).

He saw poverty as the result of structural factors beyond the individual's making or control. The solution to poverty, therefore, lay through the political process: parliament should enact legislation to alleviate the exploitation of workers and farmers, to improve their working and living conditions. He stressed the importance of the franchise not only as good in itself but also because he felt that until parliament ceases to be 'a rich man's club', workers would find it impossible to witness reforms that would remove the barriers towards their self-realisation. In addition, he also believed that the strengthening of trade unions, benefit societies and public participation in the affairs of the community would also help in dealing with the problem of poverty.

Green avoided entering into any details about the social measures necessary to deal with poverty. Only in the case of education did he set out any of the details of the programme which he had in mind – making elementary education compulsory and free, and providing bursaries for secondary and university education. He said nothing about the kind and level of social security measures needed to deal with poverty; the housing or public health measures needed to improve the nation's health; and so on. He confined himself to setting out the principles of reform and even at this level he was not always clear. He had a tendency to retreat 'into a cloud of qualifications' (Thomas, 1987, p 341) because of the diversity of human situations.

Again unlike Marx, Green was very hopeful that parliamentary democracy was capable of rectifying the excesses of capitalism and thus improving the living conditions of the general public. He did not support violence to achieve political ends in societies where people had the right to vote – to elect and to change their governments. Although he did not approve of capitalism as it stood, he did not want to see its overthrow either.

Green was at one with Marx, however, in viewing the economy in absolutist and simplistic terms – private versus state ownership rather than in the more complex ways of modern life:

> No doubt, he underestimated the complexity of modern economic life. In posing the alternatives of complete socialism or complete private enterprise, he is presenting an unreal choice. (Milne, 1962, p 158)

Drunkenness

Green was very preoccupied with the temperance issue, the social problem of drunkenness that afflicted working-class people of his time. Despite the fact that there were already licensing laws concerning the sale and consumption of alcoholic drinks, he believed that they were ineffective and needed considerable strengthening. What the existing legislation did was not so much to reduce the consumption of alcohol in the public houses but 'to prevent the drink-shops from coming unpleasantly near the houses of the well-to-do people, and to crowd them upon the quarters occupied by the poorer classes, who have practically no power of keeping the nuisance from them' (Green, 1890b, p 383). Working-class people drank to excess in their own neighbourhoods and annoyed their own communities.

Drunkenness was not simply a private problem; it was also a public issue, for it affected the welfare of the whole society. To begin with, drunkenness created 'social nuisance' in, mainly, working-class areas; secondly, it led to 'the impoverishment and degradation of all members of the family' (Green, 1890b, p 383); thirdly, it meant 'an injury to others in health, purse, and capability' (Green, 1890b, p 383); and, fourthly, heavy drinking habits 'do lay a heavy burden on the free development of man's powers for social good, a heavier burden probably than arises from all other preventable causes put together' (Green, 1890b, p 383). There was, of course, no disagreement on the damaging effects of heavy drinking; what difference of opinion existed was what, if anything, should be done about it.

Green rejected out of hand the objection that further tightening of the licensing laws meant more loss of individual freedom. He argued, first, that liberty never meant that people had the right to do as they please irrespective of the consequences of their actions on themselves and on others; and, second, that further limitation of people's tendency to drink heavily was 'in the interest of general freedom', that is, in people's ability to fulfil themselves to their benefit and to that of their fellow citizens (Green, 1890b, p 382). Some rights take precedence over others.

He had some sympathy with the view that people would grow out of the habit of heavy drinking as their living standards improved, but he did not accept that this was a better solution because it would be in line with individual liberty and it would also be a more secure and longer-lasting solution. He agreed that people's drinking habits reflect to some extent their daily life experiences:

> Better education, better housing, more healthy rules of labour, no doubt lessen the temptations to drink for those who have the benefits of these advantages. (Green, 1890b, p 385)

He felt, however, that this was a very long-term and dangerous strategy, for it did not guarantee success. In the meantime, the number of people afflicted by heavy drinking would increase while the political power of the drink industry would strengthen, making any legislation that much more difficult. Besides, he did not accept that one had to choose between legislation and the rise in living standards to deal with the problem, for they complemented each other. His difficulty was to decide what kind of legislation was necessary and enforceable, bearing in mind his view that it was futile to try to implement legislation that had no public support. He, therefore, suggested the more stringent rules of licensing that were required should be made a local responsibility by empowering 'the householders in each district of excluding the sale of intoxicants altogether from among them' (Green, 1890b, p 383). He hoped that placing the responsibility on the shoulders of the local community was a more effective way of dealing with the problem than leaving it to the central government. As in other areas of social legislation, Green was suspicious of central government partly because he feared it might become omnipotent and partly because he felt that public participation could best be exercised at the local level. This led him to put his trust in the local community without considering the problems arising from such a local scheme – some local communities might not take up the challenge; people might decide to walk the short distance between a prohibiting and a permissive local community for their drink; and so on.

Gender equality

Green's basic philosophy was most conducive to gender equality. The foundations of his philosophy – equality of opportunity, non-exploitation, the common good for all irrespective of class, ethnicity and gender – logically amounted to a non-sexist approach to gender issues. Yet Green wrote very little directly on gender and what he did write about gender issues was in the context of other issues which were more important to him.

Beginning with marriage, he argued for the equality of husband and wife, father and mother. He saw the family as the ideal context to inculcate the values that were necessary in the wider society that practised the common good. In the same way that a citizen's rights are counterbalanced by the rights of other citizens, so the rights of one spouse must acknowledge the rights of the other. Rights and duties go together in both the family and the wider society. He pointed out that the essential principle in a household was that 'the claims of the husband and wife are throughout reciprocal', which, in turn, meant that only monogamous marriage was acceptable (Green, 1890a, p 541). In a polygamous marriage, equality of husband and wife was impossible – the wife is 'a mere instrument of the husband's pleasure' (Green, 1890a, p 543).

He considered marriage to be a partnership for life – 'a unity in all interests and for the whole of a lifetime' (Green, 1890a, p 548) – and, hence, divorce was to be granted on very rare occasions. The only ground for divorce that he accepted was adultery on the part of either the wife or the husband, for he believed that there was nothing to be gained by prolonging a marriage in which one of the partners was 'unfaithful' to the other. This was a fairly radical proposal, for divorce on the grounds of adultery did not become legally possible in England until 1923 and later in many other countries.

Green was far more cautious about agreeing to cruelty being used on a par with adultery as a ground for divorce because he felt that there are degrees of cruelty, and because he feared that it could be used intentionally by one of the partners to obtain a divorce thus encouraging marriage break-up. He was prepared, however, to concede that where the degree and kind of cruelty was such as to destroy family life, 'in the interests of the children, who ought in such a case to be chiefly concerned, divorce implied less wrong than the maintenance of the marriage tie'

(Green, 1890b, pp 548–9). He was uncertain about mental illness, or 'lunacy' as it was then generally called, being used as a ground for divorce because of the ups and downs of the illness and the difficulties this posed for making rational decisions on divorce. He was, however, quite certain that incompatibility of the married partners was too flimsy a reason and should not be used as a ground of divorce – it would merely encourage incompatibility among those who wanted a divorce.

Green was usually opposed to generalisations because he felt that human situations are complex and each should be decided on its merits. He, thus, finished his discussion on divorce on the cautious note that in deciding grounds for divorce, apart from incompatibility, 'discretion should be allowed to a well-constituted court' (Green, 1890b, p 549). By today's standards, Green's views on divorce look ordinary, but by the standards of his period, they were certainly progressive.

Equally enlightened were his views on the education of girls. He supported the compulsory and free elementary education for both boys and girls, which was implemented in the Education Act of 1870. On secondary education, he championed the establishment of endowed high schools for girls on the same basis as those already in existence for boys. He was sure that such schools would not only prove successful in themselves but they would also stimulate educational standards in other secondary schools for girls. Finally, he supported, campaigned for and initiated measures that promoted the expansion of admission policies for girls to universities for he was sure that competition in education was good for girls, as it was for boys.

His progressive stand on many gender issues and his marriage into a family of feminist views brought him into the inner circle of the feminist group of the time. He was a frequent speaker to gatherings and seminars on feminist issues, 'often worked side by side with a feminist network that included not only moderates ... but radical campaigners' on such issues as education, divorce, prostitution, employment, and so on (Anderson, 1991, p 680).

On the issue of the franchise for women, however, Green remained silent despite his view that political power was integral to human dignity as well to the achievement of political ends. He advocated the participation of men and women at the local government level because he viewed local government as most significant to people's lives. There is nothing, however, in his writings to indicate support or otherwise for the right of women to vote in parliamentary elections, even though the gist of his theory would indicate support for that.

All in all, Green has to be seen as an advocate of non-sexist policies at both the personal and the political level. His philosophy and work 'entitle him to be included among the very diverse band of later nineteenth-century feminists' (Anderson, 1991, p 685), despite the fact that he wrote very little on gender issues per se. Green's progressive ideas on gender issues, however, must be seen in the context of the improving conditions of women in society and the rising tide of feminist thought and debate of the times. He was not an innovator on gender issues – but certainly part of the progressive school of thought of his time.

Liberal socialism

Green's concept of positive freedom was a timely theoretical response to the doctrine of laissez-faire: it accepted capitalism but it rejected the social destructiveness of unregulated capitalism; and it helped to legitimise government intervention in the economic and social affairs of the nation. Green's twin doctrine of positive freedom and the common good formed the basis for subsequent writers who extended it in ways that justified state intervention on a wider scale than he probably intended.

Notable among Green's followers was L. T. Hobhouse (1864–1929), whose ideas form a bridge between welfare liberalism and democratic socialism. Like Green, he defined freedom in positive terms though he used different terminology – unsocial and social freedom. He considered unsocial freedom as unworkable in contemporary society, for it allowed an individual 'to use his powers without regard to the wishes or interests of any one but himself' (Hobhouse, 1911, p 91). Only social freedom is practical in contemporary society because it requires the individual 'to choose among those lines of activity which do not involve injury to others' (Hobhouse, 1911, p 92). The individual pursues his interests but within the confines of the common good. Consequently, he saw no contradiction between individual liberty and the common good, simply because every citizen contributes to and has a share in the common good. Rights are social in character, as Green had argued:

> An individual right, then, cannot conflict with the common good, nor could any right exist apart from the common good. (Hobhouse, 1911, p 123)

Although his definitiosn of freedom and the common good are similar to those of Green, he goes beyond Green in the conclusions that he draws from them in relation to government policy. The state has a duty not simply to remove obstacles that impede a person's self-development, as Green argued, but to provide those conditions in society that enable the individual to live as a full member of society. This means that the state has a duty to ensure full employment and a living wage for those able to work; a system of social benefits adequate for subsistence to all those unable to work; and a range of public services ranging from education to municipal 'gas and water' services – in brief, a national minimum for all. The existence of subsistence poverty and the concentration of wealth, particularly of the inherited kind, were not to be tolerated in Hobhouse's welfare liberal society.

Hobhouse argued that state provision would not undermine but would stimulate individual effort and enterprise. In his words, a national minimum 'is not a narcotic but a stimulus to self help and to friendly aid and filial support' (Hobhouse, 1911, p 178). Hope and confidence rather than fear and insecurity, he felt, were the better stimuli to individual effort (Hobhouse, 1911, pp 182–3).

If the state had a right to demand decent behaviour on the part of its citizens, it also had a duty to provide the income and the services that would enable them to behave accordingly. Hobhouse was quite happy to accept that some people would call his proposals not welfare liberalism, as he intended, but socialism – the only proviso he made was that it should be democratic socialism: first, 'it must come from below, not from above'; and, second, 'it must make not for the suppression but for the development of personality' (Hobhouse, 1911, p 173). It is for this reason that Hobhouse can be seen as a bridge between Green's welfare liberalism and democratic socialism.

Democratic socialism

Democratic socialism was an emerging political force at the end of the 19th century in England and in Europe, as a reaction to both Marxist and utopian socialism. For this reason, it was based on the principles of the democratic political process, of gradualism and of practicality. The best exponent of this form of socialism in England was Fabianism – the socialism advocated by the Fabian Society established in London in 1884 by a group of upper-middle-class intellectuals, men and women, some of whom owed a clear intellectual debt to Green.

The Fabian Society took its name from the Roman general Fabius, who defeated Hannibal not by a frontal attack but by small raids and delaying tactics. In similar fashion, the Fabians did not develop a clear theoretical framework of socialism, or an exciting attacking strategy for the immediate overthrow of capitalism, in the way Marx had done. Rather, they put their faith in piecemeal and gradual reform but with a socialist aim in mind. They produced an endless list of pamphlets, organised conferences galore and put forward policy proposals on almost all aspects of life, all aiming to make the gradual transformation of capitalism to socialism not only possible but respectable as well. They were not agreed on everything but they did agree on the peaceful road to socialism. It is for this reason that some have claimed, with some justification, that 'there was no Fabian doctrine, but only a Fabian policy' (Gray, 1946, p 387).

Many Fabian policy proposals were compatible with Green's twin concept of positive freedom and the common good. Like Green, Fabians considered state intervention in economic and social affairs necessary in order both to correct the worst abuses of unregulated capitalism and to improve opportunities for the ordinary people. State intervention was not a suppression of but an enhancement of individual liberty. It was the absence and not the presence of the state in economic and social affairs that militated against public welfare.

Fabianism, however, went beyond Green in arguing for state intervention not only to remove obstacles to individual self-fulfilment but to establish minimum standards for all in education, health, housing and subsistence, as Hobhouse had argued. Fabians went even further to advocate the nationalisation of land and of industry. They believed that such measures were necessary not only on grounds of efficiency but also on grounds of social morality. If these economic and social measures were enacted, 'the idle class now living on the labour of others will necessarily disappear, and practical equality of opportunity will be maintained by the spontaneous action of economic forces with much less interference with personal liberty than the present system entails' (Fabian Society, 1887, quoted in Wanlass, 1953, p 348). It is the nationalisation of land and industry that really divides the Fabians from both Green and Hobhouse.

Fabianism gradually became the intellectual fountain–head of the British Labour Party and inevitably influenced social reform and the establishment of the welfare state in Britain in the immediate post-war, 1945–48, period. The architect of the reforms, however, William Beveridge, was a liberal and a follower of Green. Although we are not concerned here with the ideas that influenced the emergence of the universal welfare state in Britain or elsewhere in the West, it is worth making the point that the welfare state is the product of material changes in society – rising economic affluence, improving education standards, working-class political power, wars – as well as of changes in ideas and ideologies – welfare liberal, democratic socialist and feminist.

Conclusion

Clearly, Green's ideas contributed to the emergence of the welfare state in Britain, directly and indirectly. What cannot be claimed is that Green's ideas were in agreement with all the reform changes of the post-war era in Britain, including the nationalisation of such public utilities as electricity, gas, water, coal, railways and telephones. Green's actual proposals for reform did not go anywhere near that far. Although his theoretical framework in support of state intervention was flexible enough to be used by others to justify a multiplicity of social measures, he was explicitly against the nationalisation of services and industries. Green wanted to humanise, not to abolish, capitalism. Hence the description of Green as 'socialist' (Wanlass, 1953, pp 345–7) is only justifiable if socialism is so defined as to make it compatible with capitalism, as an economic system. It is more correct to see Green as a welfare liberal, whose vision was the establishment of 'an ethical "enabling and educative state" for all its active citizens' (Boucher and Vincent, 2000, p 29).

There has been, however, some convergence of political ideas over the years. First, Green's emphasis on positive freedom has been adopted by liberals, socialists, feminists and others; second, 20th-century welfare liberals have gone beyond Green's vision of the good society; and, third, most contemporary democratic socialist writers have dropped the early central socialist demand for the nationalisation of the means of production and distribution. They have made their peace with capitalism, provided it is regulated, and have thus moved closer to welfare liberalism. Welfare capitalism, today, is seen by the main political parties of advanced industrial societies as both the only possible as well as the most desirable socio-economic system.

Bibliography

Adams, J.A. (1980) *Marriage, Divorce, and Remarriage in the Bible*, Michigan: Zondervan.

Adkins, N.F. (1953) 'Introduction', in N.F. Adkins (ed) *Thomas Paine, 'Common Sense' and Other Political Writings*, New York: Bobbs-Merrill Company.

Aldridge, A.O. (1960) *Man of Reason: The Life of Thomas Paine*, London: The Cresset Press.

Allen, J.W. (1928) *A History of Political Thought in the Sixteenth Century*, London: Methuen.

Anderson, O. (1991) 'The feminism of T.H. Green', *History of Political Thought*, vol XII, no 4, pp 671–93.

Archibald, K. (1988) 'The concept of social hierarchy in the writings of St Thomas Aquinas', in P.E. Sigmund (ed) *St Thomas Aquinas on Politics and Ethics*, New York: Norton and Co.

Astell, M. (1694) 'A serious proposal to the ladies, for the advancement of their true and greatest interest', in M.R. Roberts and T. Mizuta (eds) (1995) *The Pioneers: Early Feminists*, London: Routledge.

Avineri, S. (1968) *The Social and Political Thought of Karl Marx*, Cambridge: Cambridge University Press.

Ayer, A.J. (1989) *Thomas Paine*, London: Faber and Faber.

Ball, T. and Dagger, R. (1991) *Political Ideologies and the Democratic Ideal*, New York: Harper Collins.

Bannerji, H. (1997) 'Mary Wollstonecraft, feminism and humanism', in E.J. Yeo (ed) *Mary Wollstonecraft*, London: Rivers Oram Press.

Barker, E. (1956) *From Alexander to Constantine*, Oxford: Clarendon Press.

Barker, E. (1959) *The Political Thought of Plato and Aristotle*, New York: Dover Publications.

Barker, E. (1970) *Greek Political Theory*, London: Methuen.

Barrow, R.H. (1949) *The Romans*, Harmondsworth: Penguin.

Bendix, R. (1966) *Max Weber: An Intellectual Portrait*, London: Methuen.

Berlin, I. (1969) *Four Essays on Liberty*, Oxford: Oxford University Press.

Blease, W.L. (1910) *The Emancipation of English Women*, London: Constable.

Boucher, D. and Vincent, A. (2000) *British Idealism and Political Theory*, Edinburgh: Edinburgh University Press.

Bouwsma, W.J. (1988) *John Calvin*, Oxford: Oxford University Press.

Bowen, J. (1981) *A History of Western Education, Vol. Three*, London: Methuen.

Boyd, W. (ed) (1962) *The Minor Educational Writings of Jean Jacques Rousseau*, New York: Columbia University.

Brinton, C. (1962) *English Political Thought in the 19th Century*, New York: Harper and Bros.

Bronowski, J. and Mazlish, B. (1960) *The Western Intellectual Tradition*, Harmondsworth: Penguin.

Brown, P.H. (1988) *Egalitarianism and the Generation of Inequality*, Oxford: Clarendon Press.

Bryson, V. (1992) *Feminist Political Theory*, Basingstoke: Macmillan.

Buchanan, J.M. (1979) 'The justice of natural liberty', in G.P. O'Driscoll (ed) *Adam Smith and Modern Political Economy*, Ames: Iowa State University.

Burke, E. (1790) *Reflections on the Revolution in France*, edited by J. Pocock (1987), Indianapolis: Hackett.

Burn, A.R. (1974) *The Pelican History of Greece*, Harmondsworth: Penguin.

Cameron, E. (1991) *The European Reformation*, Oxford: Clarendon Press.

Campbell, R. (trs) (1969) *Seneca: Letters From a Stoic*, Harmondsworth: Penguin.

Canavan, F. (1963) 'Thomas Paine', in L. Strauss and J. Cropsey (eds) *History of Political Philosophy*, Chicago: Rand McNally.

Carlyle, A.J. (1962) *A History of Medieval Political Theory in the West*, vol 1, Edinburgh: Blackwood and Sons.

Carter, M. (2003) *T.H. Green and the Development of Ethical Socialism*, Exeter: Imprint Academic.

Carver, T. (1985) 'Engels's feminism', *History of Political Thought*, vol VI, no 3, pp 479–89.

Caspari, F. (1968) *Humanism and the Social Order in Tudor England*, New York: Columbia University Press.

Cicero, T. (1971) *Selected Works*, trans and edited by M. Grant, Harmondsworth: Penguin.

Clark, M.T. (ed) (1988) *An Aquinas Reader*, New York: Fordham University Press.

Clayes, G. (1989) *Thomas Paine: Social and Political Thought*, London: Routledge.

Cole, G.D.H. (1993) 'Introduction', in P.D. Jimack (ed) *Jean-Jacques Rousseau: The Social Contract and Discourses*, London: Dent.

Coleman, J. (1988) 'People and Poverty', in J.H. Burns (ed) *The Cambridge History of Medieval political Thought, 1350–1450*, Cambridge: Cambridge University Press.

Coleman, J. (2000a) *A History of Political Thought: From Ancient Greece to Early Christianity*, Oxford: Blackwell.

Coleman, J. (2000b) *A History of Political Thought: From the Middle Ages to the Renaissance*, Oxford: Blackwell.

Collins, H. (1969) 'Introduction', in H. Collins (ed) *Paine: Rights of Man*, Harmondsworth: Penguin.

Compayre, G. (1907) *Jean-Jacques Rousseau and Education from Nature*, New York: Burt Franklin.

Copleston, F. (1946) *A History of Philosophy*, vol I, London: Search Press.

Cousins, A.D. (2004) 'Humanism, female education, and myth', *Journal of the History of Ideas*, vol 65, no 2, pp 213–30.

Cracium, A. (ed) (2002) *Mary Wollstonecraft's 'A Vindication of the Rights of Woman*, London: Routledge.

Crawford, P. (1993) *Women and Religion in England, 1500–1720*, London: Routledge.

Crossman, R.H. (1959) *Plato Today*, rev edn, London: Allen and Unwin.

Davis, B.D. (1966) *The Problem of Slavery in the Western Culture*, Ithaca: Cornell University Press.

Deane, H.A. (1963) *The Political and Social Ideas of St Augustine*, New York: Columbia University Press.

Dimova-Cookson, M. (2003) 'A new scheme of positive and negative freedom', *Political Theory*, vol 31, no 4, pp 508–32.

Dixon, S. (1992) *The Roman Family*, Baltimore: Johns Hopkins University Press.

Duncan, G. (1973) *Marx and Mill*, Cambridge: Cambridge University Press.

Dunn, J. (1984) *Locke*, Oxford: Oxford University Press.

Engels, F. (1845) *The Condition of the Working Class in England*, intro E. Hobsbawm (1969), London: Panther Books.

Engels, F. (1847) 'Principles of Communism', in K. Marx, F. Engels and V. Lenin (eds) (1974) *On Communist Society*, Moscow: Progress Publishers.

Engels, F. (1884) *The Origin of the Family, Private Property and the State*, intro E.B. Leacock (1972), London: Lawrence and Wishart.

Engels, F. (1887) 'The housing question', in (1962) *Selected Works of Marx and Engels*, vol I, 2nd edn, Moscow: Foreign Languages Publishing House.

Fennessy, R.R. (1963) *Burke, Paine and the Rights of Man*, Hague: Martinus Nijhoff.

Ferguson, J. and Chisholm, K. (eds) (1978) *Political and Social Thought in the Great Age of Athens*, London: Ward Lock Educational.

Ferguson, M. (1996) 'Mary Wollstonecraft and the problematic of slavery', in M.J. Falco (ed) *Feminist Interpretations of Mary Wollstonecraft*, Pensylvania: Pensylvania State University.

Finley, M.I. (1972) *Aspects of Antiquity*, Harmondsworth: Penguin.

Finnis, J. (1998) *Aquinas*, Oxford: Oxford University Press.

Fischer, E. (1973) *Marx and His World*, Harmondsworth: Penguin.

Fleischacker, S. (2004) *On Adam Smith's Wealth of Nations*, Princeton: Princeton University Press.

Frank, A.G. (1967) *Capitalism and Development in Latin America*, New York: Monthly Review Press.

Frankau, P. (ed) (1977) *A Vindication of the Rights of Woman*, London: Dent.

Freeden, M. (1991) *Rights*, Milton Keynes: Open University Press.

Fritzhand, M. (1967) 'Marx's ideal of man', in E. Fromm (ed) *Socialist Humanism*, London: Allen Lane.

Garforth, F.W. (ed) (1964) *Some Thoughts Concerning Education*, by J. Locke, London: Heinemann.

Gay, P. (1964) *John Locke on Education*, New York: Columbia University Press.

George, V. (2004) 'Globalization and Poverty', in V. George and R. Page (eds) *Global Social Problems*, Cambridge: Polity Press.

George, V. and Taylor-Gooby, P. (eds) (1996) *European Social Policy*, London: Macmillan.

George, V. and Wilding, P. (1976) *Ideology and Social Welfare*, London: Routledge and Kegan Paul.

George, V. and Wilding, P. (1984) *The Impact of Social Policy*, London: Routledge and Kegan Paul.

Gide, C. and Rist, C. (1913) *A History of Economic Doctrines*, New York: Heath and Co.

Glausser, W. (1990) 'Three approaches to Locke and the slave trade', *Journal of the History of Ideas*, vol 51, no 2, pp 199–216.

Gough, J.W. (1950) *John Locke's Political Philosophy*, Oxford: Oxford University Press.

Gray, A. (1946) *The Socialist Tradition: Moses to Lenin*, London: Longmans, Green and Co.

Green, T.H. (1883) *The Prolegomena to Ethics*, Oxford: Oxford University Press.

Green, T.H. (1890a) 'Lectures on the principles of political obligation', in R.L. Nettleship (ed) *Works of Thomas Hill Green, vol II*, 2nd edn, London: Longmans, Green and Co.

Green, T.H. (1890b) 'Lecture on "Liberal legislation and the freedom of contract"', in R.L. Nettleship (ed) *Works of Thomas Hill Green, vol III*, London: Longmans, Green and Co.

Green, T.H. (1890c) 'Two lectures on "The elementary school system of England"', in R.L. Nettleship (ed) *Works of Thomas Hill Green, vol III*, London: Longmans, Green and Co.

Green, T.H. (1890d) 'Lecture on "The work to be done by the new Oxford high school for boys"' in R.L. Nettleship (ed) *Works of Thomas Hill Green, vol III*, London: Longmans, Green and Co.

Green, T.H. (1890e) 'Lecture on "The grading of secondary schools"', in R.L. Nettleship (ed) *Works of Thomas Hill Green, vol III*, London: Longmans, Green and Co.

Guettel, C. (1974) *Marxism and Feminism*, Ontario: Canadian Women's Educational Press.

Haddock, B. (1988) 'Saint Augustine: The city of God', in M. Forsyth and M. Keens-Soper (eds) *A Guide to Political Classics*, Oxford: Oxford University Press.

Hampsher-Monk, L. (1992) *A History of Modern Political Thought*, Oxford: Blackwell.

Harmon, J.D. (1964) *Political Thought: From Plato to the Present*, New York: McGraw-Hill.

Hawkins, J.N. (1974) *Mao Tse-Tung and Education*, Hamden: Linnet Books.

Hayek, F.A. (1944) *The Road to Serfdom*, London: Routledge.

Hearnshaw, F.J. (1931) *The Social and Political Ideas of Some Representative Thinkers of the Revolutionary Era*, London: Dawsons.

Heilbroner, R.L. (1969) *The Worldly Philosophers*, London: Allen and Unwin.

Held, V. (1976) 'Marx, sex, and the transformation of society', in C. Gould and M. Wartofsky (eds) *Women and Philosophy*, New York: Putnam's Sons.

Hill, B. (1984) *Eighteenth Century Women*, London: Unwin and Hyman.

Hobbes, T. (1651) *The Citizen*, edited by B. Gert (1991), Indianapolis: Hackett.

Hobbes, T. (1658) *On Man*, edited by B. Gert (1991), Indianapolis: Hackett

Hobbes, T. (1668) *Leviathan*, edited by E. Curley (1994), Indianapolis: Hackett.

Hobhouse, L.T. (1911) *Liberalism*, London: Williams and Norgate.

Holton, J.E. (1963) 'Marcus Tullius Cicero', in L. Srauss and J. Cropsey (eds) *History of Political Philosophy*, Chicago: Rand McNally Publishing Company.

Hopfl, H. (1990) 'Jean Calvin: The disciplined commonwealth', in B. Redhead (ed) *Plato to Nato*, London: BBC Books.

Jones, C. (2002) 'Mary Wollstonecraft's vindications and their political tradition', in C.L. Johnson (ed) *Mary Wollstonecraft*, Cambridge: Cambridge University Press.

Jones, W.T. (1947) *Masters of Political Thought, Vol Two*, London: Harrap.

Jowett, B. (ed and trs) (1991) *History of the Peloponnesian War by Thucydides*, vol I, Oxford: Clarendon Press.

Kain, P.J. (1993) *Marx and Modern Political Theory*, Lanham: Rowman and Littlefield Publishers.

Keane, J. (1988) 'Despotism and democracy', in J. Keane (ed) *Civil Society and the State*, London: Verso.

Keane, J. (1995) *Thomas Paine: A Political Life*, London: Bloomsbury.

Kelly, G. (1992) *Revolutionary Feminism: The Mind and Career of Mary Wollstonecraft*, Houndmills: Macmillan.

Kenny, A. (1983) *Thomas More*, Oxford: Oxford University Press.

Kingdon, R.M. (1971) 'Social welfare in Calvin's Geneva', *American Historical Review*, vol 76, pp 50–70.

Kinnaird, J.K. (1983) 'Mary Astell', in D. Spender (ed) *Feminist Theorists*, London: The Women's Press.

Knowles, D. (1973) *The Evolution of Medieval Thought*, London: Longman.

Korsmeyer, C. (1976) 'Reason and morals in the early feminist movement: Mary Wollstonecraft', in C. Gould and M. Wartofsky (eds) *Women and Philosophy*, New York: Putnam's Sons.

Labarge, M.W. (2001) *Women in Medieval Life*, Harmondsworth: Penguin.

Lamb, C. (1973) 'Adam Smith's concept of alienation', *Oxford Economic Papers (New Series)*, vol 25, pp 275–85.

Lambert, M.D. (1961) *Franciscan Poverty*, London: SPCK.

Lawrence, C.H. (1994) *The Friars*, London: Longman.

Lee, D. (trs) (1987) *Plato: The Republic*, Harmondsworth: Penguin.

Lefkowitz, M.R. and Fant, B.F. (eds) (1992) *Women's Life in Greece and in Rome*, London: Duckworth.

Lindberg, C. (1996) *The European Reformations*, Oxford: Blackwell.

Locke, J. (1669) 'The fundamental constitution of Carolina', in D. Wootton (ed) (1993) *John Locke: Political Writings*, Harmondsworth: Penguin.

Locke, J. (1689a) 'The first treatise of government', in D. Wootton (ed) (1993) *John Locke: Political Writings*, Harmondsworth: Penguin.

Locke, J. (1689b) 'The second treatise of government', in D. Wootton (ed) (1993) *John Locke: Political Writings*, Harmondsworth: Penguin.

Locke, J. (1693a) 'Labour', in D. Wootton (ed) (1993) *John Locke: Political Writings*, Harmondsworth: Penguin.

Locke, J. (1693b) 'Some Thought Concerning Education' edited by F. W. Garforth (1964), London: Heinemann.

Locke, J. (1697) 'Methods for the employment of the poor', in D. Wootton (ed) (1993) *John Locke: Political Writings*, Harmondsworth: Penguin.

Long, A.A. (1974) *Hellenistic Philosophy: Stoics, Epicureans, Sceptics*, London: Duckworth.

Lubasz, H. (1976) 'Marx's initial problematic: The problem of poverty', *Political Studies*, vol XXIV, no 1, pp 24–42.

Luther, M. (1519) 'A sermon on the estate of marriage', in J. Atkinson (ed) (1966) *Luther's Works, Vol 44*, Philadelphia: Fortress Press.

Luther, M. (1520a) 'Treatise on good works', in J. Atkinson (ed) (1966) *Luther's Works, Vol 44*, Philadelphia: Fortress Press.

Luther, M. (1520b) 'To the Christian nobility of the German nation', in J. Atkinson (ed) (1966) *Luther's Works, Vol 44*, Philadelphia: Fortress Press.

Luther, M. (1522) 'The estate of marriage', in W.I. Brandt (ed) (1966) *Luther's Works, Vol 45*, Philadelphia: Muhlenberg Press.

Luther, M. (1523) 'Ordinance of a common chest', in W.I. Brandt (ed) (1966) *Luther's Works, Vol 45*, Philadelphia: Muhlenberg Press.

Luther, M. (1524a) 'To the councillors of all cities in Germany', in W.I. Brandt (ed) (1966]) *Luther's Works, Vol 45*, Philadelphia: Muhlenberg Press.

Luther, M. (1524b) 'Trade and usury', in W.I. Brandt (ed) (1966) *Luther's Works, Vol 45*, Philadelphia: Muhlenberg Press.

Luther, M. (1530a) 'Sermon on keeping children at school', in R.C. Schultz (ed) (1962) *Luther's Works, Vol 46*, Philadelphia: Muhlenberg Press.

Luther, M. (1530b) 'On marriage matters', in R.C. Schultz (ed) (1962) *Luther's Works, Vol 46*, Philadelphia: Muhlenberg Press.

Mack, J. and Lansley, S. (1985) *Poor Britain*, London: Allen and Unwin.

MacKinnon, C. (1982) 'Feminism, Marxism, method, and the state', in N. Keohane, M. Rosaldo and B. Gelpi (eds) *Feminist Theory*, Brighton: Harvest Press.

Mackinnon, J. (1929) *Luther and the Reformation*, vol III, London: Longmans, Green and Co.

Macpherson, C.B. (1962) *The Political Theory of Possessive Individualism*, Oxford: Oxford University Press.

Markus, R.A. (1988) 'The Latin fathers', in J.H. Burns (ed) *The Cambridge History of Medieval Political Thought, 1350–1450*, Cambridge: Cambridge University Press.

Marshall, J. (1994) *John Locke*, Cambridge: Cambridge University Press.

Marx, K. (1844) *Economic and Philosophic Manuscripts of 1844*, Amherst: Prometheus Books (1988).

Marx, K. (1845a) *The German Ideology*, ed C.J. Arthur (1974), London: Lawrence and Wishart.

Marx, K. (1845b) 'Theses on Feuerbach', in C.J. Arthur (ed) (1974) *The German Ideology*, London: Lawrence and Wishart.

Marx, K. (1849) 'Wage, labour and capital', in K. Marx and F. Engels (eds) (1962) *Selected Works (in two volumes)*, vol I, Moscow: Foreign Languages Publishing House.

Marx, K. (1852) 'The eighteenth brumaire of Louis Bonaparte', in K. Marx and F. Engels (eds) (1962) *Selected Works (in two volumes)*, vol I, Moscow: Foreign Languages Publishing House.

Marx, K. (1859) 'A contribution to the critique of political economy', in K. Marx and F. Engels (ed) (1962) *Selected Works (in two volumes)*, vol I, Moscow: Foreign Languages Publishing House.

Marx, K. (1867) *Capital, Vol I*, edited and introduced by D. McLellan (1999), Oxford: Oxford University Press.

Marx, K. (1875) 'Critique of the Gotha programme', in K. Marx, F. Engels and V. Lenin (eds) (1974) *On Communist Society*, Moscow: Progress Publishers.

Marx, K. and Engels, F. (1845) 'The holy family', in K. Marx, F. Engels and V. Lenin (eds) (1974) *On Communist Society*, Moscow: Progress Publishers.

Marx, K. and Engels, F. (1848) *The Communist Manifesto*, edited and introduced by D. McLellan (1998), Oxford: Oxford University Press.

Maslow, A. (1970) *Motivation and Personality*, New York: Harper and Row.

McClelland, J.S. (1996) *A History of Western Political Thought*, London: Routledge.

McConica, J. (1993) 'Erasmus', in K. Thomas (ed) *Renaissance Thinkers*, Oxford: Oxford University Press.

McGrath, A.E. (1988) *Reformation Thought*, Oxford: Blackwell.

McLellan, D. (1971) *The Thought of Karl Marx*, London: Macmillan.

Meacher, M. (1992) *Diffusing Power: The Key to Socialist Revival*, London: Pluto Presss.

Milner, A.J. (1962) *The Social Philosophy of English Idealism*, London: Allen and Unwin.

Moore, J. (1999) *Mary Wollstonecraft*, Plymouth: Northcote House.

Moorman, J.R. (1968) *A History of the Franciscan Order*, Oxford: Clarendon Press.

More, T. (1965) *Utopia*, trs by P. Turner, Harmondsworth: Penguin.

Morgan, M.L. (ed) (1992) *Classics of Moral and Political Theory*, Indianapolis: Hackett Publishing Company.

Muglan, R.G. (1977) *Aristotle's Political Theory*, Oxford: Clarendon Press.

Musgrave, R.A. (1976) 'Adam Smith on public finance and distribution', in T. Wilson, and A.S. Skinner (eds) **The Market and the State**, Oxford: Clarendon Press.

O'Connor, D.J. (1952) *John Locke*, Harmondsworth: Penguin.

Offen, K. (2000) *European Feminisms, 1750–1950*, Stanford: Stanford University Press.

Ogilvie, R.M. (1980) *Roman Literature and Society*, Harmondsworth: Penguin.

O'Hagan, T. (2004) 'Taking Rousseau seriously', *History of Political Thought*, vol xxv, no 1, Spring, pp 73–85.

Okin, S.M. (1979) *Women in Western Political Thought*, Princeton: Princeton University Press.

Paine, T. (1772) 'The case of the officers of the excise', in A.O. Aldridge (ed) (1960) *Man of Reason: The Life of Thomas Paine*, London: The Cresset Press; and G. Clayes (ed) (1989) *Thomas Paine: Social and Political Thought*, London: Routledge.

Paine, T. (1776) 'Common sense', in M. Philp (ed) (1995) *Thomas Paine: Rights of Man, Common Sense and Other Political Writings*, Oxford: Oxford University Press.

Paine, T. (1789) 'Letter to Jefferson', in M. Philp (ed) (1995) *Thomas Paine: Rights of Man, Common Sense and Other Political Writings*, Oxford: Oxford University Press.

Paine, T. (1791) 'The rights of man, part one', in M. Philp (ed) (1995) *Thomas Paine: Rights of Man, Common Sense and Other Political Writings*, Oxford: Oxford University Press.

Paine, T. (1792) 'The rights of man, part two', in M. Philp (ed) (1995) *Thomas Paine: Rights of Man, Common Sense and Other Political Writings*, Oxford: Oxford University Press.

Paine, T. (1794) *The Age of Reason*, New York: Prometheus Books (1984).

Paine, T. (1796) 'Dissertation on first principles of government', in M. Philp (ed) (1995) *Thomas Paine: Rights of Man, Common Sense and Other Political Writings*, Oxford: Oxford University Press.

Paine, T. (1797) 'Agrarian justice', in M. Philp (ed) (1995) *Thomas Paine: Rights of Man, Common Sense and Other Political Writings*, Oxford: Oxford University Press.

Paine, T. (1780) 'Emancipation of slaves', in D.C. Conway (ed) (1967) *The Writings of Thomas Paine*, vol II, New York: AMS Press.

Pascal, R. (1933) *The Social Basis of the German Reformation*, London: Watts and Co.

Pateman, C. (2003) 'Wollstonecraft', in D. Boucher and P. Kelly (eds) *Political Thinkers*, Oxford: Oxford University Press.

Perkin, H. (1969) *The Origins of Modern English Society, 1780–1880*, London: Routledge and Kegan Paul.

Peters, R. (1956) *Hobbes*, Harmondsworth: Penguin.

Philp, M. (ed) (1995) *Thomas Paine: Rights of Man, Common Sense and Other Political Writings*, Oxford: Oxford University Press.

Plamenatz, J. (1963) *Man and Society*, vol I, London: Longman.

Popper, C. (1966) *The Open Society and Its Enemies*, vol I, London: Routledge and Kegan Paul.

Porter, R. (2001) *The Enlightenment*, London: Palgrave.

Quinney, R. (1975) 'Crime control in a capitalist society', in I. Taylor, P. Walton and J. Young (eds) *Critical Criminology*, London: Routledge and Kegan Paul.

Raphael, D.D. (1977) *Hobbes: Morals and Politics*, London: Allen and Unwin.

Richardson, A. (2002) 'Mary Wollstonecraft on education', in C.L. Johnson (ed) *Mary Wollstonecraft*, Cambridge: Cambridge University Press.

Richter, M. (1964) *The Politics of Conscience: T.H. Green and His Age*, London: Weidenfeld and Nicolson.

Rimlinger, G.V. (1971) *Welfare Policy and Industrialization in Europe, America and Russia*, New York: Wiley.

Roberts, M.R. and Mizuta, T. (eds) (1995) *The Pioneers: Early Feminists*, London: Routledge.

Robertson, J. (1984) 'Adam Smith', in B. Redhead (ed) *Plato to Nato*, Harmondsworth: Penguin.

Roll, E. (1961) *A History of Economic Thought*, London: Faber.

Rosenberg, N. (1979) 'Adam Smith and laissez-faire revisited', in G.P. O'Driscoll (ed) *Adam Smith and Modern Political Economy*, Ames: Iowa State University.

Rousseau, J.J. (1755) 'A discourse on the origin of inequality', in P.D. Jimack (ed) (1993) *Jean-Jacques Rousseau: The Social Contract and Discourses*, London: Dent.

Rousseau, J.J. (1758) 'A discourse on political economy', in P.D. Jimack (ed) (1993) *Jean-Jacques Rousseau: The Social Contract and Discourses*, London: Dent.

Rousseau, J.J. (1762a) 'The social contract', in P.D. Jimack (ed) (1993) *Jean-Jacques Rousseau: The Social Contract and Discourses*, London: Dent.

Rousseau, J.J. (1762b) 'Emile', in B. Foxley (ed) (1963) *Emile*, London: Dent.

Rousseau, J.J. (1773) *Considerations on the Government of Poland*, ed W. Kendall (1985), Indianapolis: Hackett Publishing Company.

Russell, B. (1991) *History of Western Philosophy*, London: Routledge.

Sabine, G.H. (1963) *A History of Political Theory*, London: Harrap and Co.

Sapiro, V. (1996) 'Wollstonecraft, feminism and democracy', in M.J. Falco (ed) *Feminist Interpretations of Mary Wollstonecraft*, Pensylvania: Pensylvania State University.

Sarup, M. (1978) *Marxism and Education*, London: Routledge and Kegan Paul.

Saunders, T.J. (trs) (1970) *The Laws*, by Plato, Harmondsworth: Penguin.

Saunders, T.A. (ed) (1992) *Aristotle: The Politics*, trs T.A. Sinclair Harmondsworth: Penguin.

Sayers, S. (1998) *Marxism and Human Nature*, London: Routledge.

Sayers, S. (1999) *Plato's Republic*, Edinburgh: Edinburgh University Press.

Schumacher, E. (1974) *Small is Beautiful*, London: Abacus.

Seebohm, F. (1896) *The Oxford Reformers: Colet, Erasmus and More*, London: Longmans, Green and Co.

Seneca, L.A. (1964) *Letters from a Stoic*, trs M. Staniforth, Harmondsworth: Penguin.

Sigmund, P.E. (ed) (1988) *St Thomas Aquinas on Politics and Ethics*, New York: Norton and Co.

Simhony, A. (1989) 'T.H. Green's theory of the morally just society', *History of Political Thought*, vol X, no 3, pp 481–98.

Simhony, A. (1991) 'On forcing individuals to be free; Green's liberal theory of positive freedom', *Political Studies*, vol XXXIX, pp 303–20.

Simhony, A. (1993) 'T.H. Green: The common good society', *History of Political Thought*, vol XIV, no 2, pp 225–47.

Smith, A. (1759) *The Theory of Moral Sentiments*, ed K. Haakonssen (2002), Cambridge: Cambridge University Press.

Smith, A. (1776a) *The Wealth of Nations, Books I–III*, ed A. Skinner (1986), Harmondsworth: Penguin.

Smith, A. (1776b) *The Wealth of Nations, Books IV–V*, ed A. Skinner (1999), Harmondsworth: Penguin.

Smith, A. (1795) *Lectures on Justice, Police, Revenue and Arms*, ed E. Cannan (1986), Oxford: Clarendon Press.

Smith, P. (1920) *The Age of the Reformation*, New York: Holt, Rinehart and Winston.

Solar, J.S. (1988) 'St Thomas and property', in P.E. Sigmund (ed) *St Thomas Aquinas on Politics and Ethics*, New York: Norton and Co.

Sophia (1739) 'Woman not inferior to man', London: John Hawkins; in Roberts, M.R. and Mizuta, T. (eds) (1995) *The Pioneers: Early Feminists*, London: Routledge.

Sowell, T. (1979) 'Adam Smith in theory and practice', in G.P. O'Driscoll (ed) *Adam Smith and Modern Political Economy*, Ames: Iowa State University.

Spellman, W.M. (1997) *John Locke*, Basingstoke: Macmillan.

Spinka, M. (1953) *Advocates of Reform*, vol xiv, London: SCM Press.

Spitz, L.W. (1963) *The Religious Renaissance of the German Humanists*, Cambridge: Harvard University Press.

Staniforth, M. (trs) (1964) *Marcus Aurelius: Meditations*, Harmondsworth: Penguin.

Strauss, L. and Copsey, J. (eds) (1963) *History of Political Philosophy*, Chicago: Rand McNally Publishing Company.

Strong, T.B. (1994) *Jean-Jacques Rousseau*, London: Sage.

Sugden, R. (2002) 'Beyond sympathy and empathy: Adam Smith's concept of fellow-feeling', *Economics and Philosophy*, vol 18, no 1, pp 63–87.

Tawney, R.H. (1990) *Religion and the Rise of Capitalism*, Harmondsworth: Penguin.

Taylor, I., Walton, P. and Young, J. (1973) *The New Criminology*, London: Routledge and Kegan Paul.

Thatcher, M. (1995) *The Path to Power*, New York: Harper Collins.

Thomas, T. (1987) *The Moral Philosophy of T.H. Green*, Oxford: Clarendon Press.

Thompson, E.P. (1991) *The Making of the English Working Class*, London: Penguin.

Thompson, J.A. (trs) (1955) *Aristotle: Ethics*, Harmondsworth: Penguin.

Todd, J. (1994) *Mary Wollstonecraft: Political Writings*, Oxford: Oxford University Press.

Troeltsch, E. (1931) *The Social Teaching of the Christian Churches*, vol II, London: Allen and Unwin.

Tuck, R. (1989) *Hobbes*, Oxford: Oxford University Press.

Von Heyking, J. (2001) *Augustine and Politics of Longing in the World*, Columbia: University of Missouri Press.

Wanlass, L.C. (1953) *History of Political Thought*, London: Allen and Unwin.

Watkins, J.W. (1973) *Hobbes's System of Ideas*, London: Hutchinson.

Weber, M. (1930) *The Protestant Ethic and the Spirit of Capitalism*, London: Allen and Unwin.

Wempe, B. (2004) *T.H. Green's Theory of Positive Freedom*, Exeter: Imprint Academic.

Whittaker, E. (1960) *Schools and Streams of Economic Thought*, London: John Murray.

Wilde, O. (1954) *The Soul of Man Under Socialism*, London: Penguin.

Wilkins, A.S. (1914) *Roman Education*, Cambridge: Cambridge University Press.

Wokler, R. (1995) *Rousseau*, Oxford: Oxford University Press.

Wollstonecraft, M. (1790) *A Vindication of the Rights of Men*, London: Johnson.

Wollstonecraft, M. (1792) *A Vindication of the Rights of Woman*, London: Johnson.

Wollstonecraft, M. (1794) *A Historical and Moral View of the Origin and Progress of the French Revolution*, London: Johnson.

Wootton, D. (ed) (1993) *John Locke: Political Writings*, Harmondsworth: Penguin.

Wright-Mills, C. (1963) *The Marxists*, Harmondsworth: Penguin.

Wrightson, K. (2000) *Earthly Necessities*, Harmondsworth: Penguin.

Yeo, E.J. (ed) (1997) *Mary Wollstonecraft*, London: Rivers Oram Press.

Yolton, J.W. (1971) *John Locke & Education*, New York: Random House.

Zimmern, A. (1931) *The Greek Commonwealth*, 5th edn, Oxford: Oxford University Press.

Index